talks with authors

talks with

authors

edited by **Charles F. Madden**

Carbondale and Edwardsville

SOUTHERN ILLINOIS UNIVERSITY PRESS

FEFFER & SIMONS, INC.

London and Amsterdam

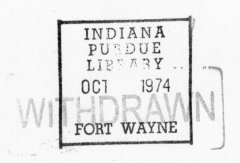
The poems by Muriel Rukeyser, "Waterlily Fire" and "George Robinson: Blues," are from *Waterlily Fire,* copyright © 1963 by Muriel Rukeyser and published by The Macmillan Company. Reprinted by permission of Muriel Rukeyser.

Copyright © 1968 by Southern Illinois University Press
All rights reserved
Library of Congress Catalog Card Number 68–10729
Printed in the United States of America
Designed by Andor Braun

preface

In the spring of 1963 at the request of The Fund for the Advancement of Education, and at the direction of President Seymour A. Smith, members of the faculty of Stephens College began to plan a series of interinstitutional courses using amplified telephone facilities. The project was related to some earlier experimentation by James Burkhart of the social studies department. In 1958 Mr. Burkhart, to give a sense of immediacy to his course in American government, arranged to have his classes carry on person-to-person telephone conversations with political figures. The dialogues were amplified so that they could be heard by all of the students in the classroom and students, using microphones, could ask their questions of these authorities. The calls added a new dimension to the study of government.

Between those early conversations and the project which these volumes reflect, came several years of continuous experimentation. One of the most dramatic concepts was the use of the conference call linking several colleges together for instruction. Mr. Burkhart, Mike Beilis of Omaha University (now with AT&T) and Edmund McCurtain of Drury College in Springfield, Missouri, were pioneers. They arranged for a three-way conference call with Dr. Margaret Mead as telephone guest lecturer and thus set a pattern which the rest of us have followed.

Sidney Tickton, then director of The Fund for the Advancement of Education, saw in these uses of the telephone an opportunity for surmounting two major problems in education: 1] the provision for top level instruction in small, liberal arts schools, and 2] barriers of finances and race in schools that were culturally deprived. He, along with a dynamic professor of education at Jackson State College in Mississippi, Dr. Jane Ellen McAllister, arranged for a summer course in Great Ideas of Antiquity to be taught by telephone by the late Dr. Moses Hadas of Columbia University. The course was made available to four schools in the Deep South—schools historically Negro: Grambling College in Grambling, Louisiana; Jackson State College in Jackson, Mississippi; Southern University in Baton Rouge, Louisiana; and Tougaloo Southern Christian College in Tougaloo, Mississippi. This experiment provided a pilot study for those of us interested in developing the programs for Stephens College. Mr. Ralph Leyden, Director of Educational Development at Stephens, planned the format for the course offerings and, working closely with Dean James G. Rice, arranged for the professors to teach the courses. Three courses were designed to use the new technique: a science seminar for college teachers, and two undergraduate offerings, Great Issues in Contemporary Society, and American Life as Seen by Contemporary Writers.

The course, American Life as Seen by Contemporary Writers, included the talks transcribed for this volume. It was taught by Dr. Harry T. Moore, Research Professor of English at Southern Illinois University, who has provided brief headnotes about each of the speakers. During the course, which was offered in the Spring Semester of 1964, he lectured regularly from his home in Carterville, Illinois, to the six college classes tied into the telephone network. His lectures provided a background for the conversations with the authors. They were brilliantly informative and incisively critical. Without Dr. Moore's lectures the academic goals of the course could not have been achieved, and the course would have lacked coherence and direction.

At each of the participating schools there were faculty and staff members whose cooperation made the course possible. Teaching the course at a participating college meant that the teacher conducted one session each week during which he discussed the assigned works, reviewed Dr. Moore's lectures, and worked with the students in the preparation of appropriate questions to ask the guest speakers. The very good questions which appear in these transcripts are evidence of the effectiveness of the teachers. (I have not tried to identify questioners by name in the transcripts of the talks.) The teachers involved were: Dr. James Livingston, Drury College; Dr. R. H. Jefferson, Jackson State College; Mrs. Moxye King, Langston University; Finley Campbell, Morehouse College; and Dr. Elizabeth Sewell, Tougaloo College.

Technicians at the colleges were responsible for setting up equipment and maintaining equipment. They were: Oral Kuehn and John Ingwerson at Stephens College; Dr. Edmund McCurtain, Drury College; Gene Mosley, Jackson State College; Achille Hebert, Langston University; W. E. Whatley, Morehouse College; and William Townsend, Tougaloo College.

Each school appointed a coordinator for the program who worked with me in handling both academic and technical matters. The coordinators were: Dr. Edmund McCurtain, Drury College; Dr. R. H. Jefferson, Jackson State College; Walter Mason, Langston University; Dr. Tobe Johnson, Morehouse College; and Dr. Naomi Townsend, Tougaloo College. I am grateful to them for their help.

In the preparation of manuscripts for this volume, and others in the series, there were hours of agonizing effort to transcribe the telephone conversations as accurately as possible. For this time-consuming and ear-shattering experience I am grateful to the secretaries assigned to the project, Mrs. Miriam McClure and Mrs. Nadine Watson, and to those from my office at Stephens College who helped at crucial moments, Mrs. Kitty Gordon and Mrs. Alice Estes.

Finally I want to express my appreciation to the authors whose conversations are included here. Their graciousness in participating in the original project has been exceeded only by their willingness to extend their participation to this publication. Each of them has read his manuscript, and I appreciate the suggestions which the authors made. I have tried to follow the suggestions and still maintain the sense of spontaneity which so joyously distinguished these sessions. Any errors which occur or any failure in communication of ideas should be laid on my doorstep.

Charles F. Madden

contents

introduction

To call a course "American Life as Seen by Contemporary Writers" sets a number of directions for the teacher and the students; to couple the course content with some new and exciting techniques of teaching opens even more possibilities. This course, offered to students in six colleges simultaneously through the use of an amplified telephone network, made full use of all such possibilities.

The course was organized to allow the students an opportunity for an encounter with the outstanding critical and creative minds of contemporary America. In choosing materials Dr. Harry T. Moore, the professor in charge of the course, decided to use works which defined certain attitudes or activities of Americans or which stylistically revealed American contributions to literature and life. The initial plan was to use only living authors but, to lend continuity and direction, the final decision was to choose major writers, living or dead, and when necessary, to select the most competent critics for the discussion. The decision was eminently wise.

Each session during the semester brought the students to a consideration of several facets of the work under study. While considering the novel the students approached a new work each week. On the first day Dr. Moore lectured and presented the writer in the context of his total output. He reviewed the place of the specific novel in the writer's work and related the novelist to others similar in time or talent. His presentation furnished a solid base for the second class period during which the students discussed the specific work with their classroom instructor. The third class session was, of course, the most dramatic and dynamic, for during this hour the students and teachers were engaged in an informal conversation with the author or critic. Although each of the telephone guests was given a period of time to make a brief presentation, many of them preferred to toss caution away and simply answer the questions posed by the students. The resulting dialogue was spontaneous and refreshing as well as extremely revelatory of creative impulse and creative labor. The mind of the artist was revealed.

My greatest disappointment in the preparation of this collection came when some of the writers who agreed to the conversations would not agree to publication. Their reasons were well communicated: most felt that a conversation transcribed and printed was too uncontrolled—the care usually exercised in their writing was missing from such a document. Most felt, too, that the time required to smooth and polish this statement would be time stolen from more important work, the new book or play or poem. I hope not to appear adversely critical—I understand these reservations—but I am disappointed nevertheless that their often delightful, always perceptive comments cannot be included in the collection. In this introduction, however, I cannot refrain from an occasional brief quotation from some of those whose complete conversations do not appear in the book.

THE TECHNIQUES OF WRITING

Listening to the artist talk about the process of writing was an unexpected value in the course. Most of the writers could not separate—or did not want to separate—the subject from the object. The novel or the poem was not seen as an abstract idea fleshed out with the techniques of novelist or poet—the two were inseparable. Most of the writers agreed too that they were not simply "seeing American life" as the title of the course suggested. They felt that there was another, more profound relationship which the artist and society experience. It was most explicitly phrased by Kay Boyle,

I believe too, that one of the many functions of a writer is to create a public and a climate. Other functions of a writer are, to be sure, to be a poet, to be a philosopher, to be a historian, but the obligation to create an intelligent and aware public, an exhilarating climate for all of us to breathe in, is the responsibility a writer must accept from the outset as peculiarly his. Because I am deeply concerned with all the tasks of the writer I feel that in our times it is not the writer who must seek to be accepted by the world in which he finds himself but it is the world that must be transformed to acceptability by the higher standards of the individual. The writer's concern must always be not only with what is taking place, although that may be of necessity the framework within which to state the tenets of his faith, but his deepest concern must be, as well, with the dimensions of what *might* within the infinite capacities of man be enabled to take place.

Miss Boyle's statement which came near the end of the course might have easily preceded statements made by John Dos Passos who was the first author to talk with us. He said, "Any writer has to adapt his style to what he is trying to write about at the moment. The material ought to form the style, I think. Anybody who is going to do anything great is always going to work up his own particular way of expressing it." He continued by describing the experimental attitudes which followed World War I—the experiments in painting by the Cubists and Futurists—and finally described his own techniques as efforts to achieve "simultaneity." He wanted, in the spirit of Eisenstein and others interested in motion picture montage, to "make the narrative stand up off the page." How better could we describe the effort to combine the breadth and depth of American life which was his subject in *U.S.A.* and *Midcentury?*

Where Miss Boyle and Mr. Dos Passos spoke of the artists' aim in general terms, some of the speakers were quite specific, singling out elements of technique which student critics often overlook. The concern of the writers for such elements underscored the seriousness with which the writer undertakes his task and his consciousness of techniques which will help him communicate his feelings. It also stimulated the critical acuity of the students. They tended after each conversation to read more carefully and with a greater awareness of the author's purposes. Vance Bourjaily, who is both teacher and novelist, clarified an important contemporary attitude with his comment on point of view.

> Like most twentieth-century writers, I had been brought up on the work of Henry James and his followers down through both Hemingway and Fitzgerald, and from this had derived, I think, a very limited idea of the possibilities of the novel as a form, without perhaps ever having thought about point of view and restricted point of view. I just automatically felt that point of view should be restricted. . . . The limits which James set, or which Lubbock tried to set after James . . . are artificial and pretentious, and deny a great deal of the vitality which is possible to a novel. It is the vitality which is so superbly present in *War and Peace*.

The efforts of the contemporary writer to reflect the complexity and vitality of individuals and of society leads to many different ways of writing. Dos Passos' effort to achieve depth in a presentation of the social reality is paralleled by Saul Bellow's treatment of psychological reality. During our conversation with Mr. Bellow a student asked him to comment on the recurrent "I want" which Henderson hears, or experiences, in the novel *Henderson, the Rain King*. Mr. Bellow's response indicated, I think, a consciousness of technique and revealed at the same time his thematic concerns. The statement shows, too, the influences of certain social developments—in this case the influence of psychological research. The "I want" was explained as follows.

> It's partly, I think, a kind of comic refusal of all the things that people are offered, comfort, prosperity, social position, machinery, money, even knowledge; and it leaves them restless. There's still the primitive voice in the individual crying, "I want," and he doesn't really understand it. This unsatisfied longing has been the

theme of much modern psychology—it isn't only I who raised this question. Such an eminent authority as Sigmund Freud tells us time and again that a human being is appeased or fulfilled only when his earliest needs are gratified.
Since the unconscious veils these earliest needs and the individual doesn't really know what they are, he tries one thing after another in an effort to find his heart's desire. It isn't easy to find his heart's desire. I wouldn't be able to tell you in so many words what that voice signifies—what it really means is that our American society does not have whatever it is that will satisfy it.

Mr. Bellow's explication which simply broadens the base for understanding Henderson and the entire structure of the novel leads one naturally to a final element of technique which should be mentioned—symbolism. This is a word which is bandied about in almost every literature course but which is said to have particular relevance in discussions of contemporary works. The students in the telephone course wanted to pursue the subject with the authors. The crux of the matter was revealed with pedagogical ease by Carlos Baker in his discussion of *A Farewell to Arms* by Ernest Hemingway. Professor Baker said,

> I am aware that to many readers the very idea of symbolism is anathema. They would like to believe that this is a simple naturalistic tale of two lovers, a Romeo and Juliet story, but, in fact, Hemingway has very carefully planned certain symbolic aspects of this book. One is the weather, another is the emblematic people, and third, the landscape itself.

The key words in this comment are "carefully planned," words which suggest a composition contrived to function on several levels. Most writers would deny this sort of manipulation of materials and Kay Boyle near the end of our series adamantly refused to admit any symbolic reading of her stories. The resolution of such diverse views was probably best expressed by Wright Morris, author of *Field of Vision*, in a talk outside of this series when he said, in effect, good writing is always symbolic and symbolic writing is always bad. He, at least in this remark, was suggesting to the reader—and the embryonic writer—that *conscious* symbolism was to be eschewed. Hemingway, Bellow, Boyle, and most of the fine writers of our time can, however, be read for more than the surface of their works. Their perception of the complexity of their characters, their understanding of their milieu reveals itself in every incident selected and in every nuance of language. This became clear through our conversations about technique.

THE SEARCH FOR IDENTITY

In treating the literary works thematically and giving at least some attention to the title of the course it was interesting to note the emergence of several major motifs. The dominant theme, the search for identity, has been treated by critics of American literature for a long time, and it was not surprising to find it looming large in our conversations. This was particularly true because the schools involved in the course were predominantly Negro and the current racial upheaval is clearly both personal and social.

Ralph Ellison discussing with us his work *Invisible Man* placed the whole issue in historical perspective.

> Since we are such a conscious culture, they [the founding fathers] wrote it all down on paper . . . as we began to name the conditions of life in this society, in this climate, and on this particular body of earth this led to a question for us. We had the ideal definition of what the society was to be, but, at the same time, we had the problem of creating ourselves into the characters known as American . . . We were in the process of making ourselves. The problem of identity has always been with us.

Mr. Ellison's comment which was part of an excellent presentation touched on identity as a problem of all Americans; Vance Bourjaily related his comments to his character Skinner Galt in *The End of My Life*, a work which some critics think is the best novel by an American dealing with World War II.

I think Skinner [protagonist in *The End of My Life*] was trying to find somebody *to be*. We use the phrase "a search for identity" about novels fairly often. It's not a very accurate phrase in my mind because it assumes that identity exists and that somehow one can find it as an accomplished and developed thing. Obviously identity doesn't exist somewhere to be found; identity—the feeling that one has achieved "self"—is something that develops very slowly perhaps through many years and through all one's youth. And identity is finally achieved, I think, from within rather than found somewhere without. Meanwhile, one is trying various systems of value; various ways of judging experience; various ways of estimating himself.

This statement by Bourjaily shows his feeling that identity is related to the psychological completeness of man—Bellow's Henderson was seeking the same kind of primitive wholeness—and the statement suggests that identity can be achieved if not found. Among the writers with whom we talked, others felt that the search itself was the valuable activity. This was particularly true of the poets. With the poets the search was never completed but was always in the process. The marvelously tenuous but real relationship presented by Muriel Rukeyser in "Waterlily Fire" or the revelation in Shapiro's "Love for a Hand" are points in the process.

RELIGIOUS THEMES

Obviously discussions of man's relation to his existence carried us into religious and philosophical realms. Both the students and faculty were surprised at the frequency with which our conversations turned to religion or to ideas with religious implications. Nearly every guest speaker aligned himself with a position which could be called religious. Richard Wilbur and Karl Shapiro spoke most directly to the subject. Shapiro was candid and informative as he discussed the influence of his Jewish background on the themes of his poetry. Particularly in the discussion of "Messias" he noted the shifting responses of the American Jew when faced with certain Hebraic traditions. In the answers to questions related to "Love Calls Us to the Things of This World" and "Beasts," Richard Wilbur articulated his position regarding man's perpetual search.

> I am talking, I suppose, about the uneasy relationship of man to nature in the largest possible sense. I present the animals in this poem as being helplessly in harmony with things, even in their acts of predation, whereas man is a torn creature—part angel, part beast—who finds it very hard to achieve perfect harmony, or a perfect sense of what he ought to be. He wavers between being a werewolf and a suitor of excellence.

INITIATION

Where Wilbur's man is a mature man seeking meaning in his existence, another of the motifs uncovered during our conversations with authors was the *rite de passage*. A number of observers have commented on the adolescent as a central figure in contemporary American literature but few have noted that the attention of the writers is focused on the transition from adolescence to manhood or on a transition which is more broadly described as a movement from innocence to understanding.

Certainly one of the clearest presentations of this process was analyzed for us in the conversation with Carvel Collins on *The Bear* by Faulkner. Professor Collins after detailing the total structure of the work—its relation to *Go Down, Moses,* the uncertainty regarding the place of Part IV, and so on—remarks that *"The Bear,* as everybody is now saying, gives an account of the initiation of the young boy into manhood." But Collins goes beyond that, he points out that Ike McCaslin "survives" as most of the "psychologically autobiographical characters" in Faulkner do not. He supports this with the observation,

> Ike has found endurance in the primitive woods and his training there, and he keeps the conscious concern which is the best characteristic of such plantation people as his

father and uncle who, however inadequately, did what they could to reduce the terrible wrong of slavery. He joins these together in the final scene at the grave site and receives then the even greater feeling of unity: that nature and the universe are one; in short, he has a basic mystical experience.

The understanding which comes to Ike McCaslin lifts him out of innocence and into maturity. The loss of innocence in this instance is a positive movement from a state of naïveté or ingenuousness to a knowledge which includes the simple but recognizes complexity.

Ralph Ellison concerned with another kind of transition included a scene in *Invisible Man* where a battle royal takes place. The scene involves a group of Negro boys battling each other for the entertainment of a group of white men. A student at Morehouse College in Atlanta asked Mr. Ellison if this were a reflection of the mixed world for the Negro—both heaven and hell. Mr. Ellison replied,

> The scene of the battle royal was a sort of initiation on the part of the hero—his initiation into reality, into the kind of reality which he was going to encounter as long as he continued to be naïve about himself and the world. I used that particular scene because it is a ritual—it is one of the rituals which we pay very little attention to in society and yet I think it reveals attitudes or, at any rate, I made it reveal attitudes.

The difference between Faulkner's Ike McCaslin and the boys in Ralph Ellison's account is clear from these two comments. Faulkner's character becomes a deeper human being; Ellison's a readier human being. One grows in spiritual awareness, the other in social awareness. Such distinctions drawn by the authors awakened students to *both* dimensions.

THE COMIC

There were other values to these conversations. The writers revealed a strain of the comic which runs through contemporary literature, the picaresque hero was readily recognized. Ellison said that humor was very important, for the American Negro, in maintaining balance. "It's an attitude toward life which looks pretty coldly and realistically at the human situation, which insists upon enduring, which insists upon, while recognizing one's limitations, trying somehow to overcome it."

The conversations are now transcribed for the reader and while the warmth of the personality does not shine through type as readily as it coursed through the telephone lines, the reader will discover in the vitality of these talks the source of the vitality in contemporary American literature. In making these available in this form I feel somewhat the way Kay Boyle did when she answered a student from Tougaloo who asked how she recognized the material which was suitable for a story. She said, "Well, you just sort of get hit in the heart by it . . . Your breath is just taken away. You feel like, 'my God, I must get that down! I must tell people that this happened.'"

Stephens College
Columbia, Missouri
May 1967

Charles F. Madden

talks with **authors**

John Dos Passos

John Dos Passos was born in Chicago in 1896, the son of a successful lawyer whose own father was a Portuguese immigrant. After going to school at Choate, John Dos Passos attended Harvard, from which he was graduated in 1916. During World War I he performed ambulance and medical corps duties, and after the Armistice traveled in Europe and the Near East. His first novel, *One Man's Initiation—1917*, was published in London in 1920; *Three Soldiers*, another war novel, appeared in New York in 1921. Mr. Dos Passos' first novel of stature, *Manhattan Transfer*, the book which first put him among the major novelists, came out in 1925. It foreshadowed the techniques of his masterwork, *U.S.A.*, a trilogy made up of *The 42nd Parallel* (1930), *1919* (1932), and *The Big Money* (1936). These books presented a concrete and vivid new image of America, its cities, and its country landscapes. In portraying the experiences of the characters involved, the novels developed new methods of overshadowing the action, with terse biographies of noted contemporaries, subjective lyric interludes, and the screaming headlines of the time. Mr. Dos Passos' next trilogy, *District of Columbia* (*Adventures of a Young Man*, 1939, *Number One*, 1943, and *The Grand Design*, 1949), met with a cooler reception from the critics and that part of the reading public which had accepted John Dos Passos as a radical or at least a liberal and now found him going toward what they considered a disappointingly conservative position. (In the interview that follows, Mr. Dos Passos refuses to accept labels and makes some interesting remarks about individualism.) Besides his novels, Mr. Dos Passos has written a miscellany of books including travel volumes such as *Journeys Between Wars* (1938) and searching investigations of the American past, including *The Ground We Stand On* (1941) and *The Head and Heart of Thomas Jefferson* (1954). In 1966 he brought out a lively autobiography, *The Best Times*. For the present telephone interview, *U.S.A.* would have been a natural choice except for its length, so *Midcentury* (1961) was chosen. This is a somewhat controversial book among readers of John Dos Passos, not all of whom place it among his best work. If *Midcentury* seems to some extent antagonistic to current practices of labor unions (while presenting a favorable short biography of Walter Ruether), it certainly does not glorify big business, which it shows—in the phrase of sociologist David Riesman—as "other-directed," and hampered by conformity. In technique, *Midcentury*, with its biographical sections, resembles *U.S.A.*, and certainly much of the story is at almost as high a level. Fortunately, in the interview John Dos Passos, among other things, talks about the technique of writing and the development of his own work in a fuller way than most authors do, and his tracing of the influence upon him of earlier experimental writers makes this discussion a particularly valuable one.

MR. DOS PASSOS: In the period of the First World War there was a great deal of experimentation in writing in both Europe and America. At that time I was particularly interested in the Italian Futurists and the French poet, Rimbaud. A number of poets were experimenting in the use of language very much the same way that the Cubists, the experimental painters, were experimenting with form and color. They were trying to produce something that stood up off the page. Some of them called it simultaneity, described it as a simultaneous chronicle, a novel full of snapshots of life like a documentary film.

I had been much affected by the sort of novel that Stendhal originated in French with his *La Chartreuse de Parme*, or Thackeray in English with *Vanity Fair*. You might call these chronicle novels. *War and Peace* is another example. In this sort of novel the story is a skeleton on which some slice of history the novelist has seen or imagined is brought back to life. Personal adventures illustrate the development of the society. Political forces take the place of the Olympians in ancient Greek drama.

About the same time I read James Joyce's *Ulysses; Ulysses* got linked in my mind with Sternes' *Tristram Shandy*. They are both subjective novels. I wanted to do that sort of thing only make it objective. I had been pretty well steeped in the eighteenth century from early youth. In college I had been taken with the crystal, literalness of Defoe's narrative and by Fielding's and Smollett's satire. I had read enough Spanish in my early life to be interested in revival of the Spanish picaresque style. I dreamed of using whatever I had learned from all of these methods to produce a satirical chronicle of the world I knew. I felt that everything should go in: popular songs, political aspirations and prejudices, ideals, hopes, delusions, crackpot notions, clippings out of the daily newspapers. It was this sort of impulse that came to a head in the series of contemporary chronicles.

Somewhere along the line I had been impressed by Eisenstein's documentary films like *Battleship Potemkin*. Montage was the word used in those days to describe the use of contrast scenes in motion pictures. I took the montage to make the narrative stand up off the page.

Drury: Mr. Dos Passos, we are interested in knowing whether or not you think individualism a lost cause in American society today. Would you comment on that?

MR. DOS PASSOS: I don't think it is ever a lost cause, actually. What's happened is we haven't been able to adjust to the very complicated industrial system that we find ourselves living in. But I don't feel it is a lost cause.

Jackson: In the March 1962 issue of *Harper's Magazine*, Daniel Aaron said, in his article entitled "The Riddle of Dos Passos," "Dos Passos has never reneged in his pledge to the 'lone individual' but his shift from a revolutionary anarchism to the kind of libertarian Republicanism represented by the late Senator Robert Taft has not carried much imaginative conviction." What is your opinion of this?

MR. DOS PASSOS: Everybody has a right to his own opinion. There isn't time enough to discuss this gentleman's opinions at the moment. He has a right to them. Naturally, I don't agree with him.

Jackson: We have another question to follow that. However, we would like you to comment on whether you consider yourself a liberal or whether you would consider yourself a conservative today.

MR. DOS PASSOS: I have been trying to avoid these classifications all my life and I will probably manage to continue doing it. This really has very little to do with my work.

MR. MADDEN: I think that is absolutely right; we ought to focus on the work as much as we can. Are there other questions from Jackson that have to do with the work?

Jackson: Do you feel that the style which you employed in *Midcentury*—you say you want the novel to stand off the page—will be employed by writers who would like to be commentators on social problems in the United States?

MR. DOS PASSOS: Well, no, because I believe everybody has to work up his own style. Any writer has to adapt his style to what he is trying to write about at the moment. The material ought to form the style, I think. Anybody who is going to do anything great is always going to work up his own particular way of expressing it.

Langston: Concerning the passage in which you say that one out of ten Americans suffer from mental illness—I understood that in your book you were concerned about economic conditions and the effect that they had on the emotional stability of a person—I would like to know, when these frustrations are put on a person, does this bring the crisis or the breaking point?

MR. DOS PASSOS: That is really a question for a psychiatrist. I think this quotation just came in sort of on the side. I don't think that *I* was saying it. It seems to me that somebody else was saying it, that I was quoting somebody in one of the passages. I don't remember the quotation myself. Where did you find it?

MR. MADDEN: I believe it occurred in one of the documentaries, if I'm not mistaken.

MR. DOS PASSOS: Oh, yes! But these would not be necessarily my opinions. They would be the opinions of whoever was speaking at the time.

Stephens: Mr. Dos Passos, do you feel that your documentaries and newsreels contribute to the plot of the story? Do you simply use these as parallels to show a rather superficial level of life that you are portraying in this book?

MR. DOS PASSOS: The whole method is based on contrast. That is what I was saying about what they call montage in the movies. It is a method of getting an effect by using contrasting scenes, contrasting styles. The whole effort was to sort of give another dimension by bringing in things that were going on at the same time as the actual narrative. Then, of course, they have a certain poetic use which is rather separate. They express a certain amount of emotion you see.

Tougaloo: A number of students say they find the book very pessimistic. There are references to sinister adolescents and to characters not motivated by anything except egocentricity. Where would you suggest, Mr. Dos Passos, that we should look for more positive views on United States society in *Midcentury?*

MR. DOS PASSOS: Well, of course, it is a satirical work and, naturally, some of it would seem rather pessimistic. On the other hand, I think you will find that the optimistic side is kept up by some of the other characters. There are some people who are really struggling to do what they can to find a desirable path of society. I mean, I was trying to paint a fairly large picture which could let many things come in.

MR. MADDEN: I have a question of my own if I may

ask it. Arthur Mizener, in his recent work *The Sense of Life in the Modern Novel,* quotes you as writing—I think in the voice of the narrator in *U.S.A.*—to F. Scott Fitzgerald, "We're living in one of the damnedest tragic moments in history." And then Mr. Mizener goes on to say, "The moment in history is not tragic. It only constitutes the circumstances in which the aware individual suffers the tragic experience of unavoidable moral choice." Would you care to comment on that?

MR. DOS PASSOS: Well, I believe that happens in almost any period in history—the question of choice always comes up. It is a part of human life, there's no avoiding that. I think that quotation was from a letter of mine to Scott Fitzgerald years ago about his story *The Crack-Up;* that very personal thing. I tried to get him to be more interested in the larger scene and less in his own personal troubles.

MR. MADDEN: Yes, I think that was the source of it, as a matter of fact. Do you think this is a particularly tragic time, or one which offers us more unavoidable moral choices than other times?

MR. DOS PASSOS: Yes, because it is a period of violent transition, and all periods of great transition are very difficult for the people who live through them. After all, in my life I have gone through two major wars and a number of small wars. I think there have been a good many periods in human history when people haven't had to go through quite that much. It is very interesting to go through such a period.

MR. MADDEN: A good period to live in then?

MR. DOS PASSOS: I don't think it is a bad period at all to live in. That was what I was trying to tell Scott in this letter; that was many years ago, of course.

Tougaloo: What about the labor union theme of the

novel? Did you choose that because it seemed to you a key issue for the 1950's, or because you knew a great deal about it and it was representative enough to carry your message?

MR. DOS PASSOS: It is a thing I have always been very much interested in. I think the way people's lives are organized is pretty basic, and the labor unions were the most direct way of describing the sort of organization which almost everybody endures. And, of course, I became very much interested in that because I had been doing quite a little study, going around talking to people, both to leaders and the rank and file. So, as the book progressed, this theme got to be more important than I had intended it to be at the beginning.

Langston: My question has to do with the clarification of one of your characters, Blackie Bowman. This character uses a language that we would associate with such a person up to the point where he uses terms like "bourgeois felicity" and "philosophical anarchy." These terms we don't ordinarily associate with the person that you have been portraying. I would like to know if this is done on purpose to give us an idea of the many aspects of this person's personality or whether it is a reflection of your own personality or your own vocabulary and style of writing?

MR. DOS PASSOS: Yes, I think it was done on purpose. You see this fellow was a "wobbly," an IWW, and naturally a good deal of that type of language would come in. He is not a thoroughly *un*educated man; he had probably read quite a little. I think if you have ever known any people of that type, you have found there is always a certain amount of sociological terminology that comes in there, too.

MR. MADDEN: This is largely due to the kind of experience that he was having where he heard speeches of this kind and actually gave some.

MR. DOS PASSOS: Exactly, yes.

Tougaloo: Why did you not attack Walter Reuther as sharply as you did the other labor leaders?

MR. DOS PASSOS (*Laughing*): I don't know that I *attacked* any of them. I suppose I have a good bit of sympathy for Walter Reuther; he is really a very attractive fellow. I don't agree with him about many things but he is one of the most attractive people in public life, I think.

MR. MADDEN: We are coming rapidly to the end of our class period. Mr. Dos Passos, I would be interested in knowing what you are doing right now. You commented that you were in Washington, or near there, working on a book.

MR. DOS PASSOS: Yes. A number of years ago I did a thing about the first half of Jefferson's life called *The Head and Heart of Thomas Jefferson*. Now I am doing a book about the second part of his life, about the end of his life. It is a historical thing.

MR. MADDEN: Dr. Moore, would you like to conclude this conversation with any comments or questions to Mr. Dos Passos?

MR. MOORE: I would like to ask Mr. Dos Passos one question. We seem to have gotten the idea that some of his work is quite pessimistic and I have a feeling, from my own reading of it and from some of the things Mr. Dos Passos has said today, that he is really an optimistic man. I mean, whether we always agree with his ideas or not, he certainly is always in there pitching, and he is really one of our most prolific, creative writers. And my thought, expressed the other day about *Midcentury*, is that it is essentially an invitation to modern man to reexamine himself. I wonder if Mr. Dos Passos agrees that that was one of his intentions?

MR. DOS PASSOS: I think the satirist is always basically optimistic. The satirist's complaint about society is always that it doesn't measure up to a fairly high ideal he has. I think that even the bitterest satirist, even a man like Swift, was probably rather an optimist at heart.

MR. MOORE: Thank you very much.

MR. MADDEN: If I may then, for the whole network, thank Mr. Dos Passos for spending this time with us. It seems to me that it has been extremely valuable. I don't know when more has been packed into thirty minutes. So, thank you very much, Mr. Dos Passos.

February 3, 1964

Horace Gregory

on Sherwood Anderson

Sherwood Anderson was born in Camden, Ohio, in 1876 and died on the Isthmus of Panama in 1941 while en route to South America on a goodwill tour. To speak for him in this series of conversations we invited the American poet, Horace Gregory, editor of a collection of Anderson's writings. Among these, we concentrated on two units for the present interview: some of the stories from *Winesburg, Ohio* (1919) and the entire novel *Poor White* (1920). Anderson began late as a writer; his first book was the novel *Windy McPherson's Son* (1916). In his Ohio childhood and youth he had been a newspaper vendor, stableboy, farmhand, Spanish-American War volunteer, and racetrack worker before becoming an advertising writer in Chicago. From 1907 to 1912 he managed a mail-order paint factory in Elyria, Ohio, until one day while dictating a letter he told his secretary he was walking in the bottom of a river—and left the factory forever. Returning to Chicago, he resumed his work in advertising. He started writing fiction and was soon publishing his stories in "little magazines"; and his career as an author began. Artistically, he never equalled *Winesburg, Ohio* and *Poor White*. The first of these projected an imaginary American place as "real" as Edwin Arlington Robinson's Tilbury Town or Edgar Lee Masters' Spoon River, while *Poor White* was virtually a capsule history of the Industrial Revolution in terms of a midwestern community. In a novel set partly on the Mississippi, *Dark Laughter* (1925), Anderson scored his one genuine popular success; but critics have not given this book a high rating, and Ernest Hemingway parodied it in *The Torrents of Spring* (1926). Anderson was usually at his best in his short stories, such as those in *Winesburg, Ohio*, and those collected in *The Triumph of the Egg* (1921) and *Horses and Men* (1923). The finest of his autobiographical books was his posthumously published *Memoirs* (1942). Anderson wrote in a rhythmic but simple style, and his work gives the impression of a man groping gently for the elusive word, often finding it and putting it tenderly in its place. With his candid approach to the subject of sex, Anderson was a pioneer among realists without becoming, as Horace Gregory shows, technically a realist.

Horace Gregory, who was born in Milwaukee in 1898, studied at the University of Wisconsin and has for many years taught at Sarah Lawrence College. His volumes of poetry include *Chelsea Rooming House* (1930), *No Retreat* (1933), *Chorus For Survival* (1935), *Medusa in Gramercy Park* (1961), and *Collected Poems* (1964). He was awarded the Bollingen Prize in 1965, one honor among many; his wife, the poet Marya Zaturenska, is a Pulitzer Prize winner. With her, Horace Gregory wrote *A History of American Poetry, 1900–1940* (1946); some of his other critical work is collected in *The Shield of Achilles* (1944), and in *The Dying Gladiators and Other Essays* (1961). In 1949 he edited *The Portable Sherwood Anderson.*

MR. GREGORY: Good morning! Perhaps it would be well for me to start with a few of the reasons why I brought together a collection of Sherwood Anderson's short stories with a reprinting of his novel *Poor White* in the Viking Portable Library. When I was very young and adventurous (I was then in prep school), I wrote a one-act play that was accepted and put on the stage—for one night only—by the Wisconsin Players of Milwaukee. That night it so happened that Sherwood Anderson, up north on a visit from Chicago, was in the audience. He was very kind in what he had to say; he encouraged me to continue writing. In 1947 when I edited the Sherwood Anderson Portable, I felt the time was long overdue for me to pay my debts of gratitude to certain writers of the Middle West, and of these, more than any other, I believed Sherwood Anderson to be a creative example, a germinating force.

Anderson was of the generation of Edgar Lee Masters, Carl Sandburg, Vachel Lindsay and a little bit younger than Theodore Dreiser. These men constituted the Middle Western renaissance. Of the entire group, Anderson was the storyteller; he had a particular kind of story to tell, poetic in its symbolic reference.

Almost all of his readers know that Sherwood Anderson became famous through writing *Winesburg, Ohio*, an inter-related group of stories, conceived, as he confessed later, in a Chicago rooming house. The people he met there became the characters in the book in which he gave them the environment of a small town in Ohio rather than the urban setting of Chicago. In these stories one sees an early stage set for an Anderson spectacle—the small town outgrowing itself and becoming a city. This was what Anderson saw as the industrialization of America. This was the overall story and theme of *Poor White*.

Anderson endowed his theme with human fears and triumphs, failures, adolescent bewilderments, and half-, but only half, won successes. Because of his wider ranges, I chose to reprint some of his later stories and all of *Poor White* rather then reprint *all* of the earlier book, *Winesburg, Ohio*. Of the later stories I believe the masterpieces are "The Man Who Became a Woman," "The Egg," and "Death in the Woods."

In my introduction to the Sherwood Anderson Portable I said that "Death in the Woods" may remind some readers of the young Wordsworth's poetry. The imagery in the story also recalls young Shelley's poem "Queen Mab," particu-larly in the poem's moonlit scene where Death makes a counterfeit of Sleep. In another story, "A Meeting South," Anderson speaks of Keats and Shelley, and I am quite certain that when Anderson was a boy he read and reread Shelley—in those days Shelley was well known to Middle Western teachers and school boys.

Anderson's teacher probably resembled Kate Swift in *Winesburg, Ohio*; in any case, her enthusiasms were con-veyed to her sensitive and gifted student. Her admirations became his; she loved the writings of George Borrow. Many years later, Anderson named George Borrow as one of the masters of his own prose, and it is highly probable that his enthusiastic teacher introduced him to Shelley's poetry.

Beyond this, there is still more evidence that Shelley's "Queen Mab" was a familiar poem to Middle Western contemporaries of Anderson's boyhood. Among Middle

Western Owenites, a colony of Utopians, "Queen Mab" was a favorite poem. Here we turn to "Death in the Woods" again and find a picture of an old woman who in death resembles a young girl. The image recalls lines from "Queen Mab"; "How wonderful is Death / Death and his brother, Sleep." Later on in the poem, Shelley used the phrase "grieving marble" which is very close to the metaphor that Anderson used in describing the old woman. If we read "Death in the Woods" as a story that is almost a poem in prose, we are right; moreover, Anderson converted his readings in Romantic poetry into something that was new, original, and his own.

A word should also be said of Anderson's association with Gertrude Stein. At first glance Gertrude Stein and Anderson seem miles apart. In actuality, the stories in her *Three Lives* were among the forerunners of the kind of prose and fiction Anderson was to write. But more important than a passing literary influence was Anderson's recognition of his affinity with Stein. Both were deeply concerned with a new simplicity in writing prose, prose that mirrored and echoed, and yet made an art of conversational speech. From totally different environments both entered the same road. They wrote their books as though each sentence (to be understood) had to be read aloud.

In addition to writing stories, Anderson was also a great teacher in his own right. It is true he never taught in a school, but he taught many writers who came after him. One of these was William Faulkner; another was Hart Crane, the poet, who also came from Ohio; another was Thomas Wolfe; another was Ernest Hemingway. Anderson's imprint on these writers was very, very great. He had a fatherly interest in them. I think it might be well for all of you who are interested to look up William Faulkner's essays on Sherwood Anderson—one of the most grateful tributes ever made by a younger writer to an elder.

Another thing that could be said of Anderson is that no writer of his generation gave so much meaning to the life of the American adolescent. In the story "The Man Who Became a Woman" we have a living portrait of the boy growing into a man. American and unsophisticated as that portrait is, it also has the essentials of universal human experience, and for that matter so has the boyish monologue "I Am a Fool." George Willard, the storyteller of *Winesburg, Ohio*, is still another portrait of an adolescent, one of the kind who leaves the Middle West and "dies with his boots on far from home."

Aside from the writing of his tales, Anderson did a great deal of writing for his two newspapers. In middle life he bought and wrote editorials for two small town newspapers, one supporting the Democratic party, the other the Republican. Was this to prove that he was nonpolitical? I think so. Although there was a measure of disillusioned idealism (which is a form of cynicism) in Anderson's makeup, the deeper fact was that he distrusted literal-minded, slogan-making political action. He sought out more enduring truths than those recited by political leaders. As a journalist he continued to observe the technological changes taking place in the United States, and, wherever he turned, the encroaching presence of the machine, machinelike thinking and machinelike feeling. What he saw raised problems that are with us now, today.

MR. MOORE: Thank you, Mr. Gregory. And now I think we are ready for questions.

Jackson: A student wants to know about the outbreak of talent in Hugh McVey in *Poor White*. The student asks if Mr. Gregory would comment on this: What were some of the forces that enabled the dead and unpolished creative ability in Hugh McVey to come alive?

MR. GREGORY: What Anderson was doing here was not being literal in any sense at all. The same question might be asked about the rise of Henry Ford. Of course, Hugh McVey was not educated at all. He was like hundreds of thousands of other Americans in his day who became inventors. This inventive streak, this interest in machinery is very American. This doesn't mean that Hugh McVey was an intellectual or really a scientist. I doubt that McVey was a real scientist at all. He was a very inventive man who had

great curiosity about machinery. This reminds me of something that I learned when I was at the University of Wisconsin. One of my classmates in mathematics was Charles A.
Lindbergh. Lindbergh was not a good mathematician, but
he was a wonderful machinist who spent all of his time
taking his motorcycle apart and putting it together again.

Morehouse: What are the influences that operated on
Anderson when he was in the formative years of his writing? I think you have mentioned the people whom he has
influenced. What are the influences on him, particularly in
American literature?

MR. GREGORY: In American literature the greatest influence on him were the writings of Mark Twain, but he was
also influenced by Herbert Spencer, by Robert Ingersoll, by
the scientists and orators of the day. And, of course, by
George Borrow the English novelist who wrote of gypsies,
who had a wonderful view of people from the earth up
which is so characteristic of Sherwood Anderson. Now, as
for Sherwood Anderson, there was remarkable *rhythm* in
his prose. The rhythm belonged to Sherwood Anderson
alone; this is something that he heard with his inner ear.

Stephens: Why does Anderson portray a man dread-
ing his poor white background? McVey makes the climb
from poverty economically and yet does not make it emotionally.

MR. GREGORY: That's a good question. What Anderson
is implying—Anderson is not so much interested in a success story. He's interested in a failure story too. Remember
the story of *The Egg* where the man was a failure? So here,
in the case of Hugh McVey, Anderson doesn't make a
completely successful hero out of Hugh McVey. As far as
Hugh McVey was concerned, although he was getting mate-
rially wealthy, his own life, his inner life, had great limitations which may be applied to the lives of many, many
Americans.

Tougaloo: Most of Anderson's characters are lonely, grotesque individuals, unfulfilled. Is this a comment on man's nature or on Midwestern society?

MR. GREGORY: Anderson's interest was always in the individual. Although he kept a broad eye open to the nature of the many human beings around him, he placed the predicament of the individual first. Let me go on a minute here to say Anderson was one who belonged to no political party, yet he held to a peculiar kind of socialism. However, his social ideas are very closely allied to a conception of himself as coming from the center of the United States, from the Middle West, as being a spokesman for all America because of this. He shares a great deal of the sense of largeness that many Middle Western writers have had. This was true of the Chicago group, those who passed through Chicago, Sherwood Anderson, Theodore Dreiser, Edgar Lee Masters, and Carl Sandburg. We also had a younger generation of Middle Western writers including T. S. Eliot from St. Louis, Missouri. Now Anderson not only thought of himself as a Middle Westerner, speaking for America, but as one who was speaking for the entire civilized world. These Middle Westerners were very egotistical. I'm one of them—I should know.

Drury: Mr. Gregory, in *Winesburg, Ohio* the selection of short stories that I read, I noticed two or three recurring scenes. One of the characters in the first selection, Wing Biddlebaum—he had actual experience with mob violence—has fear and, in the very next story, Dr. Parcival has this deep fear of mob violence—the mob is going to come and hang him. Then also Rev. Hartman has this problem with his interpretation of God; and also Jesse Bentley was mainly concerned with this search for God. Could you comment on this, please?

MR. GREGORY: I think whoever asked the question was doing some perceptive reading. Yes, there is Anderson's implied criticism of mob violence. Now, this may come from his reading of Mark Twain. You will remember that in

Huckleberry Finn there are several scenes of mob violence. Now then, from Twain we can move to William Faulkner, who through Anderson—you see I think that Anderson in this case is a transmission belt between Mark Twain and Faulkner—made memorable scenes of mob violence in America. Particularly in his novel *Intruder in the Dust* there is a brilliant portrayal of mob violence. Anderson, of course, was aware of its danger in our small, provincial centers where so little happens that people get bored. It is my belief that mob violence arises out of boredom—people who have very little to do, or have too much to do to find release for their emotions, sometimes break out into mob violence.

Morehouse: Is it clear that Anderson was influenced greatly by the Freudian revolution, particularly in his attitude toward sex? Does this explain the recurring scenes of bizarre sexuality in many of his stories?

MR. GREGORY: I think Anderson was affected by the Freudian revolution. I think many writers were. His story *The Man Who Became a Woman* was influenced by Freud. It was written about 1921 or so. Freud was being read in the twenties—not completely, not to the extent that he was ten years later. But I think that Anderson probably overheard conversation about him. I doubt if he read much Freud. At that time Freud was a name surrounded by rumors of what he had accomplished. However, there is another psychologist of whom Anderson probably knew a great deal, and that was Havelock Ellis, whose psychology of sex was known before 1921.

Morehouse: In *I'm a Fool* and in *Dark Laughter* and in *Hello Towns*, Anderson uses the Negro as a symbol of the authentic life—that is to say, of representing in contrast to the humanization, et cetera, certain reality principles. Would you care to comment on this assertion? the symbolic use of the Negro in Anderson's work?

MR. GREGORY: Yes, I think I can. I think it's the right

interpretation to say that Anderson considers the Negro a vitalizing yet ambiguous symbol in his writings. That was certainly true with *Dark Laughter*. In writing of the Negro, Anderson showed true courage. He was as ambivalent in his attitude toward the Negro, as the Negro is ambivalent toward the white man. I think that in this respect Anderson pointed the way to William Faulkner for the best in his stories about the Negro.

Morehouse: Would you say that Anderson is basically an optimist, considering the ending of *Poor White?*

MR. GREGORY: Yes, very definitely. I think that if you turn to the letters in my little *Portable Sherwood Anderson* you will see signs of that optimism there. This is where he took an opposite turn from, let us say, Theodore Dreiser. Theodore Dreiser for the most part was pretty gloomy. Anderson was comparatively cheerful. He felt that Americans go through a tremendous lot of trouble. His attitude was a little bit like that of Happy Hooligan—"Cheer up! The worst is yet to come!" But after the worst things might get a little bit better.

Langston: Mr. Gregory, will you explain the relation between religion and the acquisition of money when industrialism came in, in *Poor White?*

MR. GREGORY: I can't see any relationship between the acquisition of wealth and religion, but I can say this: that Anderson had a gloomy point of view about the danger of too much wealth too easily made in this country. To him something very dangerous was about to happen when people acquire too many material things. Now he felt—and I think that this is somewhat pointed out in his character of Hugh McVey—that wealth did not lead to happiness. Anderson himself made quite a bit of money at one time. He was a bit of a dandy—he liked fine clothes—but he was never a rich man, nor did he care for money. I doubt if his lack of concern for money had much to do with his religious beliefs. In general, he was an old-fashioned Dissenter. He was never a deeply religious writer.

Langston: Mr. Gregory, in your introduction, on page 25, you stated that it is strange to think of Anderson as a realist, as he was once classified. Under what school of philosophy would he be generally placed if not as a realist?

MR. GREGORY: You will find that answered in a letter of Anderson's in the Sherwood Anderson Portable. He dissociated himself from the realists. Notice his criticism of Sinclair Lewis. Anderson was critical of Sinclair Lewis because he felt that Lewis was too realistic, too literal-minded. Anderson is not. Let me try to make this a little bit clearer —Anderson tried many times to write an autobiography. Whenever he started to write an autobiography he wrote another work of fiction, which is something that very few writers really understand. They think they are writing their autobiographies but are actually writing fiction. In that sense Anderson was very much an antirealist. Also, Anderson was tremendously interested in the symbolic value of character. He would try very hard and he often succeeded in breaking through to a reality that is beyond mere factual realism.

Stephens: Mr. Gregory, would it be a correct assumption to say that Anderson resented the industrial revolution's rape of the small Midwestern towns, but at the same time he understood it as a part of the American tradition of progress?

MR. GREGORY: Anderson recognized the industrial revolution as part of the American development. He says very clearly—I forget just where, I think it's in another letter— that our loss in the changeover to an industrial life is a loss of individuality. Now, remember that Anderson was very fond of his grotesques, of his extraordinary American people, his exceptions to the many. He himself dressed as someone who was different. He looked like the artist that he was. Therefore, he felt that technological advances carried with them a loss of personality and distinction.

MR. MOORE: I think we ought to thank Mr. Gregory very much. It was a very lively session.

February 10, 1964

Arthur Mizener

on F. Scott Fitzgerald

Scott Fitzgerald was born in St. Paul, Minnesota, in 1896, of an Irish-American family. He died of a heart attack in Hollywood in 1940. His literary career had begun twenty years before with publication of his first novel, *This Side of Paradise* (1920), a glittering story of the new youth, much of the book reflecting Fitzgerald's experiences at Princeton. Launched as a successful author he married Zelda Sayre, whom he had met in Montgomery, Alabama, while serving as an army officer in World War I. The Fitzgeralds soon became public symbols of the glamorous twenties. Fitzgerald wanted to be a serious writer, but in order to keep up the fast pace at which he lived he had to force himself to write stories, some of them good and most of them merely slick, for the popular magazines. This work was collected in such volumes as *Tales of the Jazz Age* (1922), *All the Sad Young Men* (1926), and *Taps at Reveille* (1935). Meanwhile Fitzgerald wrote his two first-rate novels, *The Great Gatsby* (1925) and *Tender Is the Night* (1934). Both Fitzgerald and his wife collapsed under the strain of their existence; his own breakdown is described and analyzed candidly in *The Crack-Up* (1945), whose title piece was originally published serially in *Esquire*. When Fitzgerald died he had been working on a novel, *The Last Tycoon*, the existing parts of which were published in 1941 with his notes indicating how he had planned to complete the book. This novel, if finished, might have stood beside *The Great Gatsby*, that brilliant story of a magnificent fraud, and *Tender Is the Night*, that modern tragedy in which the man of great possibilities is self-destroyed. It is the latter novel, with its depth and complexities, which Arthur Mizener discusses in the following interview.

Arthur Mizener was born in Erie, Pennsylvania, in 1907, and this made him just old enough to witness parts of the life of those 1920's which F. Scott Fitzgerald celebrated. With no possible thought of a later connection, Mr. Mizener went

23

to Fitzgerald's university, Princeton, from which he received
his bachelor's and doctor's degrees, stopping meanwhile at
Harvard for an M.A. After teaching at Yale, Wells, and Carleton, he moved to Cornell University in 1951. Besides editing
two volumes of Fitzgerald's writings, *Afternoon of an Author*
(1957) and *The Fitzgerald Reader* (1963), Arthur Mizener
has published a collection of his own critical essays, *The
Sense of Life in the Modern Novel* (1964). His notable biography of Fitzgerald, *The Far Side of Paradise*, first published in 1951, reappeared in a revised edition in 1965.

MR. MIZENER: A few short years before Fitzgerald
died, in 1936, he said that he had at last given up the idea
by which he had lived his life. I don't believe that was true.
If he had, I think he would have had to allow himself to
wander through obscure American small towns for the rest
of his life the way Dick Diver does or perhaps simply to die
as Gatsby does. In any event, this dream by which he said
he had lived his life, he describes as the old dream of being
an entire man in the Goethe, Byron, Shaw tradition with an
opulent American touch, a sort of combination of J. P.
Morgan, Topham Beauclerc, and St. Francis of Assisi.

Being as American as all the rest of us, he was an idealist
who took this dream quite seriously; though some of the
time, as in this half-joking description, he could see that he
was extravagant and overly idealistic. Being an American,
too, he had a characteristic impatient insistence that the
ideal life he dreamed of should not be just a dream, but
should actually be lived in the world. That is, he was determined to make the dream real in his personal life. He was
also never contented to be a part of a society that did not
attempt to make its dream of an ideal social life actual too.

Any reader of Ftizgerald will, I think, notice that his
work, particularly his nonfiction but his fiction too, is filled
with vivid expressions of radical social ideas about American life. But these ideas never seem to be political in origin.
They were certainly never Marxist or radical in that way. I
think, actually, their source is his disappointment with
American society because it so often seems to be organized

to serve trivial, vulgar, clichéd, unimaginative ideals—
seems to have only what he called in *The Great Gatsby* "a
vast, vulgar, meretricious beauty." What I'm really trying
to say here is that I think Fitzgerald is a twentieth-century
transcendental radical; and that he cared as much about
society's being a realization of a great dream as he did
about making his personal life a realization of one.

Because he looked at America from this point of view, he
gradually developed throughout his career a subtle and, I
think, fascinating understanding of the relation between
wealth and imagination in American society. Any man like
him who wants to see the dream of a great life realized,
made actual, lived out in literal fact, would see, of course,
both the importance and the danger of wealth. It's obvious
that only the rich, successful people of the society have the
resources and the opportunities to make their individual
and collective life anything they want to make it. Only they
have the power to make their lives what Topham Beauclerc
and St. Francis of Assisi, or for that matter, Jay Gatsby or
Dick Diver, can imagine life as being. Slowly, then,
throughout a lifetime of observing them, Fitzgerald developed his subtle and fascinating understanding of the relation between the ability to make and hold great wealth in a
competitive society and the ability to imagine a great life:
between what you might call a talent for accumulation and
the gift of imagination.

The gift of imagination, what Fitzgerald calls in *The
Great Gatsby* "a heightened sensitivity to the promises of
life," he saw quite clearly was essential. Without it the great
life was impossible to conceive. But wealth is important too.
Not in and for itself, as vulgar power or mere crude display
or anything of that sort; but wealth alone makes it possible
for a man actually to live the life his imagination has
painted for him. The most famous of all anecdotes about
Fitzgerald concerns wealth. According to this anecdote,
Fitzgerald once said to Hemingway, "The rich are different
from you and me." And Hemingway answered, "Yes, they
have more money," which sounds like a snappy retort all
right, but which, in fact, shows just the kind of vulgarity
about wealth that most disturbed Fitzgerald. It may be

worth saying, parenthetically here, that this exchange of
remarks never really took place. Hemingway invented that
anecdote for a short story of his called *The Snows of Kilamanjaro*. But the big line of the story, Fitzgerald's remark
about the rich, was really written by him at the beginning of
one of his very best short stories, a story called *The Rich
Boy*. And of that sentence, Lionel Trilling once said, really
understanding it, as Hemingway did not, "for this remark
alone Fitzgerald was in Balzac's bosom in the heaven of all
novelists."

But for the rich who are distinguished from the rest of us
only by having more money and who do nothing at all with
their lives—for the rich, that is, who, as Fitzgerald put it in
The Great Gatsby, "drift here and there unrestfully wherever people played polo and were rich together"—for these
rich, Fitzgerald felt the kind of contempt that only the
disappointed idealist can feel, what he once called "the
smouldering hatred of the peasant." He hated such people
most when they were English with the unimaginative, brutal
arrogance of Lady Caroline Sibley-Biers in *Tender Is the
Night*. But he scorned them deeply too when they had the
dull, earnest, unimaginative arrogance of the untitled ducal
families of America, like the Buchanans of *The Great
Gatsby* and the Warrens of *Tender Is the Night*. Baby
Warren, with her impenetrable unawareness of what other
people are thinking and feeling, her unconscious arrogance
and assumption that whatever the Warrens want the Warrens can buy, including human beings, such as a doctor for
Nicole—this Baby Warren is a perfect example of the kind
of rich Fitzgerald despised, but he did not—this is crucially
important—he did not, as do so many social observers,
conclude that being rich made people inevitably like the
Warrens. He kept thinking of the possibility of people who
were sensitive, aware, considerate, imaginative and who
also were wealthy enough to use all these gifts in the fullest
possible way. Not that he did not see all the difficulties; no
one had a deeper sense of the psychological and social
complexity that exists for the truly sensitive rich—or a more
vivid image, as far as that goes, of the quality of life such
people might create around them. The whole opening sec-

tion of *Tender Is the Night*, I mean the opening section of
the novel in its original form, which for all the deepest and
most moving meanings of the novel is far the best form, the
whole of this opening section is written to show us how
people of great wealth, great imagination, and great self-
discipline can create a magnificent life.

As is fairly well known Fitzgerald had actually observed
this life. The little society that gathers on the beach of the
Riviera and dines with the Divers is modeled closely on the
group that actually lived there in the early twenties, around
the Gerald Murphys, to whom *Tender Is the Night* is dedicated. That dedication, if you remember, reads "To Gerald
and Sara Murphy." That remark, that dedication, referred
to an observation Picasso once made after visiting the Murphys when he said, "Wherever Sara is, there's always a
fête."

We see this beautiful life of the Divers through the eyes
of Rosemary Hoyt who had learned what personal creativity
is and, even more important, what self-discipline is from her
experience as an actress. But she is still young enough not
to understand what it costs to maintain these things all one's
life. Thus she is aware of all the beauty of the dinner party
at the Divers when "the table seemed to have risen a little
toward the sky like a mechanical dancing platform, giving
the people around it a sense of being alone with each other
in the dark universe." Then the Divers "began suddenly to
warm, and glow and expand, as if to make up to their guests
already so subtly assured of their importance, so flattered
with politeness, for anything they might still miss."

What we see in the first part of *Tender Is the Night* is the
ideal beauty of this life, the achieved perfection of this
civilization (in the highest sense of that word) because that
is all Rosemary Hoyt had the understanding to see. What
we do not see is the cost in emotional energy, in selflessness,
in self-discipline, because Rosemary is not experienced or
old enough to understand that. Thus, this is the ideal opening for a book that wishes to make us feel the value of the
fully imagined and completely civilized life. Nevertheless,
even here in this first part, behind the intelligence and the
controlled grace of the Divers that so dazzled Rosemary

Hoyt, are hints of the cost. Afterward when Rosemary asked
Dick Diver the time of day he said, "It's about half-past
one. It's not a bad time. It's not one of the worst times of
the day." For in fact Dick Diver has already begun to
exhaust his emotional and imaginative nature. He has been
carrying this world on his shoulders for six long years. Now
he is approaching emotional exhaustion exactly as he ap-
proaches literal physical exhaustion at the end of the book,
when he tries to lift a man on his shoulders on an aqua-
plane. "Did you hear I had gone into a process of deterioration?" he asks Rosemary. And when she denies it he says,
"It's true. The change came a long way back, but at first it
didn't show. The manner remains intact for some time after
the morale cracks."

The reasons the task is so exhausting are also there for us
to see in the book's first part if we only look. These are
reasons that are represented for us by individual characters.
But these characters are in turn carefully chosen to project
something about a civilization. Not just American civilization, but Western culture as a whole. Where else could so
representative a group of characters have been gathered as
on the Riviera? There's the American social climber of
another generation, Mama Abrams, "preserved," as
Fitzgerald says, "by imperviousness to experience and a
good digestion, into another generation." There is Luis
Campion, the Spaniard, letting his monocle drop into the
hair on his chest and saying to his friend, "Now, Royal,
don't be too ghastly for words." There is the American
McKisco who is writing a novel on the idea of *Ulysses*
which "takes a decayed old French aristocrat and puts him
in contrast with the mechanical age"; the McKiscos are
belligerently anxious to keep up with what they called
"what everybody intelligent knows." But McKisco is hope-
lessly defeated in his dinner-table argument by Tommy
Barban, the extremely sophisticated, anarchic, European
barbarian, who says with ruthless pleasantry, "I'm a soldier.
My business is to kill people." He does it very well. There,
finally, like a foreshadowing of what Dick Diver will become when his emotional energy is exhausted and his purpose in life gone, is Abe North, the brilliant musician who

has written nothing for seven years and who is always with great dignity quite drunk. Abe North is, incidentally, modeled after Fitzgerald's close friend, Ring Lardner. "I used to think until you're eighteen nothing matters," his wife says at one point. "That's right," Abe agrees, "and afterwards it's the same way." There, finally, is Nicole Diver's sister, Baby Warren, who concentrates in herself all the Warren arrogance and imperception. These are the rich from all parts of the Western world, representing all the characteristic types the West has produced, free to do anything they choose, and they choose to honor lack of moral imagination until they reduce all but the perverted and the stupid to despair.

These are the people who are gathered about the Divers. They are, by the heroic trick of the heart that Dick Diver works over and over again, lifted up as if by magic to something beautiful. "It was themselves," Fitzgerald says, "[Dick] gave back to them, blurred by the compromises of how many years."

But Fitzgerald does not leave to implication what this all means for the society as a whole. He tells us directly what has happened to Western civilization by showing us a scene of the battlefield of the First World War and by letting us listen to Dick Diver talk about that war. Dick says, "See that little stream; we could walk to it in two minutes. It took the British a month to walk to it—a whole empire walking very slowly, dying in front and pushing forward behind. And another empire walked very slowly backwards a few inches a day, leaving the dead like a million bloody rugs. No Europeans will ever do that again in this generation. . . . This kind of battle was invented by Lewis Carroll and Jules Verne and whoever wrote *Undine*, and country deacons bowling and marraines in Marseilles and girls seduced in the back lanes of Wurtemburg and Westphalia. . . . Why, this was a love battle—there was a century of middle-class love spent here."

This is a society that has spent its emotional capital and is living off borrowed energy—the inherited recollection of the honor the courtesy, the courage of the previous age; keeping, as Dick says about himself, the manner intact for a little while after the morale has cracked.

A little later in the novel, Dick sees a group of elderly American women in a restaurant, a group of Gold Star mothers who have come over to visit the graves of their dead sons. Watching them, Fitzgerald says, "he perceived all the old maturity of an older America. They made the room beautiful, and almost with an effort he turned back to his two women, [that is, to Rosemary and Nicole] at the table, and faced the whole new world in which he believed." A little later again, at Gstaad, Dick, according to Fitzgerald, "relaxed and pretended that the world was all put together again by the gray-haired men of the golden nineties," and "for a moment . . . he felt they were in a ship with a landfall just ahead."

In moments like this Dick Diver remembers his father, an impoverished, beautifully mannered southerner who, above all, "had been sure of what he was," as Dick never has been. As the society of which Dick was a part had exhausted the accumulated energy of its culture in the First World War, so Dick was using up the emotional energy, the expenditure of which gives meaning to his life and a reason for his exercise of self-discipline and his powers of bringing out all that is best in the people around him.

Ultimately, Dick cracks up, to use the word Fitzgerald himself used when he came to describe his own personal experience with this kind of disease. Dick suffered what Fitzgerald called in *Tender Is the Night* a lesion of vitality. He had, as Fitzgerald puts it, "lost himself—he could not tell the hour when, or the day or the week, the month or the year. . . . between the time he found Nicole flowering under a stone on the Zurichsee and the moment of his meeting with Rosemary the spear had been blunted."

This crack-up first shows as little fissures. Dick notices a pretty, but insignificant girl at Gstaad and plays to her. He is appealed to in a random way by an unknown woman at Innsbruck; he lets his heretofore submerged unconscious judgments of the people around him come to the surface in bitterness, as when he says to Mary North, "You've gotten so damn dull, Mary." He does that because he is now drinking in an uncontrolled way. There are still occasional flashes of his old will to exercise his charm on people so that they become their best selves. One comes the last time he sees Rosemary on the beach; another comes when he talks for a last time there to Mary North; but he can't keep it up. "The old interior laughter," as the book says, "had begun inside him and he knew he couldn't keep it up much longer."

The greatest of all Dick's efforts to remake people into their best selves has been his struggle with Nicole. After six years, just about as he has exhausted himself, she is cured of her schizophrenia. Becoming whole again she becomes a more intelligent version of her sister, a Warren "who welcomed the anarchy of her lover," Tommy Barban, who can, when she chooses, speak in her grandfather's voice, slowly, distinctly, insultingly. The one thing Dick Diver can save from the wreckage of his own exhaustion is, he believes, Nicole. All that remains—now she is well—is to free her from her dependence on him. By a supreme effort of will, as he sits quietly on the terrace of their house, he drives her from him. When she finally walked away, a free woman, "Dick waited until she was out of sight. Then he leaned his head forward on the parapet. The case was finished. Dr. Diver was at liberty."

This is, I think, very beautiful. We remember that Baby Warren's idea had originally been to *buy* a doctor for Nicole until Nicole got well again. Dick had laughed helplessly at that idea originally, seeing everything that was going on in Baby's mind and knowing she would never see anything of what was going on in his. Twice during the engagement only his deep love for Nicole keeps him from throwing the marriage in Baby's face, as Fitzgerald says. But now at the end, Baby and her world have won. Dick's epitaph is pronounced by Baby Warren when Nicole says, "Dick was a good husband to me for six years. . . . He always did his best and never let anything hurt me." Baby sticks her jaw out in good arrogant Warren style and says, "That's what he was educated for."

Thus the hard, brutal, anarchic world of the unimaginative rich has won and the representative of the good life, of awareness, of kindness, of understanding, has been set adrift to wander like a ghost of his former brilliant self through the little towns of upstate New York, from one of which I am addressing you at this moment. "In any case," as the last sentence of the book says, "he is almost certainly in that section of the country, in one town or another," as are perhaps all the heroes of transcendentalist American idealists. *Tender Is the Night* is a book filled with despair because Fitzgerald begins it with such a high ideal of what the American individual and American society might be if they'd only take full advantage of their opportunities.

Thank you.

MR. MOORE: Thank you, Mr. Mizener. You've really illuminated the book and Scott Fitzgerald for us. Now we are ready for our question period. Morehouse, can you come in with a question, please.

Morehouse: The first question is: What are the major influences upon Fitzgerald's style and method of writing? What influences from American and European writers?

MR. MIZENER: Gracious, that's a large order. Well, I'll do what I can with that. To tell you the truth, I believe Fitzgerald's style was largely self-developed. As a boy he read very, very widely in not-very-good literature. I suppose the only good writer, as far as the record shows, that Fitzgerald read at all intensively when he was young was Thackeray. And it is quite amusing to see the number of references to various things of Thackeray that there are in his work, but I think, perhaps, we would all agree that Fitzgerald's style is not exactly modeled on Thackeray's. While he was in college he read very widely in the authors who were fashionable at that time. He read Henry James; he read Conrad; he read above all H. G. Wells; he reviewed H. G. Wells two or three times for the Princeton undergraduate magazine. He also read some writers not of that class. In the last years he was in college and when he got out—just after he got out—he read people like James Branch Cabell. He read the popular poets of the time; he was particularly interested in Rupert Brooke, from whom he took the title of

This Side of Paradise. He once said that John Peale Bishop taught him really to understand poetry and did it by talking about Keats to him. And again we know that Keats had considerable influence on him because *Tender Is the Night* is a title which comes from a Keats's poem. All these were no doubt stylistic influences on him in one way or another but I don't believe that that influence is very direct or immediate.

The only place I think you find a direct echo of another man's style in Fitzgerald is in those passages in *The Beautiful and Damned* where he's clearly trying to write like H. L. Mencken and in the general tone of the narrator's voice in *The Great Gatsby* where the influence of Conrad shows quite clearly. Edmund Wilson has said that just before Fitzgerald wrote *The Great Gatsby* he persuaded Fitzgerald to reread Conrad and I think it's probable that the voice of Conrad is very sharply in Fitzgerald's style. He once did say that he found it very tempting, after Hemingway had become a close friend of his, to imitate Hemingway, but he felt that he had wholly resisted that influence; and I think with the exception of the conclusion of the story called "Rich Boy," which is very Hemingwayesque indeed, he did resist that influence. Does that really answer the question?

Morehouse: Yes, it was the kind of thing we have been discussing. Thank you very much.

MR. MOORE: Now it's the turn of Langston University.

Langston: I would first like to make a statement, then direct a question to Mr. Mizener concerning the character Nicole. In a short review of *Tender Is the Night* on page 142 of *Good Reading,* it is stated that Nicole discovered she no longer needed Dick. Is it more likely that her real reason for leaving her husband was her self-conscious desire to be free from all that bound her to the past?

MR. MIZENER: I don't believe so. Nicole is represented in the novel as suffering from schizophrenia and the implication is, or the clearly stated idea about her is, that she is

whole and complete—well again—not any longer schizoid at
the end of the novel. I think the implication is that she then
becomes what she was before she had become ill, a rather
more intelligent, aware, and sensitive version of her sister,
Baby Warren. She's a member of the Warren family. And
that girl is the kind of girl who wants to marry somebody
like Tommy Barban, not to marry somebody like Dick
Diver, who is really the husband of the sick Nicole and is no
longer suited to her when she gets well. I suppose if you
want to say that that means she wanted to get rid of her past
and start afresh, yes, you're right.

Stephens: On page 314 of the novel Mary North tells
Dick Diver that everybody loves him. Is the constant human
distortion of love the tragic flaw of Dick and of modern
society?

MR. MIZENER: No, I don't believe so. You will remember that there are a good many references to the question of
Dick's loving people and being loved by them. Indeed, I
think there's some suggestion in this novel that one of the
weaknesses of Dick's character is a desire to *be* loved. He
wants people at least to be fond of him and to admire him. I
think that's the purpose of that final scene when he goes out
to help Lady Caroline Sibley-Biers and Mary North when
they get in trouble with the police. He doesn't really care for
those two people, he doesn't respect them, he doesn't admire
them; but they call on him for help and he helps. Fitzgerald
wrote other stories on this subject and I think he felt that
this was a part of Dick's desire to make people better, to try
to improve them. He always went out to them and made
them happy, or he tried to. I think Fitzgerald thought that
was a weakness. It's perhaps a good weakness like Christian
mercy which will always get you in trouble and is a weakness from that point of view but is a virtue too. I do not
think Fitzgerald had any notion about modern society suffering because love is distorted in it. I think the point of
this novel is that love is defeated in it. It succeeds for the
moment when the Divers' way of life really works and then
it collapses when Dick's ability to carry on and make people

happy dies out.

Tougaloo: The only person who seems to stay stable throughout the novel is Tommy Barban. Would you say that this seems true because he is the only one who has really decided what he wants out of life?

MR. MIZENER: That's a very nice observation I think, absolutely true. He is the only man who does stay stable throughout the novel. Not only stable, but ready to meet any objection to his point of view successfully and with perfect confidence. My own inclination would be just to qualify that observation to this extent: Tommy does know exactly what he wants to do. Moreover, he succeeds in doing it. Perhaps one can say he succeeds in doing it because it's a fairly simple objective, but nonetheless it's an objective that satisfies him. I think we are to believe that Abe North, in part, knew what he wanted to do and came gradually to feel that he had destroyed himself in the process of doing it. I think what I would say here is that Tommy Barban took a very limited objective and succeeded in fulfilling it to his own satisfaction and therefore was stable and happy. Dick and Abe North are both people who took extremely idealistic objectives which were too much for any human being to fulfill and went to pieces when they couldn't fulfill them. You remember Dick Diver says, "Good men live close to the line and some of them can't stand it and they just quit"? That is, of course, what Abe and Dick, in fact, do. But I think that's a very shrewd observation on the novel.

Drury: Mr. Mizener, in your book *The Sense of Life* you comment on the lack of wholeness in this novel—that it's a group of brilliantly conceived parts. And then you said that they have the nominal unity of being events in Dick Diver's life, but that there's an incoherence that results from our not knowing, and the fact that Fitzgerald did not know either, what meaning Dick Diver's life had. Now, in the light of what you said this morning, it seemed to me that you put a great deal of meaning into it, and I just wondered if you could comment more on that. Do you really mean by this that Fitzgerald never gave up his ideals and that Dick never gives up his ideals in spite of what happens in both cases?

MR. MIZENER: It's a very mean trick of you, of course, to have gotten so far ahead of me that you've actually read *The Sense of Life* and could put me on the spot this way. Let me answer the first part of that question first because it's the easiest to answer. Fitzgerald himself said about this book in a letter to Max Perkins that he wished he hadn't had to write the last third of the book "on the bottle," as he put it, because he said "one can keep the details of the passage he is writing clearly in mind even when he's had a good deal to drink, but one cannot keep the whole book in mind." It's that sense in which I think the book tends to break apart. The parts are completely integrated in themselves and their general relation to the sense of the book is clear enough, but they aren't integrated as tightly as are the parts of what I think is a somewhat lesser book, philosophically speaking, *The Great Gatsby*. That's what I meant about the book being somewhat loosely hung together.

As far as Dick Diver's character is concerned, I think we can see—and that is what I was trying to describe today—in general what happens to Dick Diver—how his emotional energy became exhausted and he was simply incapable of living anymore up to the ideals which he set himself. But exactly what the mechanism of that process is, exactly what is going on in Dick's mind at the end of the novel, exactly how he felt about things and how he lived in those last years when he wandered around upstate New York, this we do not know.

Now, I think that was, in a sense, calculated on Fitzgerald's part. He once said about his book, "I suppose the first person who read *Hamlet* said about Hamlet, 'He's a nut, isn't he? He doesn't make any sense.'" And then in his characteristic way Fitzgerald added, "We can always find excuses in Shakespeare." Also at one time—quoting Gertrude Stein's remark that Ernest Hemingway's novels were headed straight for the museum—Fitzgerald commented, and this is an important point, that one simply must not be too clear in an explanatory way in a novel. One must keep the novel dramatic, leave things to implication. I believe he thought he was doing that about Dick Diver's character, and I think he's left us with a character that we can understand up to a point, who is absolutely fascinating as far as we do understand him, and who nonetheless leaves questions in our minds as to his profoundest attitudes and feelings. In that respect, without making any comparisons in greatness between them, I think Dick Diver is like Hamlet. I wish you hadn't asked me that question!

Jackson: One student wants to pursue the idea of Tommy Barban. It seems to him that at times Tommy Barban does not fit into this social group and he wonders whether the author had a special reason for portraying Barban as a little outside of the group.

MR. MIZENER: Yes, I think he had two reasons. One of which is perhaps incidental but interesting. Tommy Barban is modeled on a real man with whom, in fact, Zelda Fitzgerald was very intimate during the period the Fitzgeralds were living on the Riviera, and certain qualities of Tommy Barban are, I think, perhaps emphasized more than they otherwise would be in the novel because they belong to the actual man. The other thing is that Fitzgerald wanted somewhere in this novel—and I think it's a brilliant observation, at least I feel it is because this is the kind of character whom I myself recognized immediately as a European, whom I had never thought about before until Fitzgerald described him—he wanted, that is to say, the really ancient, hard-bitten, cynical kind of character who has descended into modern Europe. That kind of person is really isolated from the modern humanitarian world, I believe—that is, the world of both European socialism and American democracy. Tommy Barban is something that sort of jumped from the Renaissance or the early seventeenth century right into the present time with no influence from the intervening years. He is like Sigismundo Malatesta the great hero of Ezra Pound's *Cantos,* the medieval soldier who could be bought by anybody, who was just a professional fighter. I think he's a fascinating character in the novel and also he does represent something that exists in contemporary Western civilization.

MR. MOORE: Thank you. These questions have been so sharp and good today and the answers so full and rich that I think we're all terribly sorry we won't have time for another round. But our time is running out and I think the most we can do now is all express gratitude to Mr. Mizener for the very brilliant session and thank all of you.

MR. MIZENER: Thank you, Harry.

February 17, 1964

Carvel Collins

on William Faulkner

William Faulkner was born in New Albany, Mississippi, in 1897 and died in Oxford, Mississippi, in 1962. As a young man William Falkner (as the family name was then spelled) attended the University of Mississippi without taking a degree. He enlisted in the Royal Air Force in Canada during World War I, but was not sent overseas. His first published volume was poetry, *The Marble Faun* (1924), and his first novel was *Soldier's Pay* (1926). Many critics regard his fourth and fifth novels, *The Sound and the Fury* (1929) and *As I Lay Dying* (1930), among the finest of his works, along with *Light in August* (1932), *Absalom, Absalom!* (1936), and *Go Down, Moses* (1942). In these imaginative projections of the Deep South, Faulkner displays the general qualities as well as the particular motivations of a man creating a special literary universe. But Faulkner's countrymen were slow in appreciating him; his fellow writers in France were the first to recognize his greatness. In the United States his books were all out of print by 1946, yet only three years later he won the Nobel Prize and became one of the most celebrated of modern writers. To find one book that would introduce him representatively in the present series was difficult; we wanted to deal with various aspects—his characteristic "dark" side, his humor, his use of the past, and his sense of affirmation—as well as to present examples of his writing style. We finally selected a volume which contains two of his finest long stories, "The Bear" and "Spotted Horses," along with a somewhat less successful though not altogether ineffective tale, "Old Man." These stories and other writings of Faulkner are discussed by Carvel Collins, professor of English at Notre Dame, a leading authority on Faulkner. He has written much about this author and has edited *William Faulkner's New Orleans Sketches* (1958), *Faulkner's University Pieces* (1961), and *William Faulkner: Early Poetry and Prose* (1962), as well as *Sam Ward in the Gold Rush* (1949). Mr. Collins, who was born in West Union, Ohio, in 1912, attended Miami University, and received the M.A. and Ph.D. degrees from the University of Chicago. He has taught at Colorado State College, Stephens College, Swarthmore, Harvard, and the Massachusetts Institute of Technology. Besides the books he has edited, Mr. Collins has appeared (with Archibald MacLeish, John Mason Brown and others) in *Literature and the Modern World* (George Peabody College, 1954) and is the author of the *American Sporting Gallery* (Harvard, 1949). Mr. Collins is currently writing a full-scale biography of Faulkner.

MR. MOORE: The wire is yours, Dr. Collins.

MR. COLLINS: Fine. The three pieces which have been assigned to you in the Modern Library paperback are actually parts of three novels. The most famous of these pieces probably is "The Bear." Because twenty minutes is not very long I would like to talk a little about it and hope that matters concerning the other two pieces will come out in your question period.

"The Bear" is part of a book which was originally called *Go Down, Moses and Other Stories.* But in later editions the words "and Other Stories" were dropped from the title. I have seen a letter by William Faulkner in which he said that *Go Down, Moses* is a novel and that it should be treated as a novel. Faulkner was, like most geniuses, an experimenter, unwilling just to repeat successes—in almost all of his novels he tried for new form. "The Bear" is a chapter in a novel of a rather unusual sort.

"Old Man," another of the three assigned pieces, is also part of a novel, one titled *The Wild Palms.* Here Faulkner used another structure, an interlocking one consisting of regular alternations between sections of a story called "Wild Palms" and a story called "Old Man."

The third assigned piece, "Spotted Horses," is part of the novel, *The Hamlet,* which is organized in still a different way. Though *The Hamlet* is not made up of what at first glance appear to be separate stories like *Go Down, Moses,* or of two seemingly separate stories like *The Wild Palms,* it has struck some critics as too loosely arranged and too anecdotal to be considered a unified novel. But a closer look at the book shows that it is unified.

Now, "The Bear" because of its quality and partly because of that early form of the title of *Go Down, Moses* has been regarded as a separate story and fair game for voluminous discussion apart from the chapters of *Go Down, Moses* which surround it. In fact, it possibly has been written about more frequently than any other work by Faulkner. For purposes of our discussion today I will try to talk about it as the separate story which it is not.

I think that a major problem about the criticism of William Faulkner is that for many years there was a tradition of disrespect for his control as an artist. It started early when a leading critic said, in effect, that Faulkner had speed but no control. Ernest Hemingway once said that he thought Faulkner was the best of them all but wasted himself and that Hemingway would have been content just to have been Faulkner's manager, thus fostering or at least illustrating the impression that Faulkner lacked control. One well-known critic some years ago made the remark, surprising to us in view of the understanding we now have of the organizing genius Faulkner displays in such novels as *The Sound and the Fury* and *Absalom, Absalom!,* that Faulkner was all right in the short story form, being able to sustain unity for that long, but that he was incapable of sustaining unity through the greater length of a novel.

With the rise of the appreciation of Faulkner in recent years this opinion is no longer so widely held. But some critics still reveal the opinion that they are somehow superior to Faulkner because they can see that he did not know what he was doing in many of his works, including "The Bear." In discussing "The Bear" they reveal this opinion most frequently when they speak of the fourth of the five numbered parts. I would like to object strenuously to the view that Faulkner in "The Bear" did not know what he was doing and therefore did not make all five parts fit together as a unified work of art.

Sometimes Faulkner did write poor books or rather books much inferior to his best. *Requiem for a Nun*, for example, though it has good sections, is not a good novel as a whole. "Spotted Horses," as a section of *The Hamlet*, reminds me that though *The Hamlet* itself is a good novel the other two later parts of its trilogy, *The Town* and *The Mansion*, are not very good. So I am not sitting here telling you on the telephone that Faulkner never made mistakes, that the critics cannot castigate him for failures. He was an artist who took great chances and sometimes had failures, but his successes were magnificent.

Does "The Bear," in its fourth part, contain one of Faulkner's failures? Did Faulkner himself think so when he permitted his publishers to omit the fourth part when they reprinted "The Bear" in a book of hunting stories titled *Big Woods?* And is the critic right who says in an article which *College English* published within the past year that because the fourth part of "The Bear" is difficult and defective he has decided "The Bear" really just consists only of its other parts? I would think the answer to these questions is No. Faulkner allowed his late editor, Saxe Commins, to omit the fourth part in the *Big Woods* volume in order to keep the book at a more popular level, not too far above that of such hunting magazines as *Field and Stream;* and if one starts the elimination of the original unity of *Go Down, Moses* by pulling out from it "The Bear," I suppose one should not subsequently be too squeamish about pulling out one or more parts of "The Bear" itself. Besides, Faulkner, like a large number of writers of the first rank, was little concerned, once he had finished a work, with what was done to it by others, whether anthology editors or movie makers. As for the *College English* article which makes for us the decision that in writing *Go Down, Moses* Faulkner did not really take seriously the fourth part of "The Bear," I am ashamed I even brought it up.

That is, I think, not the way to look at it, and I would like to say what I think is one way to look at it. "The Bear," as everybody by now is saying, gives an account of the initiation of the young boy into manhood. We first see Ike McCaslin, the boy, not experienced with the annual hunt in the big woods; then he is allowed to accompany the men. In parts one, two, and three he learns from Sam Fathers, his significantly named hunting mentor, to be competent and to have not only skill but dignity and perception.

And then in part four we see the life, not in the woods but on the plowed land of the plantation. We see—as Faulkner presents it—a very defective life because some of the people owning the plantation have exploited the land and exploited other human beings, mainly their slaves. In the fifth part, we come back to the woods at an earlier stage than we had reached in the fourth (in which we even had seen glimpses of Ike McCaslin as an old man). In this very brief fifth section we see Ike having as a youth an experience which is mystical and even religious, though not in the way of organized churches. This experience is at a clearing in the woods which, much earlier, the author has said is on the dividing line between the plowed land and the primitive woods. If we count the pages, we find that parts one, two, and three are roughly, let's say, about the same length as part four. So by the time we read in the fifth part about this experience of Ike on the border between the woods and the cultivated land we have read the account of Ike in the woods in the first three parts and we have read in the fourth part an account of the plantation life of Ike's ancestors. Now, in the fifth part, we have a significant scene at the meeting line of these two areas, a scene in which Ike, one might say, pulls himself together.

Up to the time of writing "The Bear" in *Go Down, Moses* Faulkner had produced a number of characters who, like Ike McCaslin, are, in a sense, quite psychologically autobiographical. There was Quentin Compson in *The Sound and the Fury* and earlier than that, Bayard Sartoris in *Sartoris,* and there were others. They all destroyed themselves. They had found no guide to life and so committed suicide in one way or another. Both Bayard Sartoris and Quentin Compson looked at the aristocracy of the cultivated plantations and their descendants and found that of its characteristics which are here most significant one is good and one is bad. The good characteristic is self-consciousness, a belief in a certain code of behavior, a

perception about certain aspects of life. The bad characteristic is self-destructiveness. These are the characteristics of
the elder Compson, the father, the owner of the remnants of
the Compson mile of plantation in *The Sound and the Fury*.
He is terribly aware but he destroys himself by alcohol.

Quentin and Bayard turn from their aristocratic heritage
to examine people who are without the aristocrats' economic, social, and political power, people who live more
simply and anonymously and closer to the earth. But in
these people also Quentin and Bayard find two characteristics in contrast, one good and one bad. A good characteristic of these people far removed from the power and education and exploiting opportunities of the so-called aristocrats
is their endurance, which Faulkner obviously admires. But
the earlier novels and stories show that these enduring
people close to the soil lack the particular awareness which
Faulkner seems to admire in certain aristocrats. So such
Faulknerian seekers as Quentin and Bayard, having found
no answer to their questions about how to live, kill themselves.

But Ike McCaslin in "The Bear" does not kill himself. No
matter how limited and defective his adult life is later
shown to be, in subsequent chapters of *Go Down, Moses*, he
somehow does survive as the psychologically autobiographical characters in Faulkner's earlier fiction did not. A major
cause of Ike's difference is pointed up for us in the scene
which concludes "The Bear": at the clearing which the
author has gone out of his way to tell us is on the dividing
line between the plowed land and the primitive woods Ike
somehow made a partial amalgam of his training in the
woods under Sam Fathers and his aristocratic heritage from
the plantation life by rejecting the bad characteristic of
each and keeping the good characteristic of each. Ike has
found endurance in the primitive woods and his training
there, and he keeps the conscious concern which is the best
characteristic of such plantation people as his father and
uncle who, however inadequately, did what they could to
reduce the terrible wrong of slavery. He joins these together
in the final scene at the grave site and receives then the even
greater feeling of unity: that nature and the universe are

one; in short, he has a basic mystical experience.

Now this fifth section has little meaning if you throw out section four. The critic may want to see parts one, two, and three of "The Bear" as a separate account of hunting—and they are magnificent as such—but they are not the story, and a fine hunting account was not what Faulkner was writing. It is important to think of "The Bear" as a unity, a unity centered around the growing up of the young man. And for us to understand that growing up, the young man's plantation heritage—presented in the fourth part—is essential.

It is also important to think of "The Bear" as a chapter in the novel called *Go Down, Moses,* and that would take far more than another twenty minutes; but *Go Down, Moses* is a gigantic refutation of a conception which is too widely spread—that William Faulkner was hostile to integration. *Go Down, Moses,* viewed as a novel, is a moving presentation of the injustice of slavery and segregation and the unwisdom not only of slavery but of the whole idea of possession—not just possession of other men, but possession of the land. It starts with Ike McCaslin's grandfather and ends with descendants of that man's two families, one from his wife which goes down in a white line of descent and the other from one of his slaves who bore him a child. He carried his inhumanity not only into slavery but into further exploitation: he incestuously begot a child by his own slave daughter and started a predominately disinherited line which goes down the other side of the genealogical chart of this fine novel. The two lines of the chart meet in the end with the union of the descendants of both lines; and Ike McCaslin is somewhere in the middle, troubled by the great injustice which has been done and, unfortunately, powerless in the face of it.

I should like to say now in closing, before you ask what I hope is a great number of questions, that "The Bear," viewed as a separate story, seems rather optimistic at the end because Ike has won through so much. Compared with the earlier novels where the heroes—the protagonists who seem to me to be psychologically autobiographical—do not win through to anything but suicide, Ike's joining together in himself of the two good qualities of the woods and the plantation is admirable. If we vote for life over death, we certainly think it is a great thing for him to survive. But Faulkner is much more perceptive about this than we might think. Optimism is not easy to acquire, and "Delta Autumn," the chapter of *Go Down, Moses* which immediately follows "The Bear," shows that the snake near the grave mound at the end of "The Bear," which looks at Ike and turns away, is not doing what some of the critics think when they say that the snake, who is identified with ancient evil, turns away from Ike because he is pure and incorruptible and impossible to combat. Actually, it is more likely the snake sees that Ike is still tainted with evil; and when Ike calls the snake "grandfather," as he had heard Sam Fathers call a ghostly deer in an earlier chapter of the novel, we get an awareness that Ike, in spite of his winning through to survival rather than suicide, is still a descendant of his grandfather whose disregard for human beings began the recorded story of Ike's family. And in "Delta Autumn," when Ike is put to the test, he does behave, after all, as the descendant of his grandfather.

Go Down, Moses shows the size of the problem, how ingrained it is; but overwhelmingly it shows—in "The Bear" but mostly in the other chapters—the gigantic injustice about which Faulkner was not only well-informed but very much concerned. "The Bear" is a complex work in which the complexity is part of our reward; it is not difficult just to be difficult. Out of it comes a subtlety, and the subtlety is increased when we read it with all the other chapters of *Go Down, Moses* in which it is embedded.

Now, please, to your questions.

MR. MOORE: Thank you very much. That was a very illuminating presentation, and I think our students will want to read all of *Go Down, Moses* as well as a great many other works of Faulkner. Now let's take the questions in order. We'll take one from each school and then try to get back for more in rotation. The first one today is from Langston University.

Langston: In "Old Man" is the river used as a symbol
of violence to show how modern man has to contend with
the pressures of society that he neither understands nor
is able to cope with successfully?

MR. COLLINS: Well, "Old Man" is, as I said briefly a
moment ago, half of a novel called *The Wild Palms,* and
there is no question whatever that Faulkner meant the
halves to be meaningfully interlocked. The second chapter
of the whole novel called *The Wild Palms* is the first chapter
of what you have read here under the title "Old Man." I
think Faulkner is trying in the two narratives to show the
behavior of people at a very low level of so-called civilization in "Old Man" and at a higher level in "Wild Palms."
To speak directly to your question: I do not think the river
in flood—when we consider all the rest of the novel—is a
symbol of the violence of the pressures of society. I think
the river represents natural forces. In the other half of the
novel, in which the more educated people are trying to work
out their lives, I believe they are shown combating natural
forces in another way. I do not think that *The Wild Palms*
on the whole is an attack on the society which surrounds us.

MR. MOORE: Thank you. Now may we have a question
from Stephens College?

MR. MADDEN: Yes. Before we ask our question we
should give greetings to Dr. Collins. He was formerly a
member of the faculty here.

MR. COLLINS: This is just like old times.

MR. MADDEN: Yes, it is like old times. A number of
people around here send their greetings—Dr. Louise Dudley
is among them, Mrs. Haigh and others who remember your
time here.

MR. COLLINS: My regards to them.

MR. MADDEN: We have a question from a student who

comes from your part of the country.

Stephens: Does the death or fall of Old Ben and his counterpart Sam Fathers symbolically assume that this primitive element in our society is isolated and inevitably doomed?

MR. COLLINS: Well! Certainly the author has done a very good job in handling many aspects of the primitive. For one thing, Sam Fathers' life is mysteriously tied up with the life of the great bear, Ben, as you clearly suggest. When Ben is killed by Boon Hogganbeck, who is part Indian, using a knife rather than the less primitive rifle, Sam Fathers drops to the ground also. He is completely incapacitated and never does return to normal life; and it is quite likely that later Boon does him the loyal, primitive service of putting him out of his misery. Another primitive thing is shown to be dying at this time also: the big woods, which before the end of the story is sold to timbermen who begin cutting it down. Some critics, possibly influenced by lingering remnants of the historian Frederick Jackson Turner's theory about the frontier's importance in American history, seem to feel that this loss of the primitive bear, hunter, and woods is the main theme of the story. It is a great theme and magnificently presented, but it does not seem to me to be the main one. That, to me, is in "The Bear," the growth of the boy, Ike. And in the novel *Go Down, Moses* the main theme, to me, is man's exploitation of his fellowman and of the earth. Of course, the loss of these three symbols of the primitive is one with and vital to those more major themes. But I think Faulkner, much as he admired the big woods and its life, was no romantic, unquestioning disciple of Rousseau. He shows in his works that the primitive has faults as well as virtues. He also shows that within ourselves we still retain enough of the primitive to study even though the old bear, the old hunter, and the big woods are gone.

Tougaloo: We have a number of questions about style and I'm taking one typical one. What is the aesthetic function of the excessively long and involuted sentences in the work of Faulkner?

MR. COLLINS: "The Bear" itself is often spoken of as containing one of the longest sentences in literature, but if you look closely at it and other sentences in Faulkner you will find that often they actually are broken up into rather conventional segments and are not so terribly difficult to read. When there is difficulty in "The Bear" the difficulty seems to me profitable. For example, there is a place where we have trouble about the pronouns: we think a particular man is being called he. After we have gone along for a little way thinking that we are reading about that particular man we suddenly find that the pronoun has been referring to somebody else. If we take a very superficial look at this, a very academic one, we can ask why Faulkner, who knew he was referring to a different man, did not tell us so. In this instance, I think, he did not tell us because he wanted us to see the rather remarkable similarity between the two men, and to see it in a creative way rather than just to see it because he told us.

One of the functions of this method is to get the reader to become a participant. Many earlier writers of fiction more often seem to have tried to keep the reader even with the writer by giving him pieces of information like building blocks up which he can easily climb. Many serious twentieth-century writers seem more frequently to have accepted the fact that they may choose to write for a more select and competent audience—possibly, for one reason, because superficial entertainment certainly is being taken care of now by other means. So the modern author of great talent seems to feel free to deal with readers on the assumption that they are capable, in a sense, of being his partners.

The involutions of Faulkner's style and form in some of his poorer books are open to the charge of being excessively difficult. But when he is making the whole thing work well, as in "The Bear" and *Go Down, Moses,* what we might call his difficulties are really his devices for making the reader join him as an active partner in discovery. To withhold information, which Faulkner does both in big ways and in small ways by certain sentences, makes the reader participate more closely; and if he is a good reader he comes out with greater profit.

Another so-called difficulty in Faulkner arises because, in common with many writers of recent decades, he is greatly concerned with time. Often Faulkner holds something in abeyance, letting us have an idea, sense the essence of an event, and then in a parenthesis shows us a parallel event going on at the same time or earlier or later. We see the significance of the new while holding in our minds the original event; then the parenthesis ends and we come back to the first event better aware of its significance.

I think many earlier authors more nearly felt that they had answers, which they were telling the reader. In the twentieth century we, authors included, seem much less certain about answers. So more than ever a function of a major author in our time may be to ask significant questions. These authors, in a sense, are like ourselves, only much more perceptive and competent. We view them as leaders with whom we walk shoulder to shoulder—or, rather, a step or two behind—and we are to work out things with them in these difficult novels. The long sentences, the sustained significances, are taxing but they separate the men from the boys among readers, when the work is good. I do not think that the difficulty in part four of "The Bear," which contains many of these involved locutions of which you speak, is really so large. I think rather that the tension and the difficulty can bring you an aesthetic reward. I should add that so-called modern literary works are not alone in offering such difficulty; *Oedipus Rex, Hamlet,* and *Moby-Dick* are surely difficult and probably for the same reasons in spite of the rather glib remark I just made about earlier authors.

Drury: We have one student wanting to know if Faulkner's folk humor, as in "Spotted Horses," is consciously Twainian or if this type of humor is his own invention. Is there any conscious indebtedness to Mark Twain?

MR. COLLINS: Faulkner was extremely well aware of

the American tradition of humor not only from his continual reading but from his steady association with its oral
forms in the courthouse square and the hunting camps and
at the farms around Oxford, Mississippi, in the early part of
this century. He was one of the great listeners. (He was also
capable of talking very rapidly and steadily when he wanted
to and I was astonished at his ability to do so in view of his
reputation for being so silent, a reputation which he ac-
quired by being at most times a truly remarkable listener.)
One man has told me of seeing Faulkner during the Saturday nights of many years sitting on the galleries above the
courthouse square in Oxford watching the people and then
moving down among them and listening to what they had to
say.

He was himself a great storyteller in the oral tradition. A
number of young people who knew Faulkner have told me
they had heard many of his stories long before he put them
into print. They had heard them around campfires when he
would join with the children in roasting marshmallows and
frighten them with stories as they wanted to be frightened.
Some former scouts in Oxford have told me that as their
scoutmaster in the mid-nineteen twenties Faulkner was able
to keep everyone in line without shouted discipline because
those who made difficulty and spoiled the pleasure of the
whole group were not allowed to listen to Faulkner tell
stories around the campfire that night.

So he is out of the raconteur American tradition. But, as
I just said, he also had a full literary acquaintance with the
written forms related to that tradition. I used to point out
that he obviously had read Thomas Bangs Thorpe's famous
tall tale, "The Big Bear of Arkansas," on which he seems to
draw in "The Bear" just as he draws on other literary
sources, including *Moby-Dick*. And he also, as I used to
point out years ago to the amusement of some critics, obviously had read *Sut Lovingood's Yarns* by George Washington Harris, a collection of humorous tales of the general
sort from which, as Walter Blair has shown, Mark Twain
drew much of his humorous method. Subsequently, to my
personal satisfaction, Faulkner said in print that Sut Lovingood was one of his two favorite characters in literature. So

Faulkner had available not only the work of Mark Twain
but the work of writers in the tradition from which Twain
himself drew, and Faulkner had, like Twain, a long personal
exposure to the oral American folk tale. "Spotted Horses" is
a good example of the union of some of these various
sources: Faulkner's father, who operated a livery stable,
told him about a sale of Texas ponies brought into Calhoun
County, Mississippi. Presumably this account and accounts
of similar events were told over and over in Faulkner's
hearing. Faulkner, drawing on techniques absorbed from
the oral and written tradition of which Twain was a skillful
part, elaborated and refined that account into "Spotted
Horses."

Jackson: Jackson State has a couple of questions, both
of them concerning "Spotted Horses" but I'll take one of
them. Are the "gray and motionless" qualities of Mrs.
Armstid and the "watching and waiting" attitude of Mrs.
Littlejohn intended to make a statement about the role of
women in the society which Faulkner describes?

MR. COLLINS: If we look at the two women, Mrs.
Armstid and Mrs. Littlejohn, we see that Faulkner has
carefully selected representatives of two different responses
which women could make to the foolishness of the men.
Mrs. Armstid tries to stop her husband from taking her five
dollars, which she has worked so hard to get as extra
money, and spending it on a horse which will not only not
do him any good but, it turns out, will actually harm him.
She is presented, however, as essentially passive, for though
she does try to stop him and is willing to go to court for the
money, we notice, as all of you have, that she is quite
resigned to accepting her fate when Snopes will not give her
a refund. She has the courage to go ask Snopes and when he
gives her the candy worth five cents she thanks him, but
when she hears by the judge's verdict that she cannot get
anything out of Snopes she just goes home. She is an
overwhelming example of quiet fortitude.
    Mrs. Littlejohn, on the other hand—the lady running the
boardinghouse beside the sale lot—her presence is very

skillfully worked in and out through the narrative. We first see her—while the men are having a day off from work and are engaged in their foolishness about the horses—going out to heat wash water in the yard in an iron pot and going ahead with the laundry and her other work. When she pauses and looks into the sale yard she indicates that she is irritated and disgusted by the activity there. Later, when she has seen the behavior of Mr. Armstid toward Mrs. Armstid and the behavior of Flem Snopes to almost everyone, Ratliff, who has been listening as she and Mrs. Armstid washed the dishes, reports that she clattered the dishes until it finally sounded as though she threw all of the dishes at the stove. When the spotted horse comes into her house she is not at all passive—she breaks the washboard over its head and uses what is sometimes called strong language. Faulkner, without much question, seems to be showing that the two women, with their different reactions, make more sense than the men. In general, Faulkner's presentation of middle-aged and elderly women, such as Jenny Du Pre in the novel *Sartoris*, who has to watch the Sartoris men be awfully romantic about war and other things and destroy themselves in the process, shows mature women to be often most sensible and rational. There are women in Faulkner's works who are not so; he is capable of presenting a defective middle-aged woman such as Mrs. Bundren in *As I Lay Dying*. But most of his older women appear to be free from the bizarre or unwise behavior of many of the men. I think Faulkner had a conception which may be true or may be just romantic—that most women are closer to reality and closer to nature than most men. In this particular story Faulkner is trying to set up several natural things against the unnatural. Flem Snopes is the unnatural: he seems to have no emotion, he is materialistic, he is shrewdly dishonest. You will notice that when some of the men are talking about Flem Snopes and his odd, unnatural behavior, one of them, as a critic has pointed out, is chewing a twig from a flowering peach tree and even Varner, who is certainly no saint, has romantic views—for example, a primitive, folkloristic opinion about the efficacy of moonlight. The natural, rather simple people are being taken in by the materialistic Snopes throughout the novel, *The Hamlet.* Now one of the interesting things about the "Spotted Horses" episode is that Snopes in an especially diabolical way here uses very natural things—the ponies—to defeat the natural people of Frenchman's Bend. The central thing about the spotted horses is that they are about as primitive and natural as possible. They cannot be caught, they are just bright colored bits of nature which are tools in the power of the unnatural Flem Snopes. And Mrs. Armstid and Mrs. Littlejohn can only watch, the one irritated, the other resigned.

Morehouse: We'd like to know what is the full symbolism of the bear and the flood. In both stories, obviously, they represent natural forces but isn't there some other moral or metaphysical symbolism behind the bear and the flood?

MR. COLLINS: Well, I think that Faulkner, like most men of wisdom, is very much aware of man's mortality, his transitoriness, the brevity of each life. I think he is trying to have the characters—and the reader—operate and think before the background of these powerful, large, external forces which last a long time. The bear seems in some ways to be almost immortal, though, of course, the hunters kill him in the end. The suggestion is that this bear, like the one in Thorpe's "The Big Bear of Arkansas" on which Faulkner based some of this story, just dies because his time has come and he, like Sam Fathers, is through with earthly life in some large and mystical way. The fifth part of "The Bear" then stresses that, though dead, the bear goes on and that the hunt will go on in a kind of afterlife based on some conception of the happy hunting ground.

I would hazard the guess concerning the river in "Old Man" that the characters and the reader observe that it takes care of itself and goes its own way, with men merely flotsam upon it. I think one use Faulkner makes of these larger elements which last tremendously long is to give us, mere men, a truer perspective on our lives and our behavior.

MR. MOORE: Thank you. Our time is up. Thank you, Carvel Collins, for your very fine and illuminating discussion of Faulkner.

February 24, 1964

Warren Beck

on John Steinbeck

John Steinbeck was born in Salinas, California, in 1902. He grew up amid the surroundings described in his collection of stories, *The Long Valley* (1938). He attended Stanford University, but did not take a degree. After several years of working at various jobs, sometimes on California ranches such as those he has written of, he began writing novels. These attracted little attention until he had brought out his fourth book, *Tortilla Flat* (1935), a comedy of the Monterey *paisanos*. After *In Dubious Battle* (1936) and *Of Mice and Men* (1937), both set in the California hinterlands, John Steinbeck wrote his international success, *The Grapes of Wrath* (1939), the story of the migration to California of tenant farmers driven out of the Oklahoma dust bowl. Since then his books have rarely found favor with the major critics, though he has had popular successes with such books as *The Wayward Bus* (1947) and *East of Eden* (1952). Besides his imaginative writing, John Steinbeck has shown an interest in scientific subjects, particularly marine biology, and he collaborated with Dr. Edward F. Ricketts in *The Sea of Cortez* (1941). Mr. Steinbeck has also written several travel books, the most attractive of which describes his explorations in a truck with a French poodle: *Travels with Charlie in Search of America* (1962). In 1962 John Steinbeck became the seventh American to win the Nobel Prize for literature.

Since Mr. Steinbeck is a shy man who never permits interviews, we chose Professor Warren Beck to discuss *The Grapes of Wrath*. He is well known as an imaginative writer as well as a critic. Born in Richmond, Indiana, he received a bachelor's degree from Earlham College (which later gave him a Doctor of Literature degree); his master's degree is from Columbia. He is professor of English at Lawrence University and has taught at Minnesota and Colorado as well as at the Bread Loaf School of English (for eight summers). He has written the novels *Pause Under the Sky* (1947) and

Into Thin Air (1951); his four volumes of short stories include those in *The Blue Sash* and *The Rest of Silence*. Some of them have appeared in the annual volumes of the *Best American Short Stories*, and one of them is in *Best of the Best American Short Stories: 1915–1950*. On a grant from the American Council of Learned Societies, Mr. Beck is completing a study of James Joyce's *Dubliners*, though as a critic he is so far best known for his writings about American authors, particularly in *Man in Motion: Faulkner's Trilogy* (1961).

MR. MOORE: We have this morning a man who is very seasoned in all aspects of literature, the creative and the critical, and I greatly look forward to hearing him on Steinbeck. Dr. Beck will discuss Steinbeck and his work, particularly *The Grapes of Wrath*, and then I want to take questions from all of you. It gives me great pleasure, and I am honored, to introduce to all of you, Dr. Warren Beck.

MR. BECK: Thank you very much, Dr. Moore, and good morning, all 'round the circuit. I am not here, at this far northern end of the line, to utter any last word about *The Grapes of Wrath*. While I admire its intention and certain of its aspects, I have some doubts, too, about it. So I shall raise questions for you to pursue. Then briefly I shall say something about a most interesting feature of *The Grapes of Wrath*, its experimental form in an attempt at scope. I shall relate that to other such efforts to see contemporary American life through the lens of literary art, especially fiction.

To begin with, there is always the matter of title. T. S. Eliot, often a literary picker-up of more than trifles, not only named a poem after a Henry James novel but embellished it with an epigraph taken from an Elizabethan play: "Thou hast committed fornication . . . / But that was in another country; / And besides, the wench is dead." Hemingway took up the phrase "In Another Country" for the ambiguous title to one of his most telling short stories. Steinbeck took his famous novel's title from everybody

knows where, that fervidly apocalyptic poem set to a jig-
ging tune and emotionally associated ever since the
Civil War. In 1939 *The Grapes of Wrath* seemed just the
name for that book. The known phrase evoked, in an appropriate context of historical allusion, the sense of drastic
crisis, involving large numbers of people and whole sections
of the nation, in a conflict over economic interests and
human rights.

[The book was highly praised by many reviewers; it was
emphatically damned in many an editorial. A number of
public libraries banned it; and in one midwestern town it
was subjected to medieval ceremony, being publicly cast
into the flames. A magazine called *The Forum,* now defunct,
attacked Steinbeck's picture of the Oklahoma immigrants in
California as an exaggeration of their plight and a falsifica-
tion of methods of state and local officials and the operators
of the great farms; and this magazine article was reprinted
in *The Readers' Digest.* On the other hand, an objective
sociological study, *Factories in the Field* by Carey
McWilliams, gave irrefutable support for Steinbeck's treatment of the situation. And when the motion picture execu-
tive who bought the film rights to *The Grapes of Wrath* sent
out private detectives to check the matter, they reported
finding conditions worse than those Steinbeck had represented.]

Parallels are to be found in similar issues in American
life today—as to equality of rights and privileges and the
relief of dire economic needs. More particularly, automa-
tion as a specter in 1964, threatening not only industrial but
personal dislocation, has a prototype in that scene of Steinbeck's when the tractor plows straight through what had
been separate tenant farms, and the driver himself, unrecognizable until he removes his goggles, appears to that extent
dehumanized. Indeed, to my mind the most lastingly cogent
sociological observation the novel makes is just at this
point, where it is realized that in our present system, and
apparently in other imperfect societies, economic break-
downs and miscarriages of social justice have causes so
complex that neither a single villain nor a simple remedy
can be found.

At the beginning of chapter five, Steinbeck points out that despite differences among "the owner men . . . all of them were caught in something larger than themselves." As this tractor driver suggests to the tenant who threatens to shoot him, the chain of responsibility runs from him to the man who would replace him on the tractor, to the bank which is reclaiming the property, to the bank's orders from "the East." So the talk goes until it runs into ultimate complexity, still inscrutable. Says the tractor driver, "Maybe there's nobody to shoot. Maybe the thing isn't men at all." But the dispossessed farmer replies, "We've got a bad thing made by men; and by God, that's something we can change." This is characteristic of the story, which despite the appalling misfortunes of its protagonists is fundamentally optimistic. The chief sociopolitical, ethical problem raised by this novel is in what way and degree that optimism was or is valid.

At the time of its publication, however, the greatest furor over the book did not center on its large-scale theorizing, but on 1] its fidelity or falsity to facts, and 2] its propriety or impropriety of incident and language. Apparently Steinbeck had been painstaking in gathering his material and its veracity was confirmed. He knew the Okies in the Dust Bowl, on the move, and in California. Thus when he told his story realistically, he brought along a lot of gross details, and some barnyard humor. Whether he made more of this than was relevant to his story is a question of literary tastes, which you may dispute among yourselves. The liberties of the printed page have so increased since then, not only as to language but as to types of behavior represented, that we may wonder why all that former furor over Steinbeck. More properly, we may consider it not worth wondering about—an incidental fact concerning the book's reception and its place in the history of taste and license, rather than a central fact about the book itself. The present reader's problem is what the book says as a whole: what it adds up to and amounts to ideologically and aesthetically, and to what degree it is dated in its substance and import.

Now, some twenty-five years later, some readers of this novel may be disposed to borrow Eliot's epigraph and rephrase it to say "But that was in another country, and besides, those times are dead." And this might be remarked not only by a present generation of undergraduates, to whom the Depression is simply history, but by their elders who saw the economic problems of the 1930's not solved but merely superseded by World War II. Now younger and elder generations together are seeing an affluent society heavily dependent on the armament industry and an inflated stock market, but can discover huge pockets of poverty, urban and rural; and, on an international scale, since the thirties, there have been greater brutalities and more drastic displacement of persons than anything in *The Grapes of Wrath;* while politically speaking there is worse weather brewing over the whole globe than that which ruined the dust bowl farmer. The Joads set out for California. Where do we go from here? And, when we get there, that next stop, how much better off will we be? Does Steinbeck tell us something relevant still about American life?

To ask that question rhetorically is to point up a difference between Steinbeck and some of our younger fictionists. They are more sophisticated than he was, or is. Some of them, by purely aesthetic standards, are better novelists than Steinbeck. But in the main, though with exceptions, our more recent fiction writers have dealt with more limited aspects of American life. Social consciousness was the creed of American literature from the economic crash of 1929 on into the years of World War II, and the fictionist's attempt was to take the broadest possible view of representative individuals in representative socioeconomic conditions. *The Grapes of Wrath* is an eminent example. Even more ambitious was Dos Passos' trilogy *U.S.A.,* published earlier in the thirties. Hemingway, although his settings were more often European and his concerns more private, joined this tendency toward the socially based novel in *For Whom the Bell Tolls,* involving the acute, complex, political issues of the Spanish Civil War, and significantly his chief protagonist is an American. Farrell, in the *Studs Lonigan* trilogy, pondered a more limited scene, almost literally parochial, but still with a wide view of the lower middle-class urban situation as a determinant. Willa Cather, that significant and most American though presently our most neglected twentieth-century novelist, worked on a broad scale, with a social sense backed by historical perspectives. And Faulkner, our greatest novelist, while he centered his work in his mythical but realistically based Yoknapatawpha County, has studied a whole society at all levels and in all its interactions, and from the antebellum days to the present; then beyond such broad canvases as *Light in August* and *Absalom, Absalom!* he went on in a trilogy of his own, called *Snopes,* to write a great parable of modern man and society in fundamental terms of good and evil.

Most of our younger novelists have not chosen to work on such a broad scale or with such comprehensive implications about American life. Nor has the choice been entirely theirs. In fact, for the most part, they have not dared. It is no wonder if they are daunted, for what is American life as a totality? Does it exist as such or is it, if not quite nondescript, at least confusingly heterogeneous? Consequently some younger novelists and dramatists, in present uncertainties and restlessness, have narrowed their focus in one of two ways. First, they have turned again to what used to be called local color, but with a difference. Formerly, this was regional, and it fed a growing nation's wholesome curiosity about its separate parts and their distinctive vital qualities, whether of a New England village or frontier settlements or a mining camp. Nowadays fiction's local color is less regional and has more to do with separate classes—the other-directed, privately frantic dwellers in any suburbia, or quite frequently metropolitan Jewish families, for instance, or men in gray flannel or nowadays black suits on Madison Avenue, and one writer has even made a reputation in stories about Roman Catholic priests. A second narrowing of focus from society in the large is toward those characters whom unusual environment or some force still more inscrutable has actually deranged. Hence the novels or plays about the alcoholic, the psychotic, or the morally oblique. Take for instance John Updike's novel, *Rabbit, Run,* which studies a case of incorrigible irresponsibility in a way that, to me, seems to despair, not only of the bad young protagonist but of what would supposedly be corrective influences in his environment.

Our most modern specializations in fiction, however skillful, look small beside massive works such as *U.S.A.*, *For Whom the Bell Tolls*, *Snopes*, or *The Grapes of Wrath*. Conversely, Steinbeck may seem to have had the easier time of it, compared to present novelists, because to him at least the problem seemed simpler, or anyhow his examination of the subject was less searching. This judgment does not pertain to his realism, of course. The life of the Joads is fully pictured, page after page, and is viewed close-up. It is when Steinbeck tries to define what the great army of migrants is marching toward that the substance becomes thin while the rhetoric thickens.

So the critical procedure I now propose is to note appreciatively the thoroughness of Steinbeck's picturing of events in the dust bowl, on the road, and in California and, more importantly, to estimate the originality of narrative device by which he brings us close to the Joads, while not isolating them from the great numbers and varieties of other people concerned in the same course of events and the wide social problems involved. At the same time, I would examine skeptically the novel's implications about a possible solution of these problems. I raise this doubt separately so as to admit it without allowing it to eclipse what I think are the novel's virtues. Therefore let me deal first with Steinbeck's social philosophy or ideology and then with the realistic merit and technical ingenuity of *The Grapes of Wrath*.

Steinbeck's total production has been so various in its themes that it is impossible to abstract a general and fairly consistent view of it, as can be done with Faulkner, Willa Cather, Conrad, and many older novelists. In *Of Mice and Men*, two years before *The Grapes of Wrath*, he had written fatalistically of a character whose lack of intelligence made him a hopeless misfit, doomed simply becase he could not understand the facts of his environment well enough to survive. *Of Mice and Men* is a narrowly focused novel largely dependent on dialogue and, not only by its examination of a subnormal character but in its aesthetic control, is more nearly comparable to present-day fiction than *The Grapes of Wrath*. It is undeniably pessimistic, since the protagonist's friend finds that all he can do to spare him from others is a mercy killing. Even darker than the accidental fate of the subnormal individual is the cosmic view taken by the doctor in *In Dubious Battle,* who says, "There aren't any beginnings. Nor any ends. It seems to me that man is engaged in a blind and fearful struggle out of a past he can't remember, into a future he can't foresee nor understand. And man has met and defeated every obstacle, every enemy, except one; he cannot win over himself." Steinbeck's partial escape from such fatalistic denial of order is not philosophical but emotional, toward glorifying the natural vitality of the common man. In *Cannery Row,* if I understand it, Steinbeck's sentimental liking for picturesque bums and golden-hearted whores is balanced off by his layman's awe (like Sinclair Lewis') for the austere rationality of the scientist; but the bout between these two worlds of free-wheeling hedonistic irresponsibility and exclusive intellectual specialization ends ruinously in a draw and no decision.

In *The Grapes of Wrath,* however, there is an answer leading on through all difficulties, and in part it is the right answer, that is, fortitude, epitomized in the heroic character of Ma Joad. Here one compares Steinbeck with Willa Cather in her picturing of the pioneers' resoluteness. Steinbeck's theme is also Faulkner's in his emphasis on the quality of endurance, seen nowhere better than in that admirable woman Dilsey, the servant whose strength of mind and heart props up the whole deteriorated Compson family. But the strongly enduring characters encountered in Faulkner's novels simply stand their ground in specific circumstances and fixed settings, while Steinbeck's multitude of Okies are on the march and are represented in the process as developing a communal morale, even a mystique, a kind of politics that has no formal program but only a deep-felt sentiment of unity. The common quality of endurance even in the fact of the seemingly impossible is expressed by Ma Joad, "It ain't kin we, it's will we." Beyond that resoluteness the mysticism sets in.

Casy, the evangelistic fundamentalist preacher, who is troubled by the mixture in himself of religious fervor and eroticism, finds his primitive theology giving way to a primitive humanism, with a tinge of Oriental monism, as when he says, "Maybe all men got one big soul ever'body's a part of." Casey elaborates this in his prayer that is really a rambling monologue: "I got to thinkin' we was holy when we was one thing, an' mankin' was holy when it was one thing." But this is not just Casy; Steinbeck himself in chapter fourteen is formally optimistic. He says, "Man reaches, stumbles forward, painfully, mistakenly sometimes; having stepped forward he may slip back, but only half a step, never the full step back." This faith in progress Steinbeck justifies by the solidarity developed in his afflicted Okies. "This is the beginning," he says, "from 'I' to 'we,' " and then as in many of the interchapters he becomes openly the exhorter: "If you who owns the things the people must have could understand this, you might preserve yourself." But the owners cannot understand, Steinbeck says, "for the quality of owning freezes you forever in '*I*' and cuts you off forever from the '*we*.' " Such an absolute statement is not only superficial, it is incredible except as a proposal of some sort of authoritarian communal existence, either religious or political or both, in which the members will be spared being frozen forever into being just *I*, but fated to be just *we*.

However, as to the conversion from *I* to *we*, Tom Joad, we find, feels he has made it. After Tom has killed Casy's murderer and must be on his way, a fugitive, he tells Ma about it. He has "been thinkin' how it was in that gov'ment camp, how our folks took care a theirselves," and he wonders why they can't "Throw out the cops who ain't our people. All work together for our own thing—all farm our own lan'." He has absorbed Casy's mystique, thinking maybe that "a fella ain't got a soul of his own, but on'y a piece of a big one," and thus that he will always pervade the life around him. But in the first place, Tom's nostalgia for the camp overlooks the fact that there "folks took care a theirselves" under the protection of a government which had set a high wire fence around them. Then he dreams of a completely agricultural Utopia where, if they are all farming their own land, who will manufacture the wire fencing, and what authority will set it up? Moreover, to pay for this dream, he is willing to suppose "a fella ain't got a soul of his own."

This is not to say Steinbeck is a Marxist; his thinking is not systematic enough for that. But I for one get the sense that he speaks through Casy and Tom, and I believe what he thus underwrites is naïvely nostalgic and sentimental and that he is tending dangerously to give class struggles the aura of holy wars. How then shall we estimate the value of this contemporary writer's view of American life as of 1939, and for its residue of present implication? Positively and negatively, I'd say. Steinbeck is no profound thinker, no political philosopher, and his sentimentality outruns rationality when he looks at American life in the large. But he is an excellent reporter and he does dare to look closely and picture in detail; hence the impressive realism of this novel. Yet he is no mere naturalist; he does more than describe and classify. He has in great degree the fictionist's and dramatist's essential gift, empathy—the intuitive, compassionate entrance into other lives. And any example of a genuine humane compassion remains a shining value.

Finally, in its structural devices *The Grapes of Wrath* is an original experiment in the novel as an art form. I have spoken of the challenge to serious writers to try to represent American life as broadly as possible. Moreover, the depression of the thirties, with the onset of antidemocratic political tendencies in fascism and communism and the increasing omens of war, all intensified this challenge to the writer, in America as well as in Europe. There were a number of ventures in what I would call the panoramic novel, the attempt at a wider focus, more inclusive not only of numbers but of levels of society and heterogeneous and even contradictory ideological tendencies. Dos Passos, in the trilogy *U.S.A.*, made one of the most drastic experiments—he not only traced a number of individual lives, treated with the objectivity of sociological case history and as they were more or less determined by economics and politics, but he set them within a great backdrop. This included, first a number of highly colored portraits of real contemporaries presently influential on American life, all the way from Henry Ford to Rudolph Valentino; and, second, many so-called newsreels, which were scraps of headlines, advertisements, and popular songs, all jumbled together to suggest the welter of sensationalism, selfish enterprise, hypocrisy, and vulgarity which Dos Passos found predominant in American life; and third, the camera eye, subjective little prose poems expressing Dos Passos himself as he had grown up and tried to find his footing in these troubled times. The result can scarcely be called a novel; there is too much variation of form besides too much interruption of individual story line. But the movies and television have given us a new noun with which Dos Passos' *U.S.A.* can be appreciatively described; it is a documentary, and a very great documentary.

The Grapes of Wrath, as an attempt at a novel of social consciousness, is not as widely and variously documented as Dos Passos' *U.S.A.*, but far more compelling as a work of fictional art, the primary intent of which should be to create and sustain a narrative flow, a dramatic illusion. The cinema had demonstrated that a recurrent alternation between general and particular, between total environment and protagonist, between social phenomena and private lives can be made into a fluent, constantly engrossing story; and *The Grapes of Wrath,* like much modern fiction, draws directly from this newer art form. Technically, Steinbeck is successful, yet there is more to it than that. His purpose was to study the plight of large groups as people in spacious settings, but that in itself is only sociology. For fiction to have its unique effect and humanely cultivating values, it must bring the reader into contact with individual lives. Steinbeck does that, too. On these grounds we can make a basic judgment of *The Grapes of Wrath.* Perhaps Steinbeck as political theorist is as naïve and sentimental as his protagonists Casy and Tom, but the book *in toto,* by its alternation between the panoramic and the personal, implies a wisdom beyond the superficialities of Steinbeck's ideology and editorializing.

The Grapes of Wrath shows something more than the movement from *I* to *we.* It is from *I* to *we,* then back to *I,* and again to *we,* and back to *I* again, in a perpetual progressive interrelation of the individual and a complex society aspiring to democracy. Our national declaration is not for *man*, generically, but for all *men*. Interdependence is to be used not to create conformity but to protect independence. Modern history shows how social consciousness may become nothing more than an idolatry of the state and a suicide of self by submersion in totalitarian gregariousness. But social conscience, on which democracy depends, comes back in each instance to a recognition of the individual and his intrinsic inviolable worth simply as a human being. This is the difficult and sublime paradox of democracy—to set the individual and society into a fairly stable equilibrium, always equitable in its intention, neither complacent nor despairing about its shortcomings, but forever striving toward the improvement of society so that the individual may improve himself within it, not just economically, not just intellectually, but as a total human being: responsible, compassionate, just, productive, and always aspiring. That the implication of this is inherent in *The Grapes of Wrath*, and is emphasized by its art as a panoramic novel relating society and the individual, makes it, if not a great work, a good book. And while greatness is exceptional, goodness is its basis and the norm to be striven for in all things.

I think that Steinbeck has written better than he knew, in that the form of his experimental novel is its supreme function, by implying, through the alternating chapters, the practical and ethical interrelation of the individual and society, and the necessity of both personal freedom and personal responsibility in any efficiently operative and humanely just society. In this he shows the long way we still have to go.

MR. MOORE: Thank you very much, Dr. Warren Beck. That was a very profound and illuminating investigation of a book that we have all found very interesting to read, and you did more than that—you've related the work of Steinbeck to other authors we are studying in the course, Dos Passos, Faulkner, Hemingway, and Farrell. This has been a very fine, a remarkable, presentation. Thank you. And now we want to get to the questions.

Stephens: Dr. Beck, what do you think Steinbeck intended by the act of Rosasharon visiting the old man at the end of the book?

MR. BECK: It seems to me that this is an instance of Steinbeck's attempt at symbolism, which he did very crudely in the third chapter with the turtle. He is, I think, unnecessarily pointing his finger at cases, but at the end, it seems to me, he is joining the individual fates and the social problems. What she does, practically speaking, is as useful as a blood transfusion. If people find it shocking, I think they should remember that it was a shock also to her and that she did it only under the approval of that wise good woman, Ma Joad, and that she did it out of human sympathy and necessity. It therefore symbolizes things that Steinbeck has tried to unite in the story: individual suffering, individual dilemma, individual uneasiness and shock, and at the same time resoluteness, in the face of all that, to proceed with whatever is necessary, whatever one can do in the way of assistance between individuals.

Tougaloo: A student in this class from Appleton, Wisconsin, who knows Dr. Beck asks, Is Steinbeck saying that this dispossession represents the greatest spiritual violation of human dignity?

MR. BECK: Dispossession of what? You mean of property?

Tougaloo: Of the land.

MR. BECK: Well, of course, Steinbeck has a profound nostalgia, and an unrealistic nostalgia, for the small farm home which is still the ideal base for the individual life in American eyes. He is so sentimental about that that he even prefers horses to tractors. But I don't think that the book can be taken to imply that the necessary expansion of the big farm which we've seen more and more of since then is anything that fundamentally violates human rights. I don't think that's the fundamental violation. I don't quite understand how to answer the question any further than that.

Drury: We have a sudent who thinks he sees the influence of Emerson's "Over-Soul" and Whitman's "Atman." Was Steinbeck influenced by these earlier writers?

MR. BECK: There has been a great deal of talk among the critics about Steinbeck as a latter-day transcendentalist influenced specifically by Whitman and Emerson—and Thoreau as well. I don't think this is a systematic influence. Of course, you couldn't get too much of a systematic influence out of Whitman! Steinbeck is closest, I think, to Whitman rather than to Thoreau and Emerson, who were more intellectual in their transcendentalism and set forth, of course, a more organized exposition.

I've touched on the fact that he is a mystical person. I would connect him rather with two strains of influence out of the eighteenth and nineteenth centuries, the belief in the natural goodness of the common man, and also a belief in progress. At the same time Steinbeck rejects any idea of order in the universe—he's been called a nonteleological thinker, but while he's rejecting that he still has this hidden faith in progress which is to come out of the natural goodness of the common man. This is very romantic, and goes all the way back into the eighteenth and nineteenth centuries. I believe that's the predominant influence on him, and I think it is something he has breathed in rather than learned formally.

Jackson: Was there any social significance to the degradation of Casy's moral and religious life? Was it symbolic of the Okies? Or was it purely personal?

MR. BECK: Well, Tom gradually becomes a convert to Casy's mystical view of life. Early in the book he is quite different from that. You'll remember that when Casy's talking about his doubts of his own religion because he finds it connected with lust, Tom says, "I don't try to figure these things out; I just live from day to day, I do what I can, I take whatever I can get," and so on. But in his last speech, to his mother, you remember, he tells her that he feels he will be a part of all things, everywhere, where men are striving. And this is what he seems to have got from Casy. That's all I can say.

Morehouse: Ma Joad and Casy seem to represent two aspects of man's survival—one is passive and enduring and the other is active and perhaps heroic. Does this type of complementation say anything about Steinbeck's universal statement about the world today?

MR. BECK: Which one do you consider "passive and enduring"?

Morehouse: Ma Joad.

MR. BECK: She does a great deal more than Casy does; she's a great deal surer of herself; she's more purposeful. I would contest a description of Ma Joad as passive as compared with activity on the part of Casy. She is by far the more purposeful person; she is the more active person. You'll remember at the end—the last conversation between Tom and Ma Joad—if you'll look at that conversation, I think you will discover that there she is speaking in terms of the immediate and the practical—what must be done—I don't believe this is describable as passivity. I would say that she doesn't theorize; that she does not live by any ideology other than the simple human principle of holding the family together, and of maintaining human relationship and of ameliorating human suffering whenever she can by any act of her own. In other words, I have refused your question because I don't accept its premise. Could you ask it in another way?

Morehouse: Yes. Does Casy represent the concern for large areas of man's nature, universal man, and Ma Joad only the head of the family? Could you see any statement in there about man's world today, just in that type of polarity? She is the family; he is society in general.

MR. BECK: Yes. I think you can state the antithesis in that way, but this I think doesn't demonstrate anything more than differences among individuals. Ma Joad had a family on her hands and a series of responsibilities to look after. Casy was one man, he was an individual; he was more or less hanging loose and it was only Ma Joad's insistence that got him into the truck and brought him along with them, you remember. Generally speaking, one discovers this fact in life, I think, that some people are so inextricably involved in immediate and personal responsibilities that they can't look very far beyond. But after all, it seems to me that if Ma Joad by practicing her philosophy, simple as it is, can demonstrate its validity, she has made her contribution to a better society.

Langston: Do you feel that Steinbeck intended the strong religious symbolism critics have read into his *The Grapes of Wrath?*

MR. BECK: I don't know about his intentions. It certainly is not a basically Christian symbolism although it is very easy to find Christian symbolism in any kind of fiction wherever there is any sort of suffering that at the same time may seem to be sacrificial, or just unselfish. I do not agree with much contemporary criticism which overemphasizes religious symbolism. Faulkner is a case in point. I think that to overemphasize Christian symbolism in Faulkner is to minimize the larger, the more general aspects. That is a very unsatisfactory answer, I know, but you speak of a whole area of criticism and that's about all I can say about it. Could you ask a more specific question? About a passage? Or anything of the kind?

Langston: More specifically, we were thinking in terms of critics who say that Jim Casy with the initials J. C. may be analagous to Jesus Christ, and other characters are actually pointed out as apostles.

MR. BECK: I think that sort of criticism is futile. Now it may have been Steinbeck's intention—I have no way of proving it—but I think some critics have been overanxious to make that identification. They do the same thing for instance in Faulkner's *Light in August* with Joe Christmas, who has the initials J. C.

Langston: May we have another question?

MR. BECK: Surely.

Langston: One critic says the following made a difference between Steinbeck's being good and great as an author: Steinbeck concentrated on ecology, trying to put men in relation to the universe rather than sociology, man's relation to his fellows. Will you comment on this?

MR. BECK: I think that as a general statement about Steinbeck's work that will not hold. I believe it's more true of some books than others. I think, for instance, it's true of *Cannery Row*, perhaps of *The Wayward Bus*, but certainly less true of the book we're considering, where, it seems to me, he is very much concerned with men's relationship to each other. You would have to examine that statement in the light of various books, and I believe you would find it is more nearly true of some than of others. In my remarks, I said that it's pretty hard to pin Steinbeck down—he's first one thing and then another—he's not a systematic thinker, and he's been attracted by this or that or the other point of view.

MR. MOORE: Thank you very much. This has been a most profitable morning. I think we've all had a wonderful time, and we're very grateful to Dr. Warren Beck for his fine presentation.

March 2, 1964

Carlos Baker

on Ernest Hemingway

Ernest Hemingway was born in Oak Park, Illinois, in 1899 and died at Ketchum, Idaho, in 1961. After leaving high school he became for a while a reporter on the *Kansas City Star*, which trained its writers to use a terse style. Like various other American authors of his generation, Hemingway performed ambulance-corps duties in World War I; he was severely wounded in Italy just before his nineteenth birthday. After his recovery he again took up newspaper work, in Toronto and Paris, bringing out his first book, *Three Stories and Ten Poems* (1923) in the latter city. His novels, *The Sun Also Rises* (1926) and *A Farewell to Arms* (1929) brought him world fame. His stories in such volumes as *Men Without Women* (1927) and *Winner Take Nothing* (1933) established him in the front rank of writers of short fiction. Hemingway had, more than most authors, caught the mood and attitude of a generation. And he wrote of exotic places—Spain, Italy, France, Africa, and Cuba. *A Farewell to Arms* was one of the notable novels of World War I; *For Whom the Bell Tolls* (1940) projected the experiences of a guerrilla group in the Spanish Civil War. *The Old Man and the Sea* (1952), Hemingway's last popular success during his lifetime, is the story of a stubbornly courageous old Cuban fisherman. Hemingway won the Nobel Prize for literature in 1954. His posthumous best seller, *A Moveable Feast* (1964), miraculously recaptured not only the force of his early style but also his memories of Paris' Left Bank, when he was the friend (and in a sense pupil) of Gertrude Stein and Ezra Pound and was in the process of becoming one of the great literary legends of the modern world.

Professor Carlos Baker of Princeton University, author of *Hemingway: The Writer as Artist* (1952), was invited to discuss *A Farewell to Arms* for the present series. Mr. Baker, who was born in Biddeford, Maine, in 1909, attended Dartmouth, Harvard, and Princeton, at the last of which he received his Ph.D. He has specialized in editing works of the

Romantics (particularly Wordsworth, Shelley, and Keats), and is the coeditor of *The Major English Romantic Poets: A Symposium in Reappraisal* (1957) and of *Masters of British Literature* (1958). He is also the author of *Shelley's Major Poetry: The Fabric of a Vision* (1948). He has written two novels: *A Friend in Power* (1958), which has an academic background, and *Rumbelow* (1963), which deals with a literary biographer. His volume of poetry, *A Year and a Day*, was also published in 1963. Mr. Baker is now engaged in writing a biography of Hemingway.

MR. MOORE: And now if Professor Baker will talk with us for about twenty minutes on Hemingway then we can ask him some questions. Dr. Baker.

MR. BAKER: Hello, Professor Moore and all the others. You know when Professor Moore called me earlier, we reminded each other that the last time we met was in Paris just in front of the Deux Magots Restaurant some time about seven years ago. But turning to the immediate business here, we have Hemingway's *Farewell to Arms*.

I think that among the American novels that deal with the First World War, sometimes known as the Kaiser's War of 1914–1918, *A Farewell to Arms* has really borne up under the years as well as any and far better than most. Some of Hemingway's contemporaries also wrote novels about that war; and, if you've tried the experiment of picking up William Faulkner's *Soldiers' Pay* or John Dos Passos' book *Three Soldiers* and reading them, as over against the Hemingway novel, I think you can't help discovering that the *Farewell to Arms* stands up much better than the other two. It is not only fresher in its language but has more action and just more simple real interest. It has stayed singularly undated at the same time that it perfectly embodies the spirit of the time, the *Zeitgeist*, the governing ethics, you might say, of a time that seems probably to most of you far away and which, indeed, I remember dimly. But I do remember it well enough to know Hemingway hit my sense of that time extremely well.

Now another part of our pleasure in this novel might be said to come from Hemingway's ability to give us the sense of vicarious participation in the events that he depicts—one of the best reasons for reading, after all, that anyone has yet been able to discover. None of the histories of the war—the war especially as it was fought down in the Veneto, down in that region north of Venice where the Italians and the Austrians were facing one another—no history could possibly reproduce exactly how it felt to be there: to be under fire; to hear the shells that fell all around you, sometimes on you; to carry the wounded to safety, unless they hemorrhaged and died along the way. Or to go into the regimental messrooms and share wine and rough *badinage* with the Italian officers. Or the military retreat—how it is to be in a retreat and be in danger of being shot at after a drumhead court-martial. Or the acute physical discomforts of rain, cold, mud, hunger, and fear that are often the lot of the soldier. So in a sense you get a much better idea of how it was in Italy, in say 1916–1917, out of this novel than you could from any history.

Now getting to another aspect of the thing, the literary history of *A Farewell to Arms* itself, for just a few minutes. This, curiously, might have been Hemingway's first novel rather than his second. More than four years before he bought out his first novel, *The Sun Also Rises*, in 1926, he had already begun to write a story about a young American ambulance driver on the Italian-Austrian front during the First World War. Something happened to this story and he had to do it again. It was a long time before he got around to it. But a story of a young American ambulance driver had been set down, in part, as early as 1922. Nobody except his first wife ever saw this story, but it seems to have been, according to her, of course, highly romantic in manner and conception. It was also written in a prose style much more elaborate and much more adjectival than the one we usually associate with Hemingway (the familiar description of the crisp, incisive language, and so on). But the early version of the novel simply disappeared. His wife was going down to see him in Lausanne and had all his manuscripts, including this, in a suitcase. She left from the Gare de Lyon in

Paris one winter afternoon late in 1922, and she just stepped out of the train for a minute, having put her luggage aboard the train. When she came back the valise with all the typescripts and longhand copies of poems and early stories was gone. Hemingway was much dismayed and disheartened by this loss, and he didn't try to tell the Italian story until 1928, almost ten years after the events had taken place on which he based his story.

Another aspect of this history of the novel is that it's rather dramatic geographically. He began to write the novel in Paris, and then he kept on writing it in Key West, Florida: in Piggott, Arkansas; in Kansas City, Missouri; and Sheridan, Wyoming; and he finished the first draft while he was on a ranch out near Big Horn, Wyoming. During this time his second wife, Pauline, was delivered of a son by caesarean section in Kansas City, and then while he was revising his first draft his father committed suicide by shooting himself in Oak Park, Illinois. Hemingway says, "I remember all these things happening and all the places we lived in, and the fine times and the bad times we had in that year. But much more vividly I remember living in the book and making up what happened in it every day. Making the country and the people and the things that had happened, I was happier than I had ever been." This creative happiness in constructing a narrative as full of doom as this one, bears a curious resemblance to a story that's told about Thomas Hardy down in his country house near Dorchester, England. A visitor came there one day and was turned away by the writer's wife at the front door. She explained that Mr. Hardy was busily composing an extremely gloomy poem and he was enjoying himself so much that he must not be disturbed. Well, Hemingway enjoyed the business of setting down his narrative of doom, and he was far enough removed from the experience it was based on so that his pleasure was very real.

Actually, the novel seems to be based on two important events that happened to Hemingway in 1918–1919. He had not been able to forget either of them. One was the fact that he was severely wounded, that he was blown up, around midnight July 8, 1918. He was not yet nineteen when he joined the American Red Cross ambulance group stationed near Schio in northern Italy and for nearly a month he drove ambulances. But it was too tame work so he went across to the Piave front where the Italians faced the Austrians in trenches and dugouts, so close to the lines that they could hear each other talking. The boy was not doing anything in the way of fighting, he was simply handing out cigarettes and bars of chocolate to the troops. But one night, while he was engaged in this, a large Austrian trench mortar made a direct hit on the dugout where he was practicing his very limited Italian. Several of his companions were killed; one had his leg severed. Hemingway picked him up and carried him back to the main trench from the forward dugout, and took a couple of additional slugs in the legs. This was the first of two soul-shaking experiences which he could never forget and which he had been trying for ten years to put into prose fiction.

Then the second event that underlay this novel was a love affair with an American Red Cross nurse; her name was Agnes Von Kurowsky, a Polish name though she was American in origin. She was an excellent and experienced nurse, young, pretty, kind, and gay. When the boy was brought back to the base hospital in Milan, Miss Von Kurowsky was one of those assigned to his case. It was Hemingway's first head-on love affair and he threw himself into it without any caution. He managed to convince himself that he was finally and irrevocably in love in spite of the banality of the situation in which the young war hero falls in love with his nurse. Now in spite of the fact that they were often separated during the remainder of the war, Hemingway saw as much of this nurse as regulations would allow. When he sailed for New York in January 1919, he wanted to get a job, make some money, and bring her over to be married. When she rejected him by letter, he was very much hurt and reacted explosively, turning against her with masculine rage and sorrow. Yet he paid her the compliment of keeping her letters all his life—through all the time of his four marriages.

This is roughly the background of the novel. Of course, it's not all, by any means, autobiographical. For one thing, the action of the novel goes from the summer of 1915 to the spring of 1918, many months before Hemingway himself actually arrived on the scene. He had not been at the retreat of Caporetto personally; in fact, he was in the war only about five weeks in the summer of 1918. He invents also the figure of Catherine. She is based not only on his nurse, but also on his first two wives with whom he had made skiing trips to Switzerland and to Austria in the period before he wrote the novel. None of this is very surprising—any novelist must write from what he knows, taking advantage of any stories that fall into his lap by chance, and he was seeking to tell a story of love and war which had grown out of his own personal experience.

Now, moving over, for the remaining time, to the symbolic aspects of the book, I am aware that to many readers the very idea of symbolism is anathema. They would like to believe that this is a simple naturalistic tale of two lovers, a Romeo and Juliet story, but, in fact, Hemingway has very carefully planned symbolic aspects in this book. One is the weather, another is the emblematic people, and third, the landscape itself. Of course, everybody has known for a long time that in this story rain and disaster are associated carefully; and if you will read the novel with that idea in mind, if you watch the author playing with falling rain as a symbol of doom, then you must be much impressed by this symbolic aspect of this piece of fiction. Near the close of the book when Catherine is approaching her time of confinement, the weather warms up and the rains come. For a whole winter they have gloried in their isolation, these lovers, living happily up in their high mountain bastion surrounded by healthy cold air and clean snow and far from the mud and muck of war. But now at last the rains come, the time for the lying-in draws nearer, and you know that some great change is lurking just beyond their horizon. You begin to sense, perhaps, that Catherine is in mortal danger, as indeed she is.

And then, moving quickly, a second aspect of the symbolism is the way in which Hemingway endows two of Henry's friends with special moral attributes. One is the young Italian surgeon, Rinaldi, certainly a merry comrade and a capable doctor. But Hemingway is at pains to present Rinaldi as the victim of his own virtues. When Frederick Henry returns after having been away for a long time, he finds that Rinaldi has lost power, has lost strength. He is moody, he is depressed, whereas the priest, who is the other symbolic character, has gained in strength. Now, the priest is associated in the reader's mind with the region of the Abruzzi. The priest has wanted to persuade Henry to visit the Abruzzi during one of his military leaves and he paints an idyllic picture of this mountainous region—with its clear cool air, its plump game birds, and its vineyard and orchards, and its flute music and the present population who have lived there for a thousand years. And the priest says, "That's a good place up in those mountains. You can love God there without being satirized for your belief."

Well now, of course, these two men, Rinaldi and the priest, drop out of the book about halfway through—that is, after Henry and Catherine leave for Switzerland. But, it's the spirit of the priest that continues to dominate their lives for as long as they stay up in the mountainous regions of Switzerland and when they are compelled to leave their lofty station and go down to Lausanne where Catherine will die, we are reminded of the world of Rinaldi, the world of doctors and hospitals and imminent death.

The third and last manifestation of the symbolic intent of the novel is the way in which the author plays off two levels of landscape against each other. He isn't slavishly following this scheme at all, but I think in this book, as in other books, you find the continuous contrast between the mountain and lowland that appears in *Green Hills of Africa;* it appears in *For Whom the Bell Tolls;* it has already appeared in *The Sun Also Rises* and so on; and certainly we see it in some of the short stories like *The Snows of Kilamanjaro.*

So in a word this is a novel which might have been Hemingway's first, but was actually postponed for ten years by the accident of thievery. He was much better prepared to write it, of course, after the lapse of ten years than he would have been earlier. It is based on certain autobiographical factors. It is sustained from beneath by a careful arrangement of symbolic writing that I think gives the novel a good deal of its lasting power. Now I think that's about twenty minutes. I'd be glad to carry on if it is desired, but I'm very anxious to hear some questions.

MR. MOORE: Thank you very much. We draw very intelligent questions I think you'll find out, and we'll begin this morning with Tougaloo Southern Christian College.

Tougaloo: Will you comment on the symbolism of the destruction of the ants on the burning log? Is this a picture of Hemingway's attitude toward the universe?

MR. BAKER: That's a fine question but is it meant to apply to Hemingway himself and his belief, or is it the dramatic significance of it for the hero of this particular story? Can I have a little interpretation of the question?

Tougaloo: Yes, I think we are interested in Hemingway's attitude.

MR. BAKER: Well, I think Hemingway may have had this attitude at one time or another when things were going badly. Perhaps his own young man's philosophy might have been reflected by this story of the young man who is out on a hunting trip and has a campfire. He sees the ants on the log in the campfire, and he reflects on how they resemble human beings and their predicaments. They will all die eventually, yes. So will all the human beings, but a few can perhaps be temporarily saved. I think he has in mind perhaps the statement that you get in Shakespeare's *King Lear* when one of the characters says, "As flies to wanton boys are we to the gods; they kill us for their sport," the notion being that when boys kill flies they do it without rational processes, and this is how the gods act toward us. I don't believe this continues to be Hemingway's philosophy during the whole of his lifetime, but I do think that it was a notion that he had briefly during his young manhood when things went badly.

Drury: I was wondering if you would comment, Dr.

Baker, upon the judgment of some critics like Edmund Wilson and Malcolm Cowley regarding the fact that Catherine and Henry are not convincing as human personalities. They are too one-dimensional, so to speak.

MR. BAKER: I don't know. If *they* are one-dimensional characters, I don't know how you get three dimensions into a character that you create. In the first place, both of them are endowed with qualities that are drawn from real people; and Catherine herself is a composite of not only Agnes Von Kurowsky but also Hadley Richardson and Pauline Pfeiffer, Hemingway's first two wives. And then Lieutenant Henry himself, is substantially the Hemingway figure with some modification from friends. The very fact that they originate in real persons seems to me to give them some claim on credibility. I find it a little difficult to follow Edmund Wilson's critique. I don't know that he, Wilson, objects especially to any book or especially to Hemingway's heroes, although he may. I seem to remember that he made the remark that "More happens to them than they themselves are able to do." But Wilson is very much against the figures of almost all Hemingway's heroines. He even calls Maria in *For Whom the Bell Tolls* a sort of protozoan creature. I for one find it difficult to understand why they should be attacked as one-dimensional. I find them about as three-dimensional as almost any characters you encounter in fiction of our own age. What these critics probably mean is that Hemingway is not much of a character analyst. He keeps the motivations relatively simple and they are apparent; they can be shown in action or quick-moving sentences. He doesn't, in Henry James fashion, go in and out, and in and out, and around and through, and under and over the motivation of his characters. That's what they want him to do and what Hemingway himself would never conceivably do—expound at length on the motivation of his characters. I don't know if that answers the question adequately or not but at least that's an idea about it.

MR. MOORE: A good answer. Thank you.

Jackson: The relationship between Catherine and Ferguson is not so clear. Would you comment on that, please?

MR. BAKER: There's kind of womanly friendship between Catherine and her friend Fergie. Fergie likes to protect Catherine, I think, and she warns Lieutenant Henry that he is not to get Catherine with child—he is not to betray her in this way—and then that is exactly what happens. In the scene in the hotel in Stresa, when Catherine has, in effect, left the nursing service and when Lieutenant Henry himself has been threatened with execution and then gone on from there, once again the trio meets. It's what was once called, in Bradley's book on Shakespearean tragedy, a repetition of first effect. Here Fergie has warned Lieutenant Henry to stay away and not to impregnate Catherine and now you have them coming back again for a reunion. You see that Ferguson now rather reluctantly accepts the fact that these are true lovers and must go away together.

If there is an implication in the question that there's more to the association between Catherine and Ferguson than meets the eye, or some odd sexual aspect to it, I don't think this is true at all. In fact, I think more has been attributed to Hemingway in that respect than he ever meant. I don't mean with respect to these two characters but in general. Now this may not be an adequate answer again. I don't know quite how to take this question, so if you want to come back with some other comment I would be delighted to hear it.

MR. MOORE: Maybe we can take it on the next time around.

Morehouse: Hemingway states, "The world breaks everyone and afterwards many are stronger in the broken places." Could you relate this philosophy to the morality of the novel and the love element?

MR. BAKER: Well, there is the view that if you take a terrible strapping—as in this novel Frederick Henry takes a strapping when he is blown up and has his leg almost destroyed—that afterward you can be stronger because you have been through the mill, you've taken what the gods have to hand out and you in some way survived, more strongly. And I think he means to suggest, too, that Catherine has taken a strapping in the loss of her lover who has died before the novel even opens. You will remember that he wasn't wounded in any romantic way. He didn't have a bandage on him or a drop of blood on him. He didn't get wounded by a sword so that he had a chance to recover—instead of that, they blew him all to pieces. There was nothing left of him except one or two souvenirs which Catherine has retained. The implication is that she, having survived this blow from the hands of fate, is strong too in the broken places. We have two people coming together who have suffered and triumphed over suffering and then have fallen in love, and I believe that this is the kind of situation Hemingway wants to give us because he thinks it's a romantic one. Now what ultimately appears in the novel is that Catherine is going to have to die from a biological accident that has made her incapable of bearing children by normal means, and eventually, as with the ants on the log, the flames of death will come up and snuff us all out no matter how valiant, tight-lipped, or courageous we may be. It's a long road, or a short one, and death is at the end of it, Hemingway was fond of saying, and he makes this a tragedy with Catherine as the sacrificial image in it. But I think he wants us to believe that Catherine is one who has taken a licking and then survived it and has a certain degree of strength as a result of it in the same way that the hero has done.

Langston: We have two questions at Langston. The first question: Was Catherine's love for Henry a symbol of her religion or was it just a substitute for the love of the young man she had lost earlier?

MR. BAKER: Shall we take them one at a time? Was Catherine's love for Henry a symbol of her religion or was it simply a hangover of the love she had felt for the first young man?

Langston: Yes.

MR. BAKER: I think in the beginning it is quite clear in the very first major meeting between Catherine and Lieutenant Henry that she is inclined to get him mixed up with the young man who was killed. She even signifies by some of the sentences she speaks that she gets the two mixed up, and Henry reflects that he thinks maybe Catherine is a little crazy at that point. But as Lieuenant Henry begins to assume a reality of his own in her mind—in other words, as she falls in love with him as over against the young man that she had formerly loved—she begins to erect this new love into the status of a private religion. The death of the first young man has left her without any shrine in which she can worship. Now Lieutenant Henry, the substitute lover, has arrived; she feels strongly attracted toward him, and there's even one place in the novel in which she says, "You are my religion, you are all that I have to believe in," or something of that sort. So I think it's the case of dead god gone and the new god arriving for Catherine. That's what I intend to be the answer to that question. Now the next question.

Langston: The final paragraph of the novel suggests a note of despair and futility as Lieutenant Henry walks back to his hotel room in the rain. Does this suggest that he is still unable to cope with the position of man in society upset by the violence of war?

MR. BAKER: That interpretation could very well be put on the last paragraph in the novel as it was originally written, but I feel that Hemingway didn't intend that to be the application. All he meant to say was that this is the way a young man feels after he has lost his wife in childbirth; after he has driven the nurses out of her room and attempted to say good-bye to her; after he finds that a dead person is like a statue and that saying good-bye to her is like saying good-bye to a statue. Then he walks out and back to the hotel in the rain and there's an end of it. I don't believe that Hemingway would himself say that the larger implications of this final paragraph are anything but the human situation in such bereavement, and he would be likely to be quite scornful about the alleged larger significance of this paragraph.

MR. MOORE: Thank you. Now, another quotation from *King Lear*, "Though last, not least," Stephens College. Have you a question?

Stephens: Thank you. We'll move from the last paragraph in the book to the first paragraph and ask Dr. Baker if he would comment on that very famous first paragraph, particularly in relation to the stylistic devices that Hemingway has employed there.

MR. BAKER: I'd be glad to. It might be of interest to all these students that the original conclusion to Hemingway's *A Farewell to Arms* is now in print. I had a piece of good luck and was able to put it into a little anthology that I did. It's a quite different kind of conclusion from the one that is so famous about walking back to the hotel in the rain. But I throw that in—not to sell my book but simply to say if you want to look at the original conclusion and note how different it is from the conclusion that we all know so well, this is a place to look.

Now getting to the question from Stephens. I think this is, using a favorite Hemingway adjective, a lovely opening for the book, in fact the whole of chapter one which starts "In the late summer of that year we lived in a house in a village that looked across the river and the plain to the mountains." That was the summer of 1915 in Hemingway's invention. And he tells about the bed of the river where the pebbles and boulders were dry and white in the sun and where the water was clear and blue and moved swiftly in the channel. And then he brings our attention to the troops that went past and the soldiers marching and the leaves falling at the end of the summer, and afterwards the road bare and white except for the leaves. He tells about the fighting in the mountains and at night, the flashes from the artillery, establishing the fact that (as the critics of my own chapter on

A Farewell to Arms point out) fighting does take place in the mountains, after all, whereas the plain is rich with crops and fruit trees, which suggests that the plains are a good place and the mountains are a bad place. This is certainly so. But in the long run in this novel the plain of the Veneto, which is in the general vicinity of Udine and Venezia, is distinctly associated with evil; and the mountains, like the Abruzzi in Italy and the Alps in Switzerland, are associated with the idea of good.

Now there are a thousand things to say about this chapter—this short descriptive first chapter. When the soldiers marched along, muddy and wet in their capes, carrying packages of long 6.5 millimeter cartridges which bulge forward under their capes, they looked (we are told) as though they were six months gone with child. Now this is said, by some commentators, to be an anticipation of Catherine's pregnancy late in the novel. I doubt this myself, but, of course, it is always possible that Hemingway had this kind of thing in mind. Mainly what I think he wanted to do by this magnificent first chapter, these few paragraphs, is to give you the setting of the town of Gorizia, which is, as I've said, the setting for the whole first part of the novel, for the first twelve chapters of Book I.

The concluding statement that with the start of the winter came the permanent rain, and with the rain came the cholera, but it was checked and in the end only 7,000 died of it in the army—this, I think, is a clear anticipation of the connection Hemingway establishes between rain and doom throughout the rest of the book. I'm afraid that's a very inadequate answer to the question about the beginning of the book, but the book begins and ends so memorably that you could almost play a game of skipping from one to the other to see if Hemingway had maintained the tone. Is the tone of "But it was checked and in the end only 7,000 died of it in the army" comparable to the tone of "I went out and left the hospital and walked back to the hotel in the rain?" Are the two tones comparable as Hemingway performed that circular business that he sometimes attempted? For example, in *For Whom the Bell Tolls* which begins and ends with the pine needles of the forest, has he achieved a kind of circularity in coming back to the same notion, the same feel, the same emotional atmosphere that he began with?

MR. MOORE: I think we have time for one more quick question. We certainly don't want to let Dr. Baker go. Morehouse, didn't you have another question?

Morehouse: Yes. In the light of the ending would you say that Hemingway's hopelessness was seen in terms of stoicism or pessimism?

MR. BAKER: Well, I certainly don't think you could say it was any kind of worldwide pessimism at the end of the novel, nor do I believe, in the light of the original conclusion to *A Farewell to Arms,* that it's really, in a true sense, stoicism. But if I had to choose between the two I would say that it's much more stoicism than it is a world pessimism, or *Weltschmerz,* or any of those other afflictions that are so familiar in romantic literature.

MR. MOORE: Thank you. I think we still have time for one more.

MR. MADDEN: I have a question I would like to ask Dr. Baker.

MR. MOORE: Go ahead.

MR. MADDEN: I would like to have Dr. Baker comment, outside of the novel that we are studying, on Hemingway's total career and whether he sees growth in Hemingway's attitude from the first novel to the last novel or a deterioration?

MR. BAKER: All right. Do I see a growth or a deterioration as between the first novel and the last? Hemingway's own comment on this may be of some interest and perhaps is familiar to many of the listeners here. Hemingway said, when they admired *The Sun Also Rises,* that he was working with arithmetic. And when they clobbered *Across the*

River and Into the Trees, twenty-five years later, he was working with the integral calculus.

Well, I don't believe this is so, but I do believe that you can't justly say that there was a deterioration up through the time of *The Old Man and the Sea.* I think that Hemingway attempted an enormous canvas in *For Whom the Bell Tolls* and that he brought it off quite well in spite of certain flaws we might point to in the novel. In the case of *The Old Man and the Sea,* although it is a novella and a sort of a parabolical fable, his powers were still up to a very high level. Afterward, at the end of his life, he did begin to deteriorate; there is no question about it. A couple of short stories that he made the mistake of giving to the hundredth anniversary issue of the *Atlantic Monthly* seem to me to be very bad stories indeed. But Hemingway was by this time ill and aging fast, and I think this accounts for the final change that took place in the last three or four years.

MR. MOORE: Thank you again, Professor Baker. We are delighted to have had you with us today and we will read Hemingway with a new sense. Thank you.

March 9, 1964

James T. Farrell

James T. Farrell was born in 1904 on Chicago's South Side, which he has written about in various novels. He briefly attended De Paul University and then spent three years at the University of Chicago. He moved to New York, where he has for the most part lived ever since, and at first took various jobs—at a filling station, in a cigar store, in an undertaking parlor. His first book, *Young Lonigan* (1932), begun in 1929, told the story of a Chicago Irish boy in the area of 58th Street and Indiana Avenue where so many of the local Irish lived until they prospered in the twenties and moved to the South Shore area.

The Young Manhood of Studs Lonigan (1934) continued the trilogy, which was completed with *Judgment Day* (1935); the books are now published in one volume as *Studs Lonigan*, one of the finest twentieth-century American social novels. The material is not autobiographical, although Mr. Farrell was drawing upon an environment he had known all of his young life; but he observed it objectively, and Studs Lonigan is not a self-portrait. While working on the *Lonigan* trilogy, Farrell wrote *Gas House McGinty* (1933), a comic novel about employees of a Chicago express company. Besides the *Lonigan* books, Mr. Farrell has written numerous short stories and essays which have been collected in various volumes, and he has also produced several other series, the most notable of which contains the books dealing with the experiences of one of Studs Lonigan's contemporaries, Danny O'Neill, a somewhat autobiographical figure. Danny O'Neill is the central character in five novels: *A World I Never Made* (1936), *No Star is Lost* (1938), *Father and Son* (1940), *My Days of Anger* (1943), and *The Face of Time* (1953). In the following conversation, Mr. Farrell discusses other work he has planned. It should be made clear that he has never been the type of writer known as proletarian, though he has often been called an author of the proletarian school because he is a social novelist. But his milieu is the middle class, specifically the city-worker. Mr. Farrell's language is plain, based on the idiom of that environment, and the style is sometimes repetitive and flat; but this is appropriate since it suggests the unadorned and often monotonous quality of the life he is writing of, and the very buildings that house it. In In the following interview, the principal point of discussion is *Judgment Day*, last volume of the *Lonigan* trilogy. From the questions asked, it is evident that the students tended to read the first two volumes also, which helped expand the range of the conversation.

MR. MOORE: Mr. Farrell, why don't you give us your introductory comments for about ten minutes and then we'll ask you questions?

MR. FARREL: All right. I'm speaking about *Judgment Day*. *Judgment Day* was written three times in about eight months between June 1934 and February 1935. I had not originally planned *Judgment Day* to be part of *Studs Lonigan*; as a matter of fact, *Studs Lonigan* was originally conceived to be one book, one novel. When I was working on it, back in 1931, a friend of mine said to me that it was too strong for people to take at the time. I agreed with him. Volume I, *Young Lonigan*, had been the original first section. Then, after having written *Gas House McGinty*, I wrote Volume II, *The Young Manhood of Studs Lonigan*. From the very beginning I planned that this work would end with the death of Studs. That was my starting point but after having written the New Year's Eve party scene I realized there was no more I could put in that book. That was an end, so I needed a third volume.

I intended the third volume to be a fantasy in which I would reveal the dying consciousness of Studs. It would be like a wild dream. But, from day to day, when I began working on it the book wrote itself. It was very important to me for this reason: the third volume introduces the Depression and that puts Studs in history. The Depression was history, and it added significance to the *life* of Studs Lonigan. Then, along with that, I got the idea of introducing into *Judgment Day* an account of the administration of the last rites of the Catholic Church, the administration of the sacrament of Extreme Unction, this gives some meaning to the *death* of Studs. If Studs had not died in the third volume it would have been stupid to have written so much.

Now, as to the reason Studs died: You cannot say, for certain, that anything killed Studs; it's ambiguous, it had to be that. One cannot say that society killed him. It could have been he had a bad heart, that he had a heart that was weak. He might have died anyway with or without drink. One doesn't know. The real tragedy of *Studs Lonigan* is not only Studs. By his death there should be a focusing backward on the lives of many others with whom he comes in contact, who introduce the three volumes. There are many characters in *Young Lonigan*—there are over two hundred characters, I believe. Studs reacts so much, to so many things, that something more was needed.

It appears to be almost an inspiration that I thought of introducing Studs in the Depression. Needless to say, Studs is not a boy from the slums; it is not a story of the slums. Studs had by 1929 and 1930, it was revealed, saved about $5000 working as a painter for his father who was a painting contractor. He bought stock in an enterprise which was suggested to me by the Insull enterprise. Samuel Insull was the head of a vast public utilities empire which crashed during the early years of the Depression. I used the name Solomon Imbray. (I don't say it's Samuel Insull but it was like the Insull crash.) Studs buys stock in the public utilities enterprises of a man named Solomon Imbray and loses his money.

Now he might or might not have died if he had not been looking for a job in the rain. He would not have been looking for a job but for that crash. You can say that that caused his death. When we consider the death of anyone we are not absolutely certain to what degree society has played a role in it. The question of social responsibility in relation to Studs must be seen in terms of values. What values are emphasized in society and what values are not? What values are more easy to live by? In that sense you can say that there is a relationship between Studs and society. There's some social responsibility in the fate of Studs, but you cannot say that he was absolutely killed by society or that he was killed by the neighborhood in which he lived.

The main misinterpretation of this work is a misinterpretation of my own attitude. Between 1935 and the present—it has been almost thirty years since I finished *Judgment Day*, my fifth book, my fourth novel including the other Studs Lonigan books—I have thought much. I have written many other books but people still continue to interpret my ideas in terms of *Studs Lonigan* alone. That's incorrect; I've done many things since then. *Studs Lonigan* was the beginning of a life's work. I wrote the Studs Lonigan books, the three volumes, as a preparation to write the books about the O'Neills and the O'Flahertys. From them I wrote and developed more and more books. At present I am working on a series of about twenty-seven novels. You cannot take *Judgment Day*, the concluding volume of *Studs*, as a total representation of what I think or feel.

Now I would say that in *Judgment Day* there are a number of step-chapters: there's a dance marathon, an initiation into a fraternal order, the administration of the last rites of the Catholic Church, a movie—I write, in fact, practically the entire scenario of that movie; the movie is a gangster film, it suggests Al Capone—and a news reel. If you think of Studs from Volume I, there's a constant expanding outward of what is introduced into the work so that the social area grows larger.

A number of people have said that I am a naturalist who just saturates the book with facts. That's not true. The first two volumes of *Studs Lonigan* are very impressionistically presented; *Judgment Day* is different in structure. The fact that Studs is Catholic has something to do with the structure. It is necessary to describe ceremony, to describe ritual, to describe the Catholic Church in order to create atmosphere. In doing that I was not able to have what you would call a tight structure—not the structure of a story. People say that it is rambling. It isn't rambling at all; but it is not intended to be a tightly constructed story. It's a life history, and it was necessary for me to establish an environment as real as possible. That's new in American literature.

By the time I began this work I had some intellectual distance from this environment. By the time I wrote *Judgment Day* I'd been out of Chicago for several years. I wrote the book in Saratoga Springs and New York City. Technique with me is unconscious. I don't think consciously of devices. I want to present things concretely; I believe I found the right way of handling Studs. Now that's as much as I want to say.

MR. MOORE: Thank you very much, Mr. Farrell. You've illuminated the book for us and given us very interesting background material about it. Are you ready with your question, Jackson State?

Jackson: Mr. Farrell has answered three of our questions already. Would you comment on the forces that deprived Lonigan's world of spiritual vitality?

MR. FARRELL: Yes. You must consider the time. It was closer to the immigration, a first generation of Irish-Americans. There was a clannish feeling among the Irish; it came from their own experience. I might add at this point that prejudice had something to do with it. Prejudice is a poisonous attitude and *Studs Lonigan* is, I think, the first work which introduced the racial situation as exemplified in the large cities into American literature. There was a separation of groups in Stud's neighborhood where they were not entirely Irish. But he goes to the parochial school and he knows most of the Irish boys.

Then too, we must remember that this was before radio, before television, and at that time if a boy went to the eighth grade that was considered enough education. There were many fewer high school students, and there was an anti-intellectual attitude in the country as a whole. There was a suspicion among the common people—I don't like the phrase common people—among the people who were not in the educated group, that education and books were dangerous. There was a feeling, a vague feeling, about success. One got a feeling of success. I think those are factors that relate to the spiritual poverty. There was a blind faith in a kind of a predestination. If you worked hard it brought you success.

Of course, the First World War intervenes. In the beginning of Volume II of *Studs* you get the First World War, a historic dateline. After that there's an unsure moral consciousness with everything. The entire world, it would seem, was changed by that war. Then there was prohibition!

Morehouse: Were Stud's failures symbolic of his personal ineffectiveness or simply the powerlessness of the individual?

MR. FARRELL: Well, it's very hard to say. I made Studs up and I made Studs up so that he would be ineffective; I made the same point with his death. The sense of his death is that there was waste—there was wasted life. I would say this, you can have several interpretations. The attitude I have is that Studs wasn't able to carry the load of the future by himself. If he had lived there would have been waste in his life. He admitted he was very far from developing his potentialities. The thing that sets Studs off from many characters who are on the same level of education is that he has a tremendous drive for power that's wasted in dreams.

Langston: Mr. Farrell, Studs is filled with rebellion. Is this rebellion against society or against the social conditions which are responsible for man's spiritual poverty?

MR. FARRELL: Studs is not really in revolt against society. His revolt is blind; it is blind revolt. He wants to be a man and he is not a delinquent. He feels more at home with those of his own age and he doesn't want to change—he resists change very much. You know, Studs is better off than some of the boys. He has a future he thinks is sure because he has a hand in his father's business. Another factor about Studs is that he's small. If Studs were large, if Studs were tall, the book wouldn't make sense. Studs's size is involved. You have to remember this, we can explain how a character might feel but in the final analysis each human being is a mystery. Studs is real if, in his substance as a character, you believe in him as real. If a fictional character is created as a true creation of character there is a mystery in the end. I don't know why I did everything to Studs; I know why I did some of the things to him.

Stephens: Could you explain the significance of the initiation scene? Is there a parallel within our society?

MR. FARRELL: Well, there is a parallel. It's the fraternal order. That's about all I care to say on it.

Tougaloo: Does the spiritual poverty depicted in *Studs Lonigan* still prevail in our society and if so where would you see that a regeneration could come from?

MR. FARRELL: I don't know if it's worse or better. Sometimes I think it's worse, sometimes I think it's better. I believe the way you tell is to see the role that we have for Studs. At the beginning of *Young Lonigan* Studs wants to be a man—he wants to work and be independent. Today there's a different attitude among younger people. I don't know which is better or which is worse. We must recognize that there are casualties in every generation. I just don't know. You can't measure spiritual poverty—say it's more or it's less. Certainly, this is a deceptive period we live in. There's such a vagueness between the people of the country as a whole and the intellectuals, particularly those who are so critical-minded that they are sterile and judgmental. You can't draw an easy coalition of ideas and attitudes and criticisms. I don't think polls tell us much. I don't know. I would say this: I don't think America is an unhealthy country or a decadent country.

Drury: It has been said, Mr. Farrell, that the kind of black picture of personal disintegration that began in *Judgment Day* is the oblique expression of your idealism. Could you comment upon this and your idealism?

MR. FARRELL: I don't know if it's an oblique expression or not. I was carried away by *Judgment Day*. I stated in the beginning that the starting point of this trilogy was that Studs was going to die. The point is that he was conceived in dialectical contrast to the character Danny

O'Neill who was a figure in many of my works. Now it's possible I do have some idealism—I would rather not use the word idealism, it has sort of a taint on it. We live in a country where some people think they are realistic and they are not idealistic. I would say that it is an oblique expression of the fact that I have faith in man and I have faith in the future.

MR. MOORE: Thank you. Now we have a second round of questions coming up. Langston, do you have that question ready?

Langston: Yes, we have. Mr. Farrell, your technique has been found to be both realistic and naturalistic. However, some critics have termed both of these techniques as mystic primarily because, to some extent, you call for reform and an improvement which is not characteristic of traditional naturalistic writers. They note also that your determinism was used in a fashion different from earlier writers such as Dreiser and Norris. Would you comment on this?

MR. FARRELL: Well, in a way, what the critics say is their business, not mine. More than that, I never pay attention to them because I don't think most of them can quite tell me what I am doing. Even if they are right from their standpoint, I can't assimilate it. There's no reason why I should write like Dreiser and Norris. As a matter of fact, I don't. The word naturalism—I don't know in what sense it's meant. I've written an essay on naturalism, originally a lecture, which is in a book of mine reprinted recently and called *Selected Essays* by James T. Farrell. Here I point out that I am a philosophical naturalist. I'm not a determinist. The determinism in *Studs Lonigan* is not a determinism that I impress on the universe as a whole. The determinism I impose on a character as an author is when I decided, as with Studs, that he was going to die. The fact of Studs's death was in my mind all the time and controlled the entire selection of scenes and sequences. In my other work the characters are fighting their environment. I'm not as fond of determinism as they say I am.

Morehouse: Would you care to comment on the fact that the first two volumes of the trilogy are concerned with sociological factors and the last with psychological factors in Studs's environment?

MR. FARRELL: I don't make those distinctions between psychological and sociological factors of environment. Besides there is a practical relationship. It is as much psychological in the beginning as in the end. From the first page of *Young Lonigan* to the last page of *Judgment Day* there is a great deal presented of what goes on in the mind of the character, Studs Lonigan. In one sense the first two books are more psychological. I use a controlled free-association method, (there is a Freudian influence there). The idea of free association was employed more in the first two volumes. The books were not sociological investigation; there was no investigation. I remember from my boyhood many things and out of the memories I constructed, created, and developed a character. My plan of the book kept changing. I never write with an outline. I wrote it from day to day, from year to year. I did a lot of other writing at the same time. I decided that this would be a concrete story. I wasn't trying to generalize it. I had some knowledge of sociological theories and attitudes and some knowledge of psychological attitudes and philosophical views. I'd read a great deal by that time. All during the time I was writing *Studs* I read more. I was concerned with making the character real. My main concern in all my fiction is character.

Morehouse: What about the psychological relation between Studs and his mother?

MR. FARRELL: I don't have much to say. She's a mother. She resents the girl whom Studs is going to marry, and I don't know exactly what to say there except that it's one kind of relationship between a mother and her son. It's not drawn out too strongly. Studs never cared too much about his family, except to take them for granted. Studs lived more outside than inside the family. There's not a great deal of communication between him and his family. As a matter of fact, Studs doesn't communicate very much with people; Studs has a dream of himself. His dreams are more vivid than his conversation.

Stephens: Speaking of Studs as a particular individual, a concrete individual, is he also the Everyman as Alfred Kazin and others feel?

MR. FARRELL: That's for others to decide. I hoped that he would be like many others. When I wrote him I didn't care. I thought, he's going to be real. This is going to be a character in himself located at a certain time in a certain place. I didn't think of Everyman. Many people are of the opinion that Studs represents a certain element and a certain event for a majority of people—many people stated that to me. I do think that's true, but that's just my opinion.

Tougaloo: Would Mr. Farrell comment further on the role of religion in *Judgment Day*.

MR. FARRELL: Well, you see, I don't believe Studs is against religion. In *Judgment Day* I think the only role of religion is the use of the sacrament of Extreme Unction of the Catholic Church. It's a fact that gives greater meaning to Studs's death. If Studs just died at the end of Volume II, when he lies in the gutter after the New Year's Eve drinking, his death wouldn't mean much. The use of the sacrament generalizes his death. That's what I feel. I think that was a very happy inspiration. Studs is not antireligious. As a matter of fact, he has moral problems because of his religion. Every so often he goes to confession, and he goes to church almost every Sunday. Studs is deeply religious; he is not a religious spirit, he just accepts. He accepts institutionalized religion; he doesn't question anything about it.

Drury: We understand that a new novel by Mr. Farrell is coming out. Would it be appropriate to ask about that now?

MR. FARRELL: It's called *Where Time Collects* and it has about fifteen major characters but really the main character is a girl named Ann Daniels. It is set in a Midwest city which I call Valley City. This girl, who is a waitress, has a kind of purity about her and a great deal of energy and spirit. She marries a louse and both families are presented —there's constant shifting and changing in time. I no longer use the kind of chronological structure that I did in my earlier works, *Studs* and other novels. Now when I write I'm constantly going backward and forward in time. This volume is the second of my series. It introduces different characters but later the girl, Ann Daniels, meets characters who are related or connected with or associated with the characters in Volume I. This is a vast conception; at the present time I'm working on twenty-seven different volumes of this work. Volume II is, I think—this is a personal confession—the best book I've ever written as far as the writing is concerned.

MR. MOORE: Isn't this your thirtieth novel, Mr. Farrell?

MR. FARRELL: My thirtieth work of fiction.

MR. MOORE: Your thirtieth work of fiction.

MR. FARRELL: Eighteen novels and twelve volumes of fiction—of stories. I have over thirty-one thousand pages of manuscripts which are ready—almost ready, or close to ready.

MR. MOORE: May I ask, are you finished with the Bernard Carr trilogy?

MR. FARRELL: Yes.

MR. MOORE: That is just a trilogy; there will be no more volumes?

MR. FARRELL: Yes, except I have a lot of detail I can use. I'm working on several manuscripts I didn't use. One is where I have Bernard Carr and Danny O'Neill meet, and Danny O'Neill laces the devil out of Bernard Carr.

MR. MOORE (*laughing*): You had, I believe, intended to end the Danny O'Neill stories after three, but you wrote a fourth some years later, *The Face of Time*, 1953.

MR. FARRELL: There were four; that was the fifth.

MR. MOORE: Yes.

MR. FARRELL: I wrote a new beginning.

MR. MOORE: Do you have any further plans for Danny O'Neill outside of this meeting with Bernard Carr?

MR. FARRELL: No, but there are any number of stories and I've published a novelette but I've skipped now to Eddie Ryan, another name for Danny O'Neill really. It is autobiographical but it is not essentially autobiography. When you write an autobiography (I'm writing my own now) you have to stick to what is so, what is true. But in a work of fiction you can use an autobiographical character as an ideal character. You can make him good or great. I'm using Eddie Ryan, rather than Danny O'Neill, as the integrating image or figure of all my works.

MR. MOORE: Now, do any of our other colleges have a question they'd like to come in with at this time?

Tougaloo: Tougaloo does.

MR. MOORE: Go ahead!

Tougaloo: How have you achieved your immense output of work?

MR. FARRELL: Well, I just write. I write all night. You

see I'll sleep when I'm dead. I sleep three or four hours most days. I've been doing this since I was twenty-one. I'm pretty healthy so I can stand it, and I love my work. Now I write longhand. It's very hard to read but I used to write three drafts. I only write one draft now and revise that.

Morehouse: How would you compare your characters, Danny O'Neill and Studs Lonigan?

MR. FARRELL: Danny O'Neill is a parallel, is the dialectical opposite of Studs. He is tougher than Studs, but he doesn't brag about it. If you consider the way I describe the fight of Studs, there is a lot of fanfare. With Danny, he just boxes, he jabs with his left and hits with his right, comes up with a bloody nose, charges and boxes. He hits him. I would describe Studs as the dead center of mediocrity. Danny has a wider variety of experience. He has more curiosity. He's a better athlete than Studs.

Stephens: Let's try this one. Alfred Kazin has called your elaborate realism "a perfect example of that benevolent philistinism which believes that one escapes from materialism by surrendering to it" and an outgrowth of the "need of catharsis by terror, if not by pity." Would you comment on this, please.

MR. FARRELL: Mr. Kazin will have to explain that himself. I'm sorry, I don't know what he means.

Morehouse: Would you comment on two things: your use of headlines in the book and the ending of the book.

MR. FARRELL: About the headlines. I got that idea mainly from Dos Passos' *U.S.A.* I just thought it would give a sense of the horror of what the newspapers print. Also, in part, I used it to develop a plot of Solomon Imbray and the crash and to give the sense of the Depression. I used it to generalize the social atmosphere.

There is a tragedy in the atmosphere at the end. I originally planned *Judgment Day* to be a scene of the dying consciousness of Studs, a vast fantasy. Day to day *Judgment Day* wrote itself. I just jotted it down, I wrote a book that I didn't plan. When I came to Studs's death I wrote a long sequence but I could only use a page or two of it. I never could get it published, and I had a fire in my apartment in New York in 1946 and lost nearly all of that novel. I only had about twenty pages—fragments to make up twenty pages—and I put that in *Gas House McGinty*. I had a long dream sequence but I wrote that as a preparation for Studs's death. All through I introduced dreams into my writing. I used to hold myself closer to a strict presentation of reality presenting it in chronological order. I personally got a great relief from freeing myself. I was holding these in.

MR. MOORE: There's a great dream in *Gas House McGinty*, Mr. Farrell. Everybody will remember that.

MR. FARRELL: I don't read my own work but I read that the other day.

MR. MOORE: Well, it's worth reading and rereading again. I'm afraid our time is up. Good luck to your new book that comes out in June. Thank you.

MR. FARRELL: Thank you all very much. I hope I did my best anyway.

March 23, 1964

Karl Shapiro

Karl Shapiro was born in Baltimore in 1913. In school he wrote in emulation of his older brother, who had won several literary prizes. After attending the University of Virginia, which he left because he was more interested in composing poetry than in studying, Mr. Shapiro stayed away from schools for a while, then entered Johns Hopkins University and later went for one year to the Enoch Pratt Library School. His first book, *Poems* (1935), was printed by a small press in Baltimore. Drafted into the army in 1941, Mr. Shapiro continued to write poetry, publishing it in various magazines. Sent overseas in 1942, he served in Australia, New Guinea, and various Pacific islands. At this time his fiancée, Evalyn Katz (later his wife), arranged for book publication of his verses. These included *Person, Place and Thing* (1942) and *V-Letter and Other Poems* (1944), which won the Pulitzer Prize for poetry in 1945. *Essay on Rime* (1945) was a critique, in verse, of contemporary poetry as Karl Shapiro remembered it while stationed in New Guinea. *Trial of a Poet and Other Poems* (1947) has for its title piece a dialogue that projects an examination of the place of the poet in society. In 1946–47 Karl Shapiro was Consultant in Poetry at the Library of Congress, and in 1950 he went to Chicago to edit *Poetry: A Magazine of Verse*. In 1956 he became a professor of English at the University of Nebraska and editor of the magazine *Prairie Schooner*. He now teaches at the Chicago campus of the University of Illinois. Besides his poetry, Mr. Shapiro has written a good deal of criticism, some of it appearing in the collection *In Defense of Ignorance* (1960). He has continued writing verse, as in *Poems of a Jew* (1958) and *The Bourgeois Poet* (1964), the latter volume consisting of prose poems. Throughout his work, Karl Shapiro has manifested a fine control of language; it is not surprising that he has written an excellent study of prosody. But there is always sense in his language and always the declared participation of the recording and speaking consciousness, the poet himself. He can be wry, melancholy, joyous, wistful, and ironic; and he is almost always shrewdly witty. The poems of his which the students read for the present occasion are: "Teasing the Nuns," "Love for a Hand," "Messias," "Auto Wreck," and "Scyros."

MR. MOORE: Good morning. Our procedure this morning is a little different. This is the first poet we have interviewed, and it's good to have Karl Shapiro as our first poet. He has just been in Alaska. He's away from his home base at the University of Nebraska and will be speaking this morning from Carleton College in Northfield, Minnesota. Good morning, Mr. Shapiro.

MR. SHAPIRO: Hello, Harry. How are you?

MR. MOORE: Fine, thanks. How are you?

MR. SHAPIRO: Fine. I don't have any prepared statement; I'm against prepared statements. But I have a subject that I want to talk about; it fits in with the poems of mine the students have read. I notice that of the schools participating with us half or more are Negro colleges or have something to do with Negro students. I want to say something about the possibility of a Negro poetry in the United States.

I've been thinking about this for many years, editing magazines and so on. I have wondered whether we have ever had very much Negro poetry or whether we ever *will* have a body of work that could be designated, specifically, as Negro poetry. I know people like Gwendolyn Brooks, a friend of mine, and Margaret Cunningham, a poet I helped get published. But it seems to me that American Negro poetry is almost as weak as Anglo-American poetry, which is the sort of thing that most American poets write.

The trouble might be that in this country we have only one poetic orientation and that's English poetry. Everybody's brought up to study English literature and English poetry. I think that English poetry might be irrelevant to the American literary world or to the American world.

English poetry is possibly the greatest body of poetry in the full European sense, but its connection with American life and American culture seems to be pretty marginal, or at a tangent to what our life really is like. And this would apply far more to the Negro American than it would to somebody like me, whose background is not English except in so far as I grew up in the English language and knowing English literature.

Of the Negro poets that I know—and I think I know most of them—Melvin Tolson is one of the best we have in this country but he is practically unknown, even among poets.

MR. MADDEN: Mr. Shapiro, your voice seems to be dropping and we are missing the ends of your sentences.

MR. SHAPIRO: Oh, I'm sorry. I'm sitting next to a banging radiator here and that's not helping very much. I was talking about the American Negro poets I know—Melvin Tolson, Robert Hayden, Gwendolyn Brooks, and Margaret Cunningham. I think, although there have been attempts by people like Tolson to create poems out of a different kind of experience which is not the experience of the English culture, and by people like Hayden who are trying to get into the historical culture of the American Negro—slavery and so on—the kind of thing we've always had in Negro poetry in this country seems to be a pale imitation of English or Anglo-American poetry and consequently has simply disappeared into the main stream of the academic, university kind of poetry. When people think of Negro poetry they probably think of spirituals which are vastly overrated—sort of Uncle Tom on Sunday poetry—or jazz lyrics. Some of the lyric work involved with jazz is probably better, but this sort of thing has had, so far, no direct effect. So I believe it might be possible to evolve a Negro poetry in this country. I think if we should it would be completely unrecognizable and unlike anything that we have seen before.

In somewhat the same way I feel that poetry has nothing to do with racial matters. But which is American *can* differentiate itself from European aesthetics and philosophy of literature. That is something American poets have been working toward ever since this country was founded and they haven't quite got there. We have about two or three poets who are really Americans in the sense that Whitman was, but much of our poetry seems to fall back into the English tradition. Somehow the American Pegasus never quite gets off the ground.

Now, I'm not going to say more about that but, in connection with the poems that I've chosen, it crossed my mind immediately, what on earth would these poems mean to students in a southern Negro university? My answer would be, they probably don't mean a damn thing and shouldn't, but I'm willing to be challenged on that. An appreciation or understanding of these poems would be predicated on some kind of knowledge or experience of the foreign literature of England. I like these poems. I guess they are in the literary rather than a more natural tradition, whatever that would be. Now, would somebody like to take over from that point.

MR. MOORE: Yes, Karl. Thank you very much. The question period will now begin.

Stephens: Dr. Moore, I wonder if in talking about these poems we might avoid a "buckshot" questioning. Let's choose a poem and go down through the colleges to see about that one, and then another poem and so on. Do you think that might work?

MR. MOORE: Well, which shall we do first? "Teasing the Nuns"?

> *Up in the elevator went the nuns*
>   *Wild as a cage of undomestic ducks,*
> *Turning and twittering their unclipped hats,*
>   *Gay in captivity, a flirtatious flock*
> *Of water-fowl tipped with black*
>   *Above the traffic and its rearing suns.*
> *Higher and higher in the wall we flew*
>   *Hauled on by rosaries and split strands of hair,*
> *Myself in the center sailing like Sinbad*

> *Yanked into heaven by a hairy roc;*
> *Whence we emerged into a towery cell*
>   *Where holy cross was splayed upon the wall*
> *In taxidermy of the eternal. They*
>   *Bedecked in elegant bird-names dropped*
> *Curtsies, I thought, and merrily sat*
>   *And fixed their gaze on mine that floated out*
> *Between them and their poised hawk.*
>
> *"Sisters," I said.—And then I stopped.*

MR. MOORE: All right. Dr. Campbell at Morehouse, do you have any questions on "Teasing the Nuns"?

Morehouse: Yes. Mr. Shapiro, is there any progression of the bird images in the poem that is important to an understanding of the poem?

MR. SHAPIRO: I don't believe there was any conscious evolution of this bird imagery. And this thing from Sinbad, "hairy roc," I think was put in there simply as a kind of a fright image, to suggest something being yanked off the ground by some sort of beast. I think the only symbolic bird in the whole aviary is the hawk which is something like Gerard Manley Hopkins' comparison of the bird with Christ. The others are mostly just psychological images and have no particular philosophical content.

Stephens: We are particularly concerned with the last line which you have set off from the rest of the poem, and would like to suggest that there are a number of connotations possible. One reader has suggested that many people miss relationships with others because they don't take the one step that will establish the relationship. I wonder if you would like to comment on that particular line of the poem?

MR. SHAPIRO: Yes, I think the whole poem is based on that line really; and it is a kind of surprise or joke because it doesn't get anywhere. This is a poem written by a Jew who is teaching in a Catholic university. He is supposed to be telling the nuns what poetry is and then he gets up there to the top of this tower and they have all the answers to everything. He just addresses them and then doesn't know what to say. There is no communication between him and them, really.

Tougaloo: Ordinarily nuns seem to be quite different from the picture presented in "Teasing the Nuns." What's the purpose of such a gay picture?

MR. SHAPIRO: Well, maybe my unfamiliarity with nuns (*laughing*). But it seemed to me that when I was teaching these people that they were extraordinarily good-humored and seemed to be much happier than the "civilians" around. Also the fact that, in their general decorum, it struck me that the nuns were the last of the race of ladies. That is, they dress like ladies, they have manners nobody else has, and so on. The teasing has to do with teasing their ladylikeness.

MR. MOORE (*laughing*): I've noticed this too about nuns in college classes.

Jackson: Would you comment further on the phrase "their poised hawk." To whom is that reference made?

MR. SHAPIRO: Well, in each one of these rooms there is a crucifix on the wall. I take the image of the crucifix as sort of a stuffed bird and the hawk has some reference to Gerard Manley Hopkins' bird. It's poised because it's behind me. It has its wings out so to speak and it's—well, you might call it the Christian bird. It's about to attack this Jew. That's putting it a little stronger than the poem makes it, but it's something to that effect.

MR. MOORE: Now we have to get on. Our time is flying and we have the second poem in our list which is "Love for a Hand."

Two hands lie still, the hairy and the white,

And soon down ladders of reflected light
The sleepers climb in silence. Gradually
They separate on paths of long ago,
Each winding on his arm the unpleasant clew
That leads, live as a nerve, to memory.

But often, when too steep her dream descends,
Perhaps to the grotto where her father bends
To pick her up, the husband wakes as though
He had forgotten something in the house.
Motionless he eyes the room that glows
With the little animals of light that prowl.

This way and that. Soft are the beasts of light
But softer still her hand that drifts so white
Upon the whiteness. How like a water plant
It floats upon the black canal of sleep,
Suspended upward from the distant deep
In pure achievement of its lovely want.

Quietly then he plucks it and it folds
And is again a hand, small as a child's.
He would revive it, but it barely stirs,
And so he carries it off a little way
And breaks it open gently. Now he can see
The sweetness of the fruit, his hand eats hers.

MR. MOORE: Morehouse, again. Do you have a question on that poem?

Morehouse: Yes. "Love for a Hand" is I think, the perfect kind of poem where students, no matter where they are located, can relate in a very strong way. I would like to know what is meant by the image "Soft are the beasts of light." Why the image of beasts? Is that a variation of "little animals" or is that simply to bring in the subconscious world of the woman who is sleeping?

MR. SHAPIRO: I'll see if I can answer that. The little lights are moving around the room and because this whole thing is a descent into sleep, or the subconscious, everything is mysterious and a bit frightening. The little fragments of light turn into moving, living things. It is simply, I guess, an association of the depths of this kind of symbol.

Stephens: Is it possible that, by narrowing down the reference in this poem to the hand, you were trying to achieve a reflection of life that would actually make us look out in a larger sense? Why focus on this small element?

MR. SHAPIRO: On the hand?

Stephens: Yes.

MR. SHAPIRO: Well, let's see. The total image is almost like the image of drowning in which you see nothing. There's nothing visible but the hand. There's nothing for the man—this is a poem I wrote to my wife—there is nothing for the husband to hold on to but that hand, that he concentrates on. The rest of the body is missing.

Stephens: Is there anything in this that would be similar to the quality you mentioned in the line "Soft are the beasts of light." Is there a kind of liveliness to this hand which is then a reflection of the larger liveliness to which it's attached?

MR. SHAPIRO: I think this is a poem of diminishing return. There's nothing left at the end but the two hands. What the psychological significance would be I don't know, but the students can find out.

Stephens (laughter): Thank you.

Tougaloo: You spoke in a recent article against set patterns in poetry, yet this poem has interesting formal patterns and patterns of rhymes. Would you comment on that?

MR. SHAPIRO: Yes. All of the poems, I think, here are

either metrical or stanzaic. At that time I was writing in formal verse; I have since given it up. But for many years I was fascinated by conventional ways of using meter and standard line.

Drury: You have spoken many times in criticism of the intellectual approach to modern poetry. Is this poem more intellectual than the others that you have given us to think about for today?

MR. SHAPIRO: I'd say it's probably less. This is quite a personal poem. I think that I don't know what the intellectual content would be except the imagery is rather involved. But that's mostly a matter of technique. There's no ideology in this poem that I know of.

Drury: Then you see this focusing down on something that is much more personal and emotional as a way of escaping the intellectual approach that you don't like?

MR. SHAPIRO: Possibly. I think in a poem like this poets frequently ask themselves perhaps, can you write a love poem to your wife? What would it be like? This is something of that sort.

Jackson: One student has commented on the fact that the last line, "The sweetness of the fruit, his hand eats hers" might come from a metaphysical poet. We would like to ask Mr. Shapiro if he had been influenced by English metaphysical poets.

MR. SHAPIRO: Oh, I'm sure everybody has. When I was young I read all the metaphysical poets all the time, and I'm sure a lot of it fell into my bloodstream. I don't know that there is anything metaphysical about that particular line; in fact, one man wrote to me once, tried to get me to explain the poem, and then accused me of being a cannibal.

MR. MOORE: Now we are ready for the next poem.

MESSIAS

Alone in the darkling apartment the boy
Was reading poetry when the doorbell rang;
The sound sped to his ear and winged his joy,
The book leaped from his lap on broken wing.

Down the gilt stairwell he peered
Where an old man of patriarchal race
Climbed in an eastern language with his beard
A black halo around his paper face.

His glasses spun with vision and his hat
Was thick with fur in the August afternoon;
His silk suit crackled heavily with light
And in his hand a rattling canister shone.

Bigger he grew and softer the root words
Of the hieratic language of his heart,
And faced the boy, who flung the entrance wide
And fled in terror from the nameless hurt.

Past every door like a dead thing he swam,
Past the entablatures of the kitchen walls,
Down the red ringing of the fire escape
Singing with sun, to the green grass he came,

Sickeningly green, leaving the man to lurch
Bewildered through the house and seat himself
In the sacrifical kitchen after his march
To study the strange boxes on the shelf.

There mother found him mountainous and alone,
Mumbling some singsong in a monotone,
Crumbling bread crumbs in his scholar's hand
That wanted a donation for the Holy Land.

MR. MOORE: Morehouse College, do you have a question on that?

Morehouse: Yes. In your opening remarks you mentioned the fact that you had perhaps chosen poems which would not be relevant to the students in this area. "Messias" might be seen in this light more readily than the others. However, one student has pointed out that what happens in "Messias" might also have happened to a Negro in the same situation, particularly, "Fled in terror from the nameless hurt." Would you care to comment on this line considering his comment?

MR. SHAPIRO: Yes. I think that that line perhaps might carry over to a more general area of understanding, although I am here talking about, specifically, this kind of Talmud scholar who goes around collecting money so he can continue his studies—a sort of half beggar, half scholar. In this poem there is a conscious attempt to turn him into a figure who inspires fear—the father figure, the authoritarian who was either the Talmud scholar or God or the Father or any sort of authority which frightens this boy who is reading poetry. His terror is, I guess, the terror God, whether a big *G* or a small *g*, or the terror of a person who has laid down the law. In the Hebrew tradition the Bible is primarily the law.

Stephens: In the last stanza, one student has asked, what does Mr. Shapiro mean when he describes the father image as "mountainous and alone." She wonders if this is an allusion to Moses and Mt. Sinai.

MR. SHAPIRO: Yes. I think that's very good.

Langston: The second stanza of "Messias" says "Climbed in an eastern language with his beard / A black halo around his paper face." Why did you choose to use "black halo" when usually we think of a halo to be something white and shiny; and then, why do you say "paper face"?

MR. SHAPIRO: Well, this man doesn't speak English. He speaks a foreign language, and he has a black beard and his face is white. The paper, of course, has to do with the Torah or the Bible. He carries this kind of sacred halo with him that I don't particularly want. It is a black halo. Well, anyhow, that's an interesting combination of images. It seemed that his entire face was ringed, his white face and the black circle around it. It is more than visual though. There are all kinds of colors in here that have to do with religion: gold and black and white and red and green and so on.

Stephens: Another rather specific question comes from a student who would like Mr. Shapiro to comment on the line "Crumbling bread crumbs in his scholar's hand." She wonders if there is more than just the literal meaning here.

MR. SHAPIRO: I'm not sure I can answer that. This happened to be the actual image. Of course a certain kind of bread might be manna or something of that sort. But bread, I think, in the context of this poem would have strictly religious or sacramental meaning. Aside from showing the man's impatience or nervousness it might have something to do with the staff of life or the symbolic bread.

Stephens: Since this is often a Christian image, I think perhaps the use here would raise a question in her mind.

MR. SHAPIRO: Well, quite possibly I intended it to have that kind of irony because I used the term "Holy Land." Palestine was called everybody's Holy Land; and there would be that kind of contradiction set up between the two faiths.

Stephens: Then if we might ask just one more question on this poem. You mentioned the revolt from the Father. Is there also, in this poem, a revolt from the traditional religion? Is this at all a picture of the American Jew?

MR. SHAPIRO: I don't know whether I would transfer

my feelings to other people but, as far as I was concerned, this was a more personal poem and it did have some overtones of that sort.

Tougaloo: Would you comment on the title? If the old man is a father figure, is the child thinking of his own Messiah-hood and running from it?

MR. SHAPIRO: Yes, he's running from it. But there's a bit of folklore attached to this. At the Passover, one of the Hebrew ceremonies, the door is left open in case the Messiah should come, and there's a chair left vacant for him. When the boy answers the door the first thing he thinks of is that the Messiah has come, only he has the wrong connotations: he thinks he is coming to get him instead of coming to redeem him, or whatever Messiahs do. (*laughter*)

Drury: One of our students wants to know why in the fifth stanza you used the architectural term "entablatures." What value do you think that had in what you were driving at?

MR. SHAPIRO: Well, it suggests—it's such a gorgeous word—it suggests a permanency of architecture although it's nothing but perhaps little tiles on the wall. But everything suddenly begins to look hieratic.

Jackson: We would like for you to comment on the rhyme scheme. We see that you have "rang, wing, hat, light, heart, hurt, swam, came, lurch, march," like something from Emily Dickinson. Was that consciously done?

MR. SHAPIRO: I would say so, yes, to avoid exact rhyme and to get off rhyme, nuances of rhyme.

AUTO WRECK

> *Its quick soft silver bell beating, beating,*
> *And down the dark one ruby flare*
> *Pulsing out red light like an artery,*
> *The ambulance at top speed floating down*

Past beacons and illuminated clocks
Wings in a heavy curve, dips down,
And brakes speed, entering the crowd.
The doors leap open, emptying light;
Stretchers are laid out, the mangled lifted
And stowed into the little hospital.
Then the bell, breaking the hush, tolls once,
And the ambulance with its terrible cargo
Rocking, slightly rocking, moves away,
As the doors, an afterthought, are closed.

We are deranged, walking among the cops
Who sweep glass and are large and composed.
One is still making notes under the light.
One with a bucket douches ponds of blood
Into the street and gutter.
One hangs lanterns on the wrecks that cling,
Empty husks of locusts, to iron poles.

Our throats were tight as tourniquets,
Our feet were bound with splints, but now,
Like convalescents intimate and gauche,
We speak through sickly smiles and warn
With the stubborn saw of common sense,
The grim joke and the banal resolution.
The traffic moves around with care,
But we remain, touching a wound
That opens to our richest horror.

Already old, the question Who shall die?
Becomes unspoken Who is innocent?
For death in war is done by hands;
Suicide has cause and stillbirth, logic;
And cancer, simple as a flower, blooms.
But this invites the occult mind,
Cancels our physics with a sneer,
And spatters all we knew of denouement
Across the expedient and wicked stones.

MR. MOORE: Now we come back to Morehouse College

in Atlanta for a question on "Auto Wreck."

Morehouse: You begin with this very powerful opening image; in the second stanza the image is a variation of it; then in the last two stanzas we get what you might call intellectual. That is, I would assume you begin to bring in a kind of ideational statement. First, is this order of image first and then idea a deliberate pattern and secondly do you consider this the proper way to introduce intellect into the poem without destroying either the intellect or the imagistic power of the poem?

MR. SHAPIRO: Well, I would hope so. At this time this was a technique I used almost always in writing a poem. I set up the image with as much strength and clarity as I could; I devoted all my time to putting the picture in the reader's mind. Then, when it was there, I disposed of it somehow or dealt with it in some way.

Langston: We would like to ask a question on the last stanza. You have written "Suicide has cause and stillbirth, logic;/And cancer, simple as a flower, blooms." I'd like for you to explain this, please.

MR. SHAPIRO: Everything seems to have a cause except an auto wreck, or an accident, or whatever these things are. That is, there are unanswered questions about the meaning of the accidental. Does it have any meaning? Is there such a thing as pure chance? I don't answer the questions, I just ask them in a poem. I guess they're unanswerable questions. But even things like suicide are causal and cancer or whatever. We can ascribe a cause for almost anything—anything except the purely accidental.

Stephens: Our question more or less follows the question from Langston. One student notes that, in general, Mr. Shapiro, you might be called optimistic in your poetry but that this poem seems to express the philosophy of determinism, which we have run into in the prose writers. She wonders if you might like to comment on the attitude reflected here.

MR. SHAPIRO: I don't know that I can because I don't remember what my state of mind was. This poem might have been published in 1942, but it was written earlier by several years. And I don't remember what my interpretation of it was now. The philosophy of the poem would be not the same.

Stephens: Taking it one step further, a student notes that in your book *Beyond Criticisms* you say that "poetry should be neither pro-science nor anti-science, it should neither reject nor assimilate the machine. To take an abstract position about science or about anything else is to deflect art from its purpose." She comments that it seems, particularly in "Auto Wreck," that you are making a judgment about modern man and his machine. Would you comment on that?

MR. SHAPIRO: I would say not. I don't think I am taking a position and I don't think determinism would enter into these questions that are asked at the end of the poem. Rather I guess the poem's supposed to express the naïvete of man in the face of the ununderstandable.

Stephens: This is your occult mind?

MR. SHAPIRO: Yes, but everything known about the last act, the "denouement" and so on, is simply thrown around meaninglessly across the "wicked stones." "Wicked stones" is used here—certainly without any theological meaning—simply something that was in the way, a natural, blind calamity.

Tougaloo: Our question connects this poem with the next one. Both poems seem to center on the idea of death and destruction. Could you comment on this?

MR. SHAPIRO: Well, they were written about the same time and about the time the first conscription had begun.

The poem "Scyros" is about the beginning of the war, with its quotation from Rupert Brooke. I think there is a definite coloration of feeling in those poems that have to do with violent death.

Jackson: We have a question on this line "The traffic moves around with care, / But we remain." Can "But we remain" be read on two or three different levels? Is that conscious ambiguity?

MR. SHAPIRO: I don't think so. I believe I simply meant that part of this scene has come back to life but some of the people remain transfixed by the horror of it. "We remain" obviously would mean that we weren't killed in that particular wreck too. But I wouldn't know what other level of meaning you could have in this particular place.

MR. MOORE: Now we have our last poem which is a rather complicated one, "Scyros." Mr. Shapiro has mentioned Rupert Brooke and, as many of you may know, he was the British poet of the First World War who died of blood poisoning, I think, aboard a battleship in the Aegean Sea and was buried on the island of Scyros which was also an island associated with Achilles in Greek mythology.

SCYROS
snuffle and sniff and handkerchief

The doctor punched my vein
The Captain called me Cain
Upon my belly sat the sow of fear
With coins on either eye
The President came by
And whispered to the braid what none could hear

High over where the storm
Stood steadfast cruciform
The golden eagle sank in wounded wheels
White negroes laughing still
Crept fiercely on Brazil

Turning the navies upward on their keels

    Now one by one the trees
    Stripped to their naked knees
To dance upon the heaps of shrunken dead
    The roof of England fell
    Great Paris tolled her bell
And China staunched her milk and wept for bread

    No island singly lay
    But lost its name that day
The Ainu dived across the plunging sands
    From dawn to dawn to dawn
    King George's birds came on
Strafing the tulips from his children's hands

    Thus in the classic sea
    Southeast from Thessaly
The dynamited mermen washed ashore
    And tritons dressed steel
    Trolled heads with rod and reel
And dredged potatoes from the Aegean floor

    Hot is the sky and green
    Where Germans have been seen
The moon leaks metal on the Atlantic fields
    Pink boys in birthday shrouds
    Look lightly through the clouds
Or coast the peaks of Finland on their shields

    That prophet year by year
    Lay still but could not hear
Where scholars tapped to find his new remains
    Gog and Magog ate port
    In vertical New York
And war began next Monday on the Danes.

MR. MOORE: Now Morehouse College do you have a question about "Scyros"?

Morehouse: The first stanza was the most puzzling. We were able to work out most of the poem except the first stanza. We would like to know whether that "me Cain" was really the author or simply a symbolic person. Secondly, is the mentioning of England, Paris, China, King George, Ainu, Thessaly, etc., to establish the international conflict or international disaster which we are feeling at this moment? And thirdly, why the image of "white negro?" It is a very good paradox but does it have anything to do with the total poem?

MR. SHAPIRO: Let me answer the second one first. This had to do with the way this war began to break out in unexpected places all over the world. And let me come back to the white negro thing in a minute. I didn't get your first question. What did it have to do with Cain?

Morehouse: In the first stanza, what does it mean?

MR. SHAPIRO: The first two lines?

Morehouse: Really the entire first stanza.

MR. SHAPIRO: Well, the soldier is about to be drafted into the army so the doctors are, of course, punching him around with needles, and the officer in charge already assumes that this man is going to be a soldier. He has a mark of Cain on him before he gets going. And that image of the "sow of fear" comes from the image of fear. The President is shown here as somebody who is either dead or blind to what's really happening. I meant to use braid simply as a metaphor for generals and admirals; the President had come to confer with his chiefs. Does that explain that?

Morehouse: The soldier opens it up wide; now it's become quite clear. Now the "white negro" image?

MR. SHAPIRO: Yes. Now I don't know whether I'm the inventor of that famous expression or not, this is before Norman Mailer; but I didn't mean what Mailer means by it.

I prefer his meaning. I was simply talking about the mixtures of people in this country who suddenly drop their hedonism and become part of this whole nightmare of war. Brazil is simply any place not necessarily Brazil— beginning to become involved in the holocaust. There are also overtones in here—this creeping on Brazil—of what the South Americans call imperialism.

Stephens: Ours is a technical question. One of the students would like to ask Mr. Shapiro to comment on the fact that this poem is without punctuation. Is this a way of indicating the meaninglessness of war and yet the relationship of incidents happening all over the world?

MR. SHAPIRO: The advantage of not using punctuation is that you do something to the rhythm to keep it at a steady flow and you do something to the meaning by making the meanings less important than the images. I think that was why I didn't want it. While you are on the subject, the meter of this poem I took from Milton's "Nativity Ode." This was the kind of a literary irony I was playing around with.

Tougaloo: The poem gives a strong feeling of being in a universe of mixed sense and nonsense. You just mentioned the word nightmare and maybe that covers, but what was the impression you meant to convey?

MR. SHAPIRO: Nonsense is a rather mild word for this kind of war. I was trying to do this thing as closely as I could with some rather surrealist technique and I've never done much of that. The attempt here in the imagery, in the "dynamited mermen" and so on, and "tritons dressed in steel," is to use violent visual imagery in order to express the violence. Sometimes things are sort of pretty like "Pink boys in birthday shrouds." These are young men who are being trained as aviators and who usually dressed in these colorful things or flew through colorful clouds.

Drury: One of our students would like for you to

comment upon the prophet in the last stanza.

MR. SHAPIRO: Yes. The prophet is Rupert Brooke and the poem is named after the place where he is buried. Rupert Brooke in this poem is treated somewhat ironically. He was the last of the patriotic poets, and Sir Winston Churchill dropped a flag over Scyros not long ago when he flew over there because of Rupert Brooke and his famous poem about the soldier. But after Brooke the poets began to wake up and from that time on there were no more patriotic poets; they were all antiwar poets. The countries at war are trying to find a prophet such as Rupert Brooke who can please them and be a kind of a spiritual leader but they can't wake him up.

MR. MOORE: We have several minutes. Is there anybody who wants to come in with a question on one of these poems that has been left unsettled?

Morehouse: I have noticed in the four selections that there is a tremendous exuberance and almost overpowering imagistic projection, yet the poems are controlled by certain rhythmic, and in some cases rhyme and structural, patterns. I would like to know, Mr. Shapiro, whether this is an influence upon you of someone or whether you arrived at this combination of imagistic exuberance and a certain amount of formal control on your own. Would you comment on this?

MR. SHAPIRO: Were you speaking of a particular poem?

Morehouse: "Scyros" is in my mind, also "Messias," and also the hands poem.

MR. SHAPIRO: Well, all of my poetry up to that time was saturated in the great English tradition, and specifically poets like the metaphysical poets who impressed me by their technique more than by what they were saying. I was saturated too with modern English poets such as W. H.

Auden and Spender who were beginning to break some of the more rigid forms. But in the "Scyros" poem, there was a deliberate intention of taking a stanzaic form (I left out Milton's last line of versification) that seemed to me to fit quite well what I was talking about: my kind of nativity. I am talking about the nativity of death. It makes a perfectly reasonable or rational irony.

Morehouse: Do you feel that you have been influenced by Imagists, Lowell and that school?

MR. SHAPIRO: No, not at all until recently. I think in my early poetry I was less influenced by them than I should have been.

MR. MOORE: Thank you very much. I am afraid our time is up. I think we've had some wonderfully intelligent and searching questions and magnificent answers. I believe we all know a great deal more, not only about these poems which we've studied of Mr. Shapiro's, but also about the entire process of poetry and the process of the poets. We all owe Mr. Shapiro a vote of thanks for a very fine explication of these poems.

April 6, 1964

Muriel Rukeyser

Muriel Rukeyser was born in New York City in 1913. She writes that, because her father was a builder, she has always felt "a part of the building, tearing down and rebuilding of the city, with all that implies." She attended Vassar for two years, following each year with a summer session at Columbia. She became a reporter, covering many of the outstanding events of the thirties. She was even arrested at the second Scottsboro trial in Alabama, which provided the background for her poem "The Trial." Sent to Barcelona in 1936 to report on the People's Olympics, she arrived in Spain on the day the Spanish War started and was able to provide firsthand accounts of the conflict. Miss Rukeyser's close contact with world events gave her early poems a particular concreteness in addition to their pervasive lyricism. Her first book, *Theory of Flight* (1935), was based partly upon her experiences at an aviation school. In introducing *Theory of Flight* as one of the volumes in the Yale Younger Poets series, Stephen Vincent Benét wrote, "The mind behind these poems is an urban and a modern one. It has fed on the quick jerk of the newsreel, the hard lights in the sky, the long deserted night-street." For *U.S. 1* (1938), Miss Rukeyser traveled on that highway down the Atlantic seaboard. She has twice tried the experiment of linking photographs with verse commentary to give the poems in question a close relationship to their subjects. She has written a biography, *Willard Gibbs* (1942), which investigates the life of an American scientist. *One Life* (1957) is an altogether different kind of biography, one dealing with Wendell Willkie. It is made up of poems, prose passages, and such items as newspaper headlines. Miss Rukeyser has called this book "a story and a song." She has continued to write poems, collected in such volumes as *Waterlily Fire* (1963), has published several translations, and is the author of a novel with an Irish setting, *The Orgy* (1965). Miss Rukeyser's later poetry has far less social content than her earlier work; today the rich lyric strain that was always found in her verse appears more emphatically, and she manipulates words, phrases, and rhythms with

energetic skill. The poems discussed in the following interview are: "George Robinson: Blues," "Double Dialogue,"
and "Waterlily Fire."

MR. MOORE: We're delighted today to have that fine
poet Muriel Rukeyser, speaking to us. You'll notice from
the three poems that we have that she's an extraordinarily
versatile poet and that she has kept up her activity beautifully with this marvelous recent poem "Waterlily Fire." It
shows the continuing intensity in her work. Miss Rukeyser,
we're very glad to have you with us this morning.

MISS RUKEYSER: Thank you very much, Mr. Moore. I
am happy to talk about poems and particularly the materials of poems today. And I am very glad that the level of
this is going to be raised in ten minutes or so; that there will
be an exchange.

The materials of the poems are very serious, as you know.
There's an extraordinary relationship, not only with experience, but with the understanding of one's own experience in
such a way that something in the nature of that experience,
based in the unknown reader's life, can be given, can be
shared. Auden said once that living poets have been criti-
cized with that dirty word obscure. He said there *are* difficulties here. He said you'll know them if you've ever tried to
share one experience with one person. It's not only one's
own experience that is material here but the deep place
where the nature of understanding can be shared. It seems
to me that one goes fuzzy, one goes what is called obscure if
one dives, for this is a curious nervousness in the face of
poetry, the actual fear of poetry. This is not clear to all of
us, even to those of us who have committed all of our lives
to poetry. The sense of the fear of this, all around us, is
sometimes more acute than the sense of the poetry itself. It's
an enormous tragedy, a tragedy that's certainly not confined
to poetry, but poetry is an index and there are other in-
dexes. It seems to me the very deep expression of the Negro
at this moment, expression of the passions that are under-

neath the life of this country, is like the expression of poetry. I sometimes think of Wordsworth, about the poem and the writer of the poem as a state funeral. This is a social expression, wild, naked, clearly under passion, having to be understood. The writer of the poem and the reader of the poem share the same thing here. You, as readers, and you who are going to be writers of poems, the future writers of poems, share this with anyone who has written. We are all trying to come to fuller consciousness of our own lives by means of each other's lives.

Now the materials that I have used in these poems are perhaps of several different kinds, perhaps not, perhaps they are all of one kind. The first one is "George Robinson: Blues." George Robinson is a man unknown in his name, a man in West Virginia, a Negro involved in a fight, a fight of despair, an attempt at hope in the middle of hopelessness, a fight whose meeting took place in a tool-repair shop, so that the sound of the belts, the sounds of the machinery, cover or protect the sound of the meeting, where the men were dying while the women and children were helpless. This was before your lifetime. They were dying for the sake of the tunnel that was being built—really *not* for the tunnel that was being built, really because the imagination had not gone far enough then to insure them of the protection that they could have with the masks used against saturating dust that makes the hardening of the lungs, the hardening of the imagination.

The second poem, "Double Dialogue," is based on a real dialogue. I say "Homage to Robert Frost" and I mean it not really in homage to his poems as much as to himself. One evening, one night, one whole night, after a reading when he had asked me to stay, he talked to me about the last night in his son's life, the night before his son shot himself. The double dialogues were the two conversations, with the son speaking to Frost and Frost telling me about it afterward.

The parts of "Waterlily Fire" are based on these materials and many more besides, definitely and indefinitely. The first part, The Burning, speaks of the actual burning of the painting, of the building in which the burning of the painting of Monet's "Waterlilies" took place. The fire was in a fireproof building, the Museum of Modern Art in New York, and I found myself going to an appointment there and somehow getting in past the guards into the building and out again looking for Richard Griffith, my friend and curator of the museum's film library. I had no business going past the guards. I don't know how I did. This is the place in which before this fire there had been another building. I had had a job in that building and knew the street well. The city is the city I was born in. The pouring of the city, the concrete, the tearing down of buildings, the pouring of new buildings is very much tied up with my childhood because my family was busy with the sand and gravel business, the concrete business. The materials here go from childhood, growing up in a city, to the history before that, to a television interview (that came into my room as these TV incidents come into one's room now), to a dream, and finally, to an actual incident in the last area drill New York had, during which some of us stayed outside in City Hall Park. And, along with that, I've used an idea that comes to us from India: the idea of life as the "long body," as one's own body, an image in procession from infant to child to young grown-up to grown-up—all the changes—the changes of oneself and the procession of images. Mr. Moore, can you go on now?

MR. MOORE: Yes. Thank you very much. We will now call upon the different colleges for questions. We'll take each poem in order. The first one this morning is "George Robinson: Blues."

Gauley Bridge is a good town for Negroes, they let us stand
        around, they let us stand
around on the sidewalks if we're black or brown.
Vanetta's over the trestle, and that's our town.

The hill makes breathing slow, slow breathing after you
        row the river,
and the graveyard's on the hill, cold in the springtime blow,
the graveyard's up on high, and the town is down below.

*Did you ever bury thirty-five men in a place in back of
        your house,*
thirty-five tunnel workers the doctors didn't attend,
*died in the tunnel camps, under rocks, everywhere, world
        without end.*

*When a man said I feel poorly, for any reason, any weak-
        ness or such,*
letting up when he couldn't keep going barely,
the Cap and company come and run him off the job surely.

I've put them
DOWN from the tunnel campus
to the graveyard on the hill,
tin-cans all about—it fixed them!—

TUNNELITIS
holds themselves up
at the side of a tree,
I can go right now
to that cemetery.

*When the blast went off the boss would call out, Come let's
        go back,*
*when that heavy loaded blast went white, Come, let's go
        back,*
Telling us hurry, hurry, into the falling rocks and muck.

*The water they would bring had dust in it, our drinking
        water,*
the camps and their groves were colored with the dust.
*We cleaned our clothes in the groves, but we always had
        the dust.*

*Looked like somebody sprinkled flour all over the parks
        and groves,*
it stayed and the rain couldn't wash it away and it twinkled
that white dust really looked pretty down around our ankles.

As dark as I am, when I came out at morning after the

> *tunnel at night,*
> *with a white man, nobody could have told which man was*
> *white.*
> *The dust had covered us both, and the dust was white.*

MR. MOORE: Stephens College, a question on "George Robinson: Blues"?

Stephens: Yes. The students here have noted, of course, the rhythmical quality of the poem and the part of the title that follows the colon. Would Miss Rukeyser care to comment on any possible influence of Vachel Lindsay and the group of people who tried to incorporate blues rhythm into poetry?

MISS RUKEYSER: This is a free fantasy on the blues form, of course. In true blues you are likely to get the repetition of the third line being the repetition of the second. You are likely to get a long, thrown-out first line, cast far out. This is not only in the blues, you find it in the African songs which Miriam Makeba has been singing, and you find it picked up by many American poets who have been drawn to this repeating rhythm with its care for the repetition, the knocking of the blood, the beat that comes through against the verbal meaning. There's an old anthology called *Blues* that will show you the song form. You have it now, of course, in so many poems that are so deep in American poetry by now that it's become its own form. This is one of the loosest possible variations on it, I think.

Tougaloo: Does your poem "George Robinson: Blues" exhibit your concern for social justice and equality?

MISS RUKEYSER: I don't know what it exhibits. I would have to ask you what it exhibits. I'm speaking from the other side of it. I care here about George Robinson. George Robinson was a real man to me. He speaks for a great many things—not only the dust—much more for the men, and the women and children behind them. It seems to me that social justice comes in here as a matter of what is happening to lives—the way in which horizons are opened up, the way in which they are thrown away. Of course, the rage for justice comes into these things. I hope it comes in as a pattern for life.

Drury: Since the rhythms are so important here I wonder if you would mind reading a portion for us, especially the shifts from the longer spans to the shorter.

MISS RUKEYSER: All right. I'll be glad to: "George Robinson: Blues." (Miss Rukeyser reads the poem.)

MR. MOORE: Thank you. Jackson State College?

Jackson: One student has suggested that the last line probably suggests the idea of the certain inevitable involvement that the white man and the black man will have. Would Miss Rukeyser comment on the last line, please?

MISS RUKEYSER: I'm very glad you spoke of that. Looking back at the poem, I would say that it makes no comment on this point, because it's so external. It is a covering with dust. If it really works—if the last line really works, it does it by so strong an omission that I hope you get a suggestion of the opposite—that this likeness is inner, and not outer. I think if this sort of thing works, it works, as it does for me in the plays of Tennessee Williams, when you get so strong a suggestion of perfect love, of married love, of the love that is absolutely left out of the writing that the suggestion of the opposite comes through. But I would leave that to you.

Morehouse: We have two questions. Is it possible that the dust could also mean death? The dust was white, does the covering on both men have some reference to death or dying, or doom?

MISS RUKEYSER: I don't know. The dust was white. The dust was fatal to most people. I think this is part of the texture, of the way the poem is received.

Morehouse: Our second question has to do with your rhyme scheme, the way you structure your phonetic element. In the first section you have very strong lines—brown, town, blow, below. Then, at the end, it begins to fade away and your last four stanzas have rather weak or repetitious rhyme—dust, dust, white, white. Is this deliberate?

MISS RUKEYSER: Yes, it's deliberate in this way. One trains oneself, one prepares oneself, for it, and what I wanted was the suspended ending, an ending in which recurrence would do it. It should be read with a southern voice and a man's voice—mine is a northern voice and a woman's voice and it's not right for it. It should be read in George Robinson's voice, or George Robinson's voice as you imagine it.

DOUBLE DIALOGUE
Homage to Robert Frost

In agony saying: "The last night of his life,
My son and I in the kitchen: At half-past one
He said, 'I have failed as a husband. Now my wife
Is ill again and suffering.' At two
He said, 'I have failed as a farmer, for the sun
Is never there, the rain is never there.'
At three he said, 'I have failed as a poet who
Has never not once found my listeners.
There is no sense to my life.' But then he heard me out.
I argued point by point. Seemed to win. Won.
He spoke to me once more when I was done,
'Even in argument, father, I have lost.'
He went and shot himself. Now tell me this one thing:
Should I have let him win then? Was I wrong?"

To answer for the land for love for song
Arguing life for life even at your life's cost.

Langston: In your poem, "Double Dialogue," what is the significance of the space before the last two lines?

MISS RUKEYSER: Well, the poem is a sonnet, of course, of a kind, and the space—I would hope to use space in many ways—to let air in, to let time in, to prepare for a change in the nature of what follows. I would hope to make space give us some sort of metric silence in a poem so that it can be used musically. This, of course, is used in the mind to prepare for the two lines which are my own conclusion. The dialogue ends and I go on with it.

Stephens: One of the students has asked this question: Does Miss Rukeyser mean by "arguing life for life even at your life's cost," that there must be a higher value even beyond life itself?

MISS RUKEYSER: I would be glad, I think, if that were picked up in that way, although I speak very slowly. I think the arguing life includes all the potentials of life and that you are speaking of the potential of life in its religious sense, if I take you right. I am speaking directly about what I took the meaning of Frost and his talk with his son to be, and the painful, bitter answer to the bitter question "Should I have let him win?" I think a great many things have won if that argument is carried all the way through.

Stephens: May I follow that up then by asking if, in Robert Frost's life, you see a parallel? Is this why we have a double dialogue? Is there a parallel in the questions and arguments that he is having with life?

MISS RUKEYSER: I meant it literally: the two conversations, with Frost and his son and Frost with me, but I think it carries further. I think it is in the argument of life with life, in a sense, and it produces something.

Stephens: Thank you.

Drury: I was wondering if Miss Rukeyser agrees with Lionel Trilling that Frost is a "poet of terror"?

MISS RUKEYSER: I tried to make a defensive statement

at the beginning that this was related—not so much to Frost's poems but to the way he was speaking that evening. I think that he has reaped some of the things he was talking about; that he has simplified out many things and that he has suggested many things in their opposites, but it was his personal quality, the biographical quality, to which I was speaking in this poem.

Jackson: Before I gave out the poems to my class I read this poem aloud without allowing the students to know who had written this poem. When I asked them, all of them said Robert Frost.

MISS RUKEYSER: Oh?

Jackson: I wonder, was there a conscious effort on Miss Rukeyser's part to write in the idiom and style of Frost?

MISS RUKEYSER: It was really to bring through the way that Frost was speaking that night. I have written many sonnets—more when I was in high school and college than since—and I have written in very strict form (mostly very early) and it seemed to me that this form was closer to what Frost was doing. The way to get his voice in, without imitating him, was to do it in this way.

Morehouse: One student has pointed out that you have a way by which you balance the prose with a poetic quality—the repetition of "he said," the way in which "win" goes to "won," etc. Was this again deliberate manipulation on your part of the prose conversation but, at the same time, an awareness of the poetic end you are trying to get?

MISS RUKEYSER: I think you are speaking for the way of poetry, in which the climbing sounds will produce the emotions. I've cared about this very much; people have asked me why I've rhymed so little and I think they've done this with poet after poet who rhymes very much and uses rhymes within the line and who works with the sounds as they climb. I work in a form which I call held rhyme, in which all the rhymes are modulations of one central sound and move toward a tonic, if you like, which is the last word of the poem. I feel that recurrence itself is a romantic thing—I very much like working with it in the actual repetition of phrases sometimes and in the climbing of one sound.

Morehouse: I think it was Frost who said that to leave rhyme out of poetry was like playing tennis with the net down, but I think you compensate for this by your handling of phonetic structure. Is this true?

MISS RUKEYSER: I think really you will find many, many rhymes in what I do. They may not be at the ends of the lines. I've done something else that I care about. I'll tell you about one line, for instance, that I think speaks of what I'm trying for. I once wrote a poem called "Ajanta" which has been reprinted rather widely and the first line of this poem is this: "Came in my full youth to the midnight cave." Now I've thought of that line itself as an arch form—in which "came" and "cave" balance and in which "in my" and "midnight" balance and in which "full youth" and "to the" balance "came in my full youth to the midnight cave." I care very much about the close meaning of the structure.

MR. MOORE: Thank you. Now before we leave this poem is there anyone else from any of the schools who has a question on "Double Dialogue"?

Stephens: At the risk of repetition, I'd like to follow up one thing. In setting aside the last two lines of the sonnet we start with "to answer" and we can go back to "was I wrong to answer for the land"—this is one way that it can be read, as though this were an extension of the first dialogue or the dialogue with Frost. Then it might have other possibilities—a possibility of poetic comment from the poet herself in which she notes the effect of this incidence on Frost's life and on what he was doing. Should we read it both ways, Miss Rukeyser?

MISS RUKEYSER: I, myself, at this time would prefer the second way and I imagine that is the real reason for the leaving of the space. These are the lines that describe Frost's whole—the essence of what he was doing—even absolutely wrung in agony and grief.

MR. MOORE: Thank you and now "Waterlily Fire."

WATERLILY FIRE
for Richard Griffith

I.   The Burning

Girl grown woman   fire   mother of fire
I go the stone street turning to fire.   Voices
Go screaming   Fire   to the green glass wall.
And there where my youth flies blazing into fire
The dance of sane and insane images, noon
Of seasons and days.   Noontime of my one hour.

Saw down the bright noon street the crooked faces
Among the tall daylight in the city of change.
The scene has walls   stone   glass   all my gone life
One wall a web through which the moment walks
And I am open, and the opened hour
The world as water-garden   lying behind it.
In a city of stone, necessity of fountains,
Forced water fallen on glass, men with their axes.

An arm of flame reaches from water-green glass,
Behind the wall I know waterlilies
Drinking their light, transforming light and our eyes
Skythrown under water, clouds under those flowers,
Walls standing on all things stand in a city noon
Who will not believe a waterlily fire.
Whatever can happen in a city of stone,
Whatever can come to a wall can come to this wall.

I walk in the river of crisis toward the real,
I pass guards, finding the center of my fear
And you, Dick, endlessly my friend during storm.

The arm of flame striking through the wall of form.

II.   The Island

Born of this river and this rock island, I relate
The changes   :   I born when the whirling snow
Rained past the general's grave and the amiable child
White past the windows of the house of Gyp the Blood.
General, gangster, child.   I know in myself the island.

I was the island without bridges, the child down whose
*   blazing*
Eye the men of plumes and bone raced their canoes and fire
Among the building of my young childhood, houses;
I was those changes, the live darknesses
Of wood, the pale grain of a grove in the fields
Over the river fronting red cliffs across—
And always surrounding her the river, birdcries, the wild
Father building his sand, the mother in panic her parks—
Bridges were thrown across, the girl arose
From sleeping streams of change in the change city.
The violent forgetting, the naked sides of darkness.
Fountain of a city in growth, an island of light and water.
Snow striking up past the graves, the yellow cry of spring.

Whatever can come to a city can come to this city.

Under the tall compulsion

*   of the past*

I see the city

*   change like a man changing*

I love this man

*   with my lifelong body of love*

I know you

*   among your changes*

talks with authors

> *wherever I go*

Hearing the sounds of building

> *the syllables of wrecking*

A young girl watching

> *the man throwing red hot rivets*

Coals in a bucket of change
How can you love a city that will not stay?
I love you
> *like a man of life in change.*

Leaves like yesterday shed, the yellow of green spring
Like today accepted and become one's self
I go, I am a city with bridges and tunnels,
Rock, cloud, ships, voices. To the man where the river met
The tracks, now buried deep along the Drive
Where blossoms like sex pink, dense pink, rose, pink, red.

Towers falling.   A dream of towers.
Necessity of fountains.   And my poor,
Stirring among our dreams,
Poor of my own spirit, and tribes, hope of towers
And lives, looking out through my eyes.
The city the growing body of our hate and love,
The root of the soul, and war in its black doorways.
A male sustained cry interrupting nightmare.
Male flower heading upstream.

Among a city of light, the stone that grows.
Stigma of dead stone, inert water, the tattered
Monuments rivetted against flesh.

Blue noon where the wall made big agonized men
Stand like sailors pinned howling on their lines, and I
See stopped in time a crime behind green glass,
Lilies of all my life on fire.

Flash faith in a city building its fantasies.

I walk past the guards into my city of change.

III.   Journey Changes

Many of us   Each in his own life waiting
Waiting to move   Beginning to move   Walking
And early on the road of the hill of the world
Come to my landscapes emerging on the grass

The stages of the theatre of the journey

I see the time of willingness between plays
Waiting and walking and the play of the body
Silver body with its bosses and places
One by one touched awakened into into

Touched and turned one by one into   flame

The theatre of the advancing goddess   Blossoming
Smiles as she stands intensely being in stillness
Slowness in her blue dress advancing standing I go
And far across a field over the jewel grass

The play of the family stroke by stroke acted out

Gestures of deep acknowledging on the journey stages
Of the playings the play of the goddess and the god
A supple god of searching and reaching
Who weaves his strength   Who dances her more alive

The theatre of all animals, my snakes, my great horses

Always the journey   long   patient   many haltings
Many waitings for choice and again easy breathing
When the decision to go on is made
Along the long slopes of choice and again the world

The play of poetry approaching in its solving

Solvings of relations in poems and silences
For we were born to express   born for a journey
Caves, theatres, the companioned solitary way
And then I came to the place of mournful labor

A turn in the road and the long sight from the cliff

Over the scene of the land dug away to nothing and many
Seen to a stripped horizon carrying barrows of earth
A hod of earth taken and emptied and thrown away
Repeated farther than sight.   The voice saying slowly

But it is hell.   I heard my own voice in the words
Or it could be a foundation   And after the words
My change came.   To enter.   The theatres of the
*   world.*

IV.   Fragile

I think of the image brought into my room
Of the sage and the thin young man who flickers and asks.
He is asking about the moment when the Buddha
Offers the lotus, a flower held out as declaration.
"Isn't that fragile?" he asks.   The sage answers:
"I speak to you.   You speak to me.   Is that fragile?"

v.   *The Long Body*

This journey is exploring us. Where the child stood
An island in a river of crisis, now
The bridges bind us in symbol, the sea
Is a bond, the sky reaches into our bodies.
We pray   :   we dive into each other's eyes.

Whatever can come to a woman can come to me.

This is the long body   :   into life from the beginning.
Big-headed infant unfolding into child, who stretches and
*   finds*
And then flowing the young one going tall, sunward,
And now full-grown, held, tense, setting feet to the ground,
Going as we go in the changes of the body,

As it is changes, in the long strip of our many
Shapes, as we range shifting through time.
The long body   :   a procession of images.

This moment in a city, in its dream of war.

We chose to be,

Becoming the only ones under the trees

when the harsh sound

Of the machine sirens spoke. There were these two men,
And the bearded one, the boys, the Negro mother feeding
Her baby. And threats, the ambulances with open doors.
Now silence. Everyone else within the walls. We sang.

We are the living island,

We the flesh of this island, being lived,
Whoever knows us is part of us today.

Whatever can happen to anyone can happen to me.

Fire striking its word among us, waterlilies
Reaching from darkness upward to a sun
Of rebirth, the implacable.   And in our myth
The Changing Woman who is still and who offers.

Eyes drinking light, transforming light, this day
That struggles with itself, brings itself to birth.
In ways of being, through silence, sources of light
Arriving behind my eye, a dialogue of light.

And everything a witness of the buried life.
This moment flowing across the sun, this force
Of flowers and voices body in body through space.
The city of endless cycles of the sun.

I speak to you   You speak to me

> *Langston:* I would like to know what "crooked faces"

in "Waterlily Fire" is supposed to mean. I could see crooked faces in the shadows of night, but not in the bright, noon street. Will you please comment on this?

MISS RUKEYSER: I have thought very often of the street full of people hoping for unity in themselves as being broken into pieces. It seems to me one of the crimes of our life, of the order we live in, is to require a partial response from people. If you look at their jobs, you know, you see how often they are partial responses to things that are demanded of people to make the jobs go. If you look at people in their professions, in the way they work, in the way they live, when they compromise, when they cut down on their fullness, when they destroy by forgetting, when they destroy by distorting, the fragmenting of the person—I meant it in that way, in the way of distorting—you see this very clearly on some streets. You see it, of course, as a projection of yourself in certain things. It was the setting up of this kind of distortion of a belief in some idea of security rather than the idea of living in change, living in movements, living in the procession of images that is the long body, that makes the main idea. I was interested in what is not so secure in life but necessary, to go on living, to go on moving and breathing as a living thing.

MR. MOORE: Thank you. Now, Stephens College, your question on "Waterlily Fire."

Stephens: Yes, I hope, Dr. Moore, that we'll be able to have several rounds on this poem. It is long and complex. The first question is an overall question. Your poem "Waterlily Fire" seems at once to be a search for the self through a series of individual images and, at the same time, a recognition of the illusiveness of that self by the setting apart of psychological fragments. Will you comment on that?

MISS RUKEYSER: Yes, I'll try to. I'll go straight to the word illusive. It seems to me that these things are illusive if one thinks of them as a fixed goal but if one sees it in move-

ment, in life, as the long body, for example, it is a continual
search but it is a continual finding also. We've talked so
much about search and I wish to live in search, but I wish
also to find from time to time; I think one finds if one—well,
it goes all the way back—this is not in any way a contemporary thing. I think it's this thing of knowing that one lives in
relation to the known and one also lives in relation to the
unknown. It is knowing that these are moving, that one is a
moving being in a moving world, in a moving universe. The
stability is in relationship. This may be a very female way
of talking about it. I think it is a way that transcends such
things as illusive, and even such qualities as female, but it is
a question of moving—being able to dance these things
out—to live in relationships that are all moving but that
have their own stability, a kind of musical stability, a spiritual stability.

Stephens: Would this be related to the painting in any
way, as one observes that particular painting? There was
constant change and yet a fixed item.

MISS RUKEYSER: Thank you very much. I hope so. Of
course, you have here the destruction of the painting and
the fact that it was demolished. In working with people who
are writing poems I've tried something more than once:
having someone go outside the room who was willing to go
out and try to write a poem and bring it back. At that point
I'd tear it up (as I would do only in this exercise) and ask
the people where the poem is now. Where it is is in them.
And then, of course, I'd put the poem together again.

Stephens: It sounds like a good experiment.

MR. MOORE: I join Stephens in hoping we can have
several rounds with this particular poem with such interesting complexity and rewarding richness.

MISS RUKEYSER: Thank you. I like that. I'll keep my
answers short.

MR. MOORE: Well, please make them as full and deep as you wish. Tougaloo College, your question on "Waterlily Fire."

Tougaloo: One of our students says this, "As I read this poem I felt that the destruction of the painting gave the poet a feeling that by this one change her whole life and the life of the city might be altered," and she quotes "lilies of all my life on fire" and "I walk past the guards into my city of change." Would you comment on this?

MISS RUKEYSER: Yes. I believe that student is right. And I think of Dylan Thomas' saying that to write a poem changes this world. I believe that everything does. I believe that it is a question of noticing, of absorbing in one's own life, of allowing it to move in its own movement and I don't think that that change can be denied. I think there is also a clear relationship that moves along in the middle of change. I think that if you see everything as static you run into the whole other trap. When William James lectured once in Boston, he asked for questions and a Boston lady got up (this was before any phone relationships) and said, "What does the world rest on?" He said, "Well, what *does* the world rest on?" fascinated, and she replied, "A rock." And he asked, "What does that rest on?" She said, "Young man, let me make myself clear, it's rock all the way." I think that idea of stability and security is the thing that makes for the fragmentation.

Drury: One of the students would like a comment on the punctuation in this poem. I assume he means the arrangement on the page in general—the pauses.

MISS RUKEYSER: Yes. I've had a lot of trouble with printers about that and I finally had a rubber stamp made that I put on the pages of my manuscript that says, "Please believe the punctuation." I do mean that; it has to do with breathing, with certain qualities in the lines, and with what I hope to work toward in my idea of metric styling.

Jackson: One student has suggested that the water images are probably symbolic of the healing power of life and probably the fire symbols are meaningful as destructive forces. Would you comment on that Miss Rukeyser?

MISS RUKEYSER: I think if you once start that you have to take it much farther, and do the whole constellation of water meanings and fire meanings in which they go farther than the ones we know and farther into the whole balance of destruction and creation.

Morehouse: The fire seems to be really a double symbol of energy, force, and passion on the one hand and destruction on the other. The destruction comes through a kind of growth—growth is destruction rather than just a symbol of negative destruction. Would you comment on that?

MISS RUKEYSER: Yes. I think that *is* the comment. I think that it starts in all these places and goes on and on.

Morehouse: A second point is about general technique. Do you become the city? Is that your objective correlative to your emotions and feelings?

MISS RUKEYSER: There's one place where that's said bluntly, "I was the island without bridges," in the second part called "The Island" in which the idea of the city as change, particularly as pouring and being destroyed and pouring again and the bonds of the city. I think that I would agree with that—but you know, not as bluntly as that. I wouldn't *say* that. If anybody asked me to explain it, I don't think I'd explain it.

Langston: I would like to know in your poem "The Island" where you say, "I am a city with bridges and tunnels / Rock, cloud, ships, voices," whether you are using this as a metaphor, whether you are using these as a symbol. What are they really speaking of?

MISS RUKEYSER: I would like to throw that right back. What do you think? I'm sorry, I apologize for that but I'm very interested in what you're saying, the way it comes through. Unfair of me, I know.

Langston: I'm not sure.

MISS RUKEYSER: It's all right to be not sure. It's all right.

Langston: I thought it probably would mean that, just as "I am a city," I am a person with views and bridges, probably as a symbol for things that you go through in everyday life—mishaps and everything.

MISS RUKEYSER: Oh good, I'm very glad you did that, because nobody talked about dailiness at all and I hoped very much that it would move here from the quality of dailiness to whatever depth of symbolic quality you want to take it. I wasn't just being unfair in giving it back to you, I was hoping that that would come through. Thank you very much.

Stephens: If one were to summarize a response to the poem, could it be that of the realization of the delicateness and fragility of all human relationships? Would this be a major idea in the poem?

MISS RUKEYSER: Well, I wouldn't want to leave it as delicacy without giving also the polarity of that, without saying, in all this delicacy there is tensile strength, in all this fineness of noticing there is perception and response and fineness of action as response. I would hate to leave the delicacy alone as a quality although I would never let it go. I believe that these things are very fragile, are both "thingy" and without the qualities of things. But the "thingy" quality, the daily quality, the momentary quality, in all its fragility and all its strength is to be preserved and the way in which it can truly be noticed is an art, the way in which it can truly be said.

Stephens: I think perhaps in this question there is at least a recognition of the relationship between your much earlier poem, "Effort at Speech," and the repetition of the final lines of that poem in part four of this poem.

MISS RUKEYSER: Yes. Yes. And when I came to make the book, *Waterlily Fire,* I felt that if I began with "Effort at Speech" and ended with the "I speak to you, you speak to me," that would show a way in which it had come through for me.

Stephens: There is in your mind a real relationship here, too, then.

MISS RUKEYSER: Yes. Yes, indeed.

Stephens: Thank you.

Tougaloo: We'd like to take up your last point again, this "I speak to you, you speak to me" which is repeated and with which the poem ends. Would we be right in seeing that one of the permanent things behind the fringe, the meaning and hope of life is human communication?

MISS RUKEYSER: Yes. Surely, not only communication, but what comes out of it, the fact "there" is another ending place and "there" is another beginning place and I hope that in the end readers seem to sense this which is without punctuation, that the beginning is open to us.

Jackson: This is just a comment from an observation by a student. The student says that when one looks at this picture by Monet, one is constantly aware of the intensity of the light and of the intensity of the changing blues and greens in the colors of the picture. We have observed throughout Miss Rukeyser's poem that she has several greens and blues. They seem to be her favorite colors. On the last page we have that very, very striking image of "eyes drinking light." The student observes that when she looks at this picture again after reading this poem—it seemed that her eyes were drinking light.

MISS RUKEYSER: I am very happy that that comes through.

MR. MOORE: Thank you. Morehouse College.

Morehouse: Miss Rukeyser, I notice that in your discussion, in your response to questions about the imagery, you were willing to let the images take on a light of their own—other than what you had intended. Is this a proper evaluation of your attitude?

MISS RUKEYSER: Yes, I think it is. I hope very much that the hypothetical reader, the unknown reader, the reader for whom one writes, will do this through a kind of listening that is very much bringing his entire life to the moment. But I hope for that in every part of life, it's not simply a question of poetry here. It is my hope for the way in which I would hope to live and the way in which I would hope other people would live that they would bring their entire life to believe in experience, bring their entire life to this moment in which we now are with its "be true" moments, moving moments, the moment which has never been written.

Morehouse: The second question grows out of that. Would you say then that "The arm of flame striking through the wall of form" could be the destination of a higher form—at least for me it is. I feel that this is what you are really elaborating on.

MISS RUKEYSER: It's certainly the trigger, in a way, the private image for the poem.

MR. MOORE: Thank you. I think we have time for another question or so. Is there someone who has one that he would like to come in with?

Stephens: Yes.

MR. MOORE: All right, Stephens.

Stephens: On the bottom of our copy there are some lines which would seem, in a sense, to be descriptive of the technique employed, where you use the lines: "The play of poetry approaching in its solving / Solvings of relations in poems and silences." Would this be related to the form of this poem?

MISS RUKEYSER: Yes. Yes, I hope so. And many of the questions that you have asked about form, about silence, well, about punctuation, which is silence.

Morehouse: I notice the very rich texture of your writing—imagery especially. Would you say that you have been influenced by Whitman and Amy Lowell in any way?

MISS RUKEYSER: Make it Whitman and D. H. Lawrence.

MR. MOORE: I'm afraid that our time is up.

MR. MADDEN: That comment on Lawrence should make you happy, Harry.

MR. MOORE: Thank you.

MISS RUKEYSER: It won't make Amy Lowell happy.

MR. MADDEN: May I make one comment?

MR. MOORE: Go ahead.

MR. MADDEN: In part four (I've already talked with Miss Rukeyser about this) the "thin young man" to whom she refers is a friend of Stephens College, Huston Smith. He will be here tomorrow and I plan to show him this poem in case he has not seen it yet and talk it over with him. I'm sure he'll be quite happy.

MISS RUKEYSER: I wish I could hear you do that because the interview was a marvelous one and it evoked this section of the poem.

MR. MOORE: Well, I think we're all sorry that this most interesting and fruitful session is coming to an end. We're certainly indebted to Miss Rukeyser for giving us a wonderful experience this morning. Thank you.

April 10, 1964

Anne Sexton

Anne Sexton, born in Newton, Massachusetts, in 1928, now lives in Newton Lower Falls, not far from her birthplace. She attended Boston University without taking a degree; while there studied poetry with Robert Lowell. Since 1957 her verse has appeared in journals such as the *Antioch Review*, the *Hudson Review*, and the *Partisan Review* as well as in such mass-circulation magazines as *Harper's* and the *New Yorker*. In 1959 Mrs. Sexton was granted the Robert Frost Fellowship to study at the Bread Loaf School, and in the following year she brought out her first book of poems, *To Bedlam and Part Way Back*, followed in 1962 by *All My Pretty Ones*, and in 1966 by *Live or Die*, which won the Pulitzer Prize. In 1962 she became the first traveling fellow in poetry of the American Academy of Arts and Letters. Mrs. Sexton has taught a class in the writing of verse at the Radcliffe Institute for Independent Study and has been elected a Fellow of the Royal Society of Literature of the United Kingdom. With Maxine Kumin she has written *Eggs of Things*, a book for elementary school children. In her poetry for mature readers, Mrs. Sexton is unusually candid, and a good deal of her verse is a direct rendering—in dexterous technique—of raw experience, combined with the poet's reflections. The circumstances of her life have not always been happy, and yet she is often a poet of the joy of existence as found in natural phenomena. Her New England background is one of the salient features of her writings and its geography—Boston and the Maine coast and Cape Cod—continually manifests itself. But this poet seems concerned most of all with family life, and some of her most skillful poems are family portraits which are examined with a tinge of nostalgia, a sense of guilt, and, most predominant, a harrowing ability to see the skull beneath the skin. In the conversation which follows, Mrs. Sexton undertakes a rare approach by giving over her introductory time to an intimately technical discussion of the creation of one of those poems. Her works selected for study on the present occasion are: "All My Pretty Ones," "Flight," "The Division of Parts," "I Remember," and "Young."

151

MR. MOORE: We've had a great deal about the Midwest and the South; now we're going to New England. Mrs. Sexton is, as you know, one of the most highly thought of younger poets. She's going to take about ten minutes to present a very interesting project here before we have our questions. Mrs. Sexton.

MRS. SEXTON: Well, I thought instead of making general comments I'd try to make a few specific comments on how one poem started, got off the ground. Every poet has a lot of unwritten poems in him, and every poem that does exist is one where he got lucky, where he was stubborn enough to drag a poem into existence. For me each poem has its own sound or its own voice or its own form, whatever you want to call it. Until I find it I'm crawling in the dark or through mud. The poem I thought I would look at in detail is "All My Pretty Ones," which is among the copies of my work that everyone has.

I have here, on my desk, six pages of beginning worksheets of "All My Pretty Ones." I thought I would read you parts from each page so you might see, line by line, how very badly it began, and how it almost never got written. I'm not sure of the time lapse as I read it. I have these five or six pages and perhaps they cover a week of attempt. I don't remember.

The title was given to me by a friend who stole it from Shakespeare in the first place. She wrote me a condolence note after my father's death and I received it, I think, as I was working on the poem. She said in her letter, "Oh no, Anne, your mother in March and your father in June. All your pretty ones at once?" And then she added, "Anne, the quote is from *Macbeth*, in case you don't know." (I have little formal education and little informal education.) So I read to the end of *Macbeth*—almost the end—looking for it, and I found it. Macduff hears that his wife and children

have been slaughtered and he cries out, "All my pretty ones.
Did you say all? Oh hell kite, all? What, all my pretty
chickens and their dam at one fell swoop." Later he says, "I
cannot but remember such things were that were most pre-
cious to me." Then I knew what my title was. "All My
Pretty Ones" was the name for my dead. I began badly,
with raw emotion and bitterness, with no good lines at all
and no form, nothing but the need to give reality to feeling.
So the first page goes thusly, and I apologize for the rough-
ness but I thought people might like to see how rough it can
be. What I did was roll the blank sheet into my typewriter
and sit there and look at it. Here it goes.

> *Somehow, God knows why, you died*
> *last week*

Then I go down two spaces.

> *Somehow, God knows how,*
> *I'm the only parent now.*

> *On the June morning they put*
> *my two young parents*

That's no good. I go down three spaces.

> *God knows, it's queer enough*
> *to have them gone*

I don't like that. I go down five spaces.

> *Father, the worst is over,*
> *the boozey rich man that you were*

Well, I kind of like that but it isn't right yet. Down two
spaces.

> *My mother's ashes waited*
> *patiently at the crematory*
> *for the ground to melt*

I give up and I roll that page out. I never pick up a lot of those things again.

Now, on the second page I seem to be looking at longer lines and I'm struggling away again.

> *Today they dug two squares in the family plot.*
> *My parents are ashes for the ground.*
> *It is June. At five A.M. the same old birds*
> *move in their nests and begin to sing.*

And I go down three spaces.

> *As if the gospel were true,*
> *the pitying neighbors come to comfort me . . .*
> How they loved each other!
> Now they are in heaven together.
> *Father, what do they know of you?*
> *That a second shock came boiling through*
> *your blood.*

You will note that this line is picked up in the poem. I don't lose this one. Going on:

> *That you went just three*
> *months after mother. They call that love?*
> *Father, before you had the manic time*
> *to marry that pretty widow*
> *(you were lonely you said)*
> *I cried against your shoulder and three*
> *days later you were suddenly, in Gloucester, dead.*

I kind of liked that, a little. I go down two spaces and continue.

> *Now you will never marry anyone again.*
> *For the last time the newspaper buried you*
> *in large print just like the other*
> *large rich men.*
> *It seems it ought to be against the law*

> *to have everyone die at once.*
> *It is the usual June morning. The birds sing.*
> *Time itself is the fatal flaw.*
> *And to be left . . .*
> *that's the, difficult thing.*

Well, you notice how I go off. I get very prosy and far too angry. I'm still talking to myself, which is what you do when you write a poem, I'm afraid.

Now on the next page I start trying to round into form, thinking that will help me. It's not form for the sake of "hooray I can write in form," or complicated form, but one that will help me find my voice. At this point I've gotten a copy of my father's will and I have a little legal thing here. I start out "Whereas father" which I must have gotten right from the will.

> *Whereas father you fell suddenly*

And this has a rhyme scheme. Not the one I ended up with. It goes a-b-c-d-e a-d-b-c-e-c.

> *Whereas father you fell suddenly*
> *on June third in the expected sea air*
> *of this unlucky year of our Lord*
> *nineteen hundred and fifty-nine*
> *leaving me to shuffle through another will*
> *leaving me with your famous alcoholic tendency*
> *to drink down with your blood your glass of wine.*

You see in the poem I pick these things up later.

> *Leaving me to watch over this cursed share*
> *of the residence you could not afford;*
> *twenty pairs of shoes, half a woolen mill,*
> *a gold key, a Cadillac, an English Ford.*

I go on with the rhyme scheme, going down about seven spaces.

> *And whereas the jinx rides in my head*

of your father, president of the bank
who went out shrieking in a straight jacket
of you, good God the duke you tried to be,
good God the drunk you were; good God, the man
you were the day you stopped . . . sober, jinxed instead
by a second shock boiling through your head, a refugee
from a bottle for ten years, shrieking at death you sank
from your staff because you had no wife. Back set
at your daughters you turned to anyone else's plan
and now we are your sober girls in your wage bracket.

That still wasn't right. The next page is quite long and quite repetitious. I'll read just a little bit of it. It's a different form. In the middle it says:

leaving me, witness to your prime,
leaving before you had the time
to marry that pretty widow, Mrs. Ricker,
(You were lonely you said)
I cried, grew disobedient, sicker
and three days later you were dead.

Then it goes on, with a different rhyme scheme, but it still isn't right. The next page says at the top "All My Pretty Ones." You see, I must have gotten the letter and read *Macbeth*. I start off this way:

Whereas father
I'm still hung up on that "whereas."
Whereas father, the jinx rides us apart

Now I have the rhyme scheme, a-b a-b-c-d c-d e-e. It doesn't make any difference what rhyme scheme it is; it's what it will do for what you're trying to say.

Whereas father, the jinx rides us apart
where you followed mother to her cold slumber;
a second shock boiling its stone to your heart,
leaving me here to shuffle and disencumber
you from the residence you could not afford:

> *a gold key, your half of a woolen mill,*
> *twenty pairs of shoes, an English Ford,*
> *the love and legal verbiage of another will,*
> *a box of picture albums that must go,*
> *filled with nameless folk whom I do not know.*

You see I'm beginning to get it, but look at that ending! That's terrible! Now the next page: it goes on, "All My Pretty Ones." I always start all over again to get the feeling. The only thing that is different now from the final version is that I changed twenty pairs of shoes" to "twenty suits from Dunne's." I drop the "whereas" and it goes this way:

> *Father, this year's jinx rides us apart*
> *where you followed our mother to her cold slumber;*
> *a second shock boiling its stone to your heart,*
> *leaving me here to shuffle and disencumber*
> *you from the residence you could not afford:*
> *a gold key, your half of a woolen mill,*
> *twenty suits from Dunne's, an English Ford*
> *the love and legal verbiage of another will,*
> *boxes of pictures of people I do not know.*
> *I touch their cardboard faces. They must go.*

And that's how it began. That's all I will say. Are you there?

> MR. MOORE: Yes, that's a very interesting presentation. And now, we will have questions from the different colleges in rotation.

ALL MY PRETTY ONES

> *Father, this year's jinx rides us apart*
> *where you followed our mother to her cold slumber;*
> *a second shock boiling its stone to your heart,*
> *leaving me here to shuffle and disencumber*
> *you from the residence you could not afford:*
> *a gold key, your half of a woolen mill,*
> *twenty suits from Dunne's, an English Ford,*
> *the love and legal verbiage of another will,*

boxes of pictures of people I do not know.
I touch their cardboard faces. They must go.

But the eyes, as thick as wood in this album,
hold me. I stop here, where a small boy
waits in a ruffled dress for someone to come . . . ..
for this soldier who holds his bugle like a toy
or for this velvet lady who cannot smile.
Is this your father's father, this commodore
in a mailman suit? My father, time meanwhile
has made it unimportant who you are looking for.
I'll never know what these faces are all about.
I lock them into their book and throw them out.

This is the yellow scrapbook that you began
the year I was born; as crackling now and wrinkly
as tobacco leaves: clippings where Hoover outran
the Democrats, wiggling his dry finger at me
and Prohibition; news where the Hindenburg went
down and recent years where you went flush
on war. This year, solvent but sick, you meant
to marry that pretty widow in a one-month rush.
But before you had that second chance, I cried
on your fat shoulder. Three days later you died.

These are the snapshots of marriage, stopped in places.
Side by side at the rail toward Nassau now;
here, with the winner's cup at the speedboat races,
here, in tails at the Cotillion, you take a bow,
here, by our kennel of dogs with their pink eyes,
running like show-bred pigs in their chain-link pen;
here, at the horseshow where my sister wins a prize;
and here, standing like a duke among groups of men.
Now I fold you down, my drunkard, my navigator,
my first lost keeper, to love or look at later.

I hold a five-year diary that my mother kept
for three years, telling all she does not say
of your alcoholic tendency. You overslept,
she writes. My God, father, each Christmas Day

with your blood, will I drink down your glass
of wine? The diary of your hurly-burly years
goes to my shelf to wait for my age to pass.
Only in this hoarded span will love persevere.
Whether you are pretty or not, I outlive you,
bend down my strange face to yours and forgive you.

Stephens: Since we have been looking at "All My Pretty Ones," I wonder, Dr. Moore, if we might start with that?

MR. MOORE: Yes, go ahead.

Stephens: You've done so beautifully in getting us into the first stanza that I hate to jump to the last line, but one of my students asks, in "All My Pretty Ones" is your "strange face" strange to him because you have not yet achieved the understanding of the age to come?

MRS. SEXTON: Yes, I think so. I think that's exactly right. I think I am very much of a stranger at this point. It even reflects his strange face, you see. My strange face is my condition, my present. You know, suddenly, as I said in one of the versions, I am a parent now. *My* strange face.

Stephens: You are strange to him?

MRS. SEXTON: Yes. And to myself; I would say it's also got a kind of sexual thing there. You can understand that; you know, to kiss him then, to kiss death itself. My *strange* face. It was always pretty strange to him. Only now was I trying to love him, and to forgive him for actually not being pretty.

Tougaloo: In the second stanza, about your father's old pictures, are you saying that the past of a dead person is of no use to the living, or has to be remade in someway?

MRS. SEXTON: Well, it has to be remade in so far as it's useful. As I was looking at this picture album I didn't know who everyone was. There was no one left to ask. You see? I didn't know. Who was this little boy? Was it my father? I think so. Was that my father's father? I didn't know. They can't be of use to me. It was too late to ask. So I say, "they are no use to the living."

Tougaloo: And they must go.

MRS. SEXTON: They must go, yes.

Drury: We have a general question that might be appropriate at this time. Mrs. Sexton, you spoke, in your comments on this poem, to the effect that what was wrong with some of the first drafts was that you were talking to yourself. One of the controversies in twentieth-century literature has to do with the personal character of so much of our literature. One of the students is wondering if you would comment upon the personal quality of your poetry and upon the general controversy.

MRS. SEXTON: Well, my poetry is very personal (*laughing*). I don't think I write public poems. I write very personal poems but I hope that they will become the central theme to someone else's private life. This is a very personal poem, of course; I bring in all these intimate details. But I hope that I give it a rather authentic stamp; that's always my hope. It's hard to defend writing this way when you can't write any other way, you see. The writer is stuck with what he can do. Any public poem I have ever written, that wasn't personal, was usually a failure. Does that answer the question at all?

Drury: Yes, it does. Thank you.

Jackson: In the third stanza you say "But before you had that second chance, I cried on your fat shoulder." Was there any special significance to the word "fat" or were you just being descriptive?

MRS. SEXTON: Well, he did have fat shoulders and I

think I loved him for it. I believe I was being descriptive. I don't think it had any other meaning.

Morehouse: I have a question concerning your technique. I notice that you list details one after another which seem to add up, not only to an image, but to evoke emotion. Would you care to comment on whether or not this is an operation technique in all of your poetry. What are you trying to accomplish by piling them up in that way?

MRS. SEXTON: I think a feeling of authenticity, that this is real. That's exactly what I'm trying to do.

Morehouse: Are they also to carry some kind of emotional weight?

MRS. SEXTON: Yes. Well, I think they gather up. You know, it is like piling stones one on top of the other.

Morehouse: So in your description of the snapshots we are to get not only a vision of the snapshots themselves, but we are also to understand how they refer to the father?

MRS. SEXTON: That's right, exactly. And you feel the very weight of them, the weight of throwing such a thing out, you see. If you don't pile them up, how else do you reveal the very heaviness of them to the reader?

Langston: Mrs. Sexton, in the first stanza you said, "leaving me here to shuffle and disencumber / you from the residence you could not afford." Then, in the third stanza, you say, "this year, solvent but sick, you meant / to marry that pretty widow in a one-month rush." Is that a contradiction?

MRS. SEXTON: Well, he couldn't afford it, but he was solvent. I realize I'm drawing a rather fine line there. "Solvent but sick" means going down the drain a little bit, but solvent in the world's eyes, anyway. Did I answer that? I have a feeling I didn't.

Langston: He was not really poor.

MRS. SEXTON: No, he wasn't poor. Look at all the money he was spending. But he couldn't really afford all these things. It was madness to spend money this lavishly, but he was solvent.

MR. MOORE: Stephens, would you like something further on this?

Stephens: We'd like to follow up the question from Drury, asking about the personal quality. One of the criticisms that we hear of contemporary poetry is that it is so academic. One of the great values of Mrs. Sexton's poetry is that it is personal. Through this personal quality we feel what has generally been described as universality. Are you making a conscious effort to get back to basic elements or is this simply the only way, as you say, you can do it?

MRS. SEXTON: I think it's just my style. I think if I had written twenty years ago I'd have written this way, whether it were stylish, whether it were a good thing to do or a bad thing to do. I can just do my own thing and that's the way I do it. I have been quite aware of criticism about this, naturally, because I do it; but I can't seem to change. I don't think I'm aiming at anything from an intellectual standpoint. I didn't make up my mind to write personal poems. When I started to write everyone told me, "These are too personal. These should not be published. You can't write that way." I tried to make them better poems, but they still had to be just my kind of poems. You might call it an accident.

Stephens: Don't change them at all. Don't listen to what they say.

MRS. SEXTON (*laughter*): I can't.

MR. MOORE: I wonder if we have any more questions on this poem. Tougaloo?

Tougaloo: Yes. In the last stanza, the middle section: "My God, father, each Christmas Day / with your blood, will I drink down your glass / of wine?" Could you comment on that? I noticed it occurred in one of your earlier drafts.

MRS. SEXTON: Yes, I think I mean will I inherit this . . . Christmas Day is a day of great celebration, you know, and I feel with his blood, which, in a way, is contaminated, in a way, is beautiful—will I drink down the same glass? In a way I am asking, will I inherit your glass, your wine, and your tendency. Just preceding it I say, "telling all she does not say / of your alcoholic tendency. You overslept, / she writes. My God, father" Where will I do this? When will this happen to me?

Tougaloo: Are the blood and the wine fused?

MRS. SEXTON: Yes, I think so. I'm sure that no poet can say they weren't.

Stephens: This is a reference to the sacrament?

MRS. SEXTON: Very likely. Only on an unconscious level. You just can't get away from it, you see.

Stephens: And your father becomes you?

MRS. SEXTON: That's right.

MR. MOORE: Morehouse.

Morehouse: Yes. The diary comes in in a strange way. One student asks, if you see your father's life so realistically and poetically at the same time, why this sudden shift to the diary which seems to be a repeated censuring of his nature?

MRS. SEXTON: Well, because I am cataloging these leftover objects and the diary was of a time past that I lived through, you know. But these were bad years. They tell of the worst in him.

Morehouse: Then would it be a comment on the mother's reaction to the father?

MRS. SEXTON: Of course, of course. And the family's reaction. But what Mother put down was not really the truth; it was a euphemism. And reading through the diary I thought, "Where did this happen?" and yet I would only read "He overslept." Her saying that personified the alcoholism. The worst of him.

Morehouse: Is there any relationship in the poem between the expenditure of the money and the alcoholism? Are we supposed to see this as a cause and effect relationship?

MRS. SEXTON: I don't think so. I think that's too simple, too pat an explanation.

Langston: Did your opposition to your father's marriage have anything to do with his death?

MRS. SEXTON: Of course I felt that. Not rationally, but I felt it. It's not, perhaps, as implicit as I hoped, but in the poem I don't want him to marry and then he dies. It's kind of Oedipal or something, but it's distinctly there, my guilt.

MR. MOORE: Thank you. Stephens do you want to take up "The Division of Parts" now?

Stephens: Yes, although I would be interested in further comment on that last point. Mrs. Sexton's poet's guilt might be there but this question pointed to a direct relationship and I don't think that was intended, was it?

MRS. SEXTON (*silence*): I'm thinking. Yes, I think a direct relationship.

Stephens: A direct relationship.

MRS. SEXTON: Well, somewhat. Certainly the act makes it direct anyway.

THE DIVISION OF PARTS

1.

Mother, my Mary Gray,
once resident of Gloucester
and Essex County,
a photostat of your will
arrived in the mail today.
This is the division of money.
I am one third
of your daughters counting my bounty
or I am a queen alone
in the parlor still,
eating the bread and honey.
It is Good Friday.
Black birds pick at my window sill.

Your coat in my closet,
your bright stones on my hand,
the gaudy fur animals
I do not know how to use,
settle on me like a debt.
A week ago, while the hard March gales
beat on your house,
we sorted your things: obstacles
of letters, family silver,
eyeglasses and shoes.
Like some unseasoned Christmas, its scales
rigged and reset,
I bundled out with gifts I did not choose.

Now the hours of The Cross
rewind. In Boston, the devout
work their cold knees
toward that sweet martyrdom
that Christ planned. My timely loss
is too customary to note; and yet
I planned to suffer

and I cannot. It does not please
my yankee bones to watch
where the dying is done
in its ugly hours. Black birds peck
at my window glass
and Easter will take its ragged son.

The clutter of worship
that you taught me, Mary Gray,
is old. I imitate
a memory of belief
that I do not own. I trip
on your death and Jesus, my stranger
floats up over
my Christian home, wearing his straight
thorn tree. I have cast my lot
and am one third thief
of you. Time, that rearranger
of estates, equips
me with your garments, but not with grief.

2.
This winter when
cancer began its ugliness
I grieved with you each day
for three months
and found you in your private nook
of the medicinal palace
for New England Women
and never once
forgot how long it took.

I read to you
from The New Yorker, ate suppers
you wouldn't eat, fussed
with your flowers,
joked with your nurses, as if I
were the balm among lepers,
as if I could undo

a life in hours
if I never said goodbye.

But you turned old,
all your fifty-eight years sliding
like masks from your skull;
and at the end
I packed your nightgowns in suitcases,
paid the nurses, came riding
home as if I'd been told
I could pretend
people live in places.

3.

Since then I have pretended ease,
loved with the trickeries of need, but not enough
to shed my daughterhood
or sweeten him as a man.
I drink the five o'clock martinis
and poke at this dry page like a rough
goat. Fool! I fumble my lost childhood
for a mother and lounge in sad stuff
with love to catch and catch as catch can.

And Christ still waits. I have tried
to exorcise the memory of each event
and remain still, a mixed child,
heavy with cloths of you.
Sweet witch, you are my worried guide.
Such dangerous angels walk through Lent.
Their walls creak Anne! Convert! Convert!
My desk moves. Its cave murmurs Boo . .
and I am taken and beguiled.

Or wrong. For all the way I've come
I'll have to go again. Instead, I must convert
to love as reasonable
as Latin, as solid as earthenware:
an equilibrium

I never knew. And Lent will keep its hurt
for someone else. Christ knows enough
staunch guys have hitched on him in trouble,
thinking his sticks were badges to wear.

4.

Spring rusts on its skinny branch
and last summer's lawn
is soggy and brown.
Yesterday is just a number.
All of its winters avalanche
out of sight. What was, is gone.
Mother, last night I slept
in your Bonwit Teller nightgown.
Divided, you climbed into my head.
There in my jabbering dream
I heard my own angry cries
and I cursed you, Dame
keep out of my slumber.
My good Dame, you are dead.
And Mother, three stones
slipped from your glittering eyes.

Now it is Friday's noon
and I would still curse
you with my rhyming words
and bring you flapping back, old love,
old circus knitting, god-in-her-moon,
all fairest in my lang syne verse,
the gauzy bride among the children,
the fancy amid the absurd
and awkward, that horn for hounds
that skipper homeward, that museum
keeper of stiff starfish, that blaze
within the pilgrim woman,
a clown mender, a dove's
cheek among the stones,
my Lady of my first words,
this is the division of ways.

And now, while Christ stays
fastened to his Crucifix
so that love my praise
his sacrifice
and not the grotesque metaphor,
you come, a brave ghost, to fix
in my mind without praise
or paradise
to make me your inheritor.

Stephens: We will go to "The Division of Parts." One of the main things is the use of religious symbolism.

MRS. SEXTON: I'll do my best.

Stephens: If you could just comment generally about it then maybe others will have questions.

MRS. SEXTON: I'd rather have questions. Well, what I did was spend a long time reading over the New Testament. I guess I had a lot of religious feeling—it was this Good Friday thing—it was the whole act of sorting out my mother's possessions. I don't know how my mother could have become like Christ to me, but I got it all mixed up. And, you see, I felt like the soldier who divided Christ's garments and I used this. That led me into this religious symbolism. A poet doesn't just say, "Well now, I'm going to speak in symbols," you know. It just gets all enmeshed in your mind and you try to feel your way through it. I even have a nursery rhyme. It's in there too.

Stephens (laughter): Yes, I wonder if you would comment on "the blackbirds."

MRS. SEXTON: Yes. Well, you know, "I am the queen alone in the parlor still" goes with it, and "the king is in the counting house counting out the money, the queen is in the parlor eating bread and honey." The maid is—I don't know where she is—but hanging out the clothes and the blackbird, I don't know that it exactly bites off her nose, but this was the ominous symbol. "I am the queen alone in the parlor still," means I have inherited all these material goods.

Stephens: The clothes are in the closet, aren't they?

MRS. SEXTON: That's right.

Tougaloo: We would like to pick up this question of the symbolism. You present your mother and Christ as very similar and yet different. Could you comment more fully on their relationship?

MRS. SEXTON: You mean on how they are alike?

Tougaloo: Yes. Well, alike and different.

MRS. SEXTON: Well, I don't think I fully saw how different they were until the end of the poem when I realized it was a very bad metaphor. But to me, my mother's long suffering—(*pause*) I didn't want to believe, you see. I didn't want to believe in Christ rising. I didn't want to believe in anything. I felt that I had inherited all these things—I cast my lot—I had gotten them all: the division of parts, the division of money, and all that she had gone through. I say, "I trip / on your death and Jesus, my stranger / my Christian home." Jesus was a stranger to me and I trip always on this death, her death, as in the resurrection. And then, of course, on Good Friday Jesus is on the cross and I am speaking of this.

Drury: One of our students is interested in the division image as it occurs in the fourth section of the poem where you say "Divided, you climbed into my head" and then at the end the "division of the way." Could you explain this a little more?

MRS. SEXTON (*pause*): Divided at this point between life and death, I think, when she climbs into my head. She has been divided because I have divided her. She has been divided into three parts. She is now just her three daughters and I am one part of this division. Then I think by the division of ways I mean the parting, that I must go my own way and Christ must stay where he is and I must be the inheritor. It comes to an acceptance of the division.

Jackson: This may have been answered, but I would like to ask it. Does the poem imply that the dead mother is symbolic of Christ in that they both left legacies? Also is there the idea that the inheritor took the material gifts that were left by her mother but not the spiritual gifts that her mother tried to instill in her?

MRS. SEXTON: Exactly. A very good question, well put. I'm not sure that I was consciously aware of this analogy.

Morehouse: We have a question about the third section. We'll try first the general approach. Just what is the meaning of the third section? That has caused us some confusion also.

MRS. SEXTON: Well, "Since then I have pretended ease" because I have tried to live, to go on with my life; to live with need, but not enough to shed the daughterhood, nor to sweeten him as a man. That's the regular life going on. I'm not succeeding at being a woman at this point. I am still poking at this dry page and trying to write this poem that will exorcise my feeling, fumbling for a childhood, catching at love. But Christ is still waiting and I haven't gotten over my loss. I haven't succeeded in continuing. I bring in this section because it is part of living.

Morehouse: Our second question concerns the witch image and the "Convert! Convert!" Is that your mother calling to you in some remembered past?

MRS. SEXTON: Possibly. She could call, or Christ might call through her in some way that the dead can speak back, that I would be converted to the magic of the resurrection.

Morehouse: Finally, are you perhaps the persons of the poem, one of the blackbirds in a kind of inverse sense, in the sense of despair, and guilt and shame sort of mixed together?

MRS. SEXTON: I doubt it. I think the blackbirds are really a symbol of evil. In some way, in my mind, they are tied up with the cross. They seem to me almost like the nails of the cross, a very dark omen.

Langston: Will you explain the symbolism in section four, the last lines of the first stanza.

MRS. SEXTON: "My good Dame, you are dead. And Mother, three stones" — is that what you mean?

Langston: Yes.

MRS. SEXTON: Her tears have become stones. This is my way of facing the very deadness of her body. Then I say, get out of here, get out of my dreams, you are dead! But then, almost in horror, I see that three stones slip from her eyes, as though she were crying. At this point she becomes almost as beautiful as Mary, after I have sworn at her. Does that answer the question?

Langston: Yes, thank you.

MR. MOORE: Our time is going all too rapidly in this wonderful session. Now, a question from Stephens College.

Stephens: You say about the last three lines of stanza one of part four, this is almost like the Virgin. Then you pick it up in "my Lady of my first words"?

MRS. SEXTON: That's right. That's right.

Stephens: This is a part of the same image?

MRS. SEXTON: Yes.

Stephens: In terms of the time of composition did this precede "All My Pretty Ones" by any great number of weeks or months?

MRS. SEXTON: Oh yes. By four months. When I wrote "Division of Parts" my father had not died.

Stephens: We wondered at picking up "Dame" in that section; the relation of this to the quotation from *Macbeth*.

MRS. SEXTON: No, I hadn't read it. You see I was writing this on Good Friday and my mother was recently dead. My father didn't die until June and I didn't read *Macbeth* until then.

I REMEMBER

> By the first of August
> the invisible beetles began
> to snore and the grass was
> as tough as hemp and was
> no color—no more than
> the sand was a color and
> we had worn our bare feet
> bare since the twentieth
> of June and there were times
> we forgot to wind up your
> alarm clock and some nights
> we took our gin warm and neat
> from old jelly glasses while
> the sun blew out of sight
> like a red picture hat and
> one day I tied my hair back
> with a ribbon and you said
> that I looked almost like
> a puritan lady and what
> I remember best is that
> the door to your room was
> the door to mine.

MR. MOORE: Tougaloo, do you want to ask a question

about "I Remember"?

Tougaloo: Yes. We would like to discuss the punctuation in this poem. Did you *not* use punctuation to show the continuity of things during the period you are talking about or were there other more formal reasons?

MRS. SEXTON: I'll tell you exactly why I did it this way. I feel both this and "Young," although this even more, are supposed to be breathless poems. Of course it's not possible, they should be said in *one breath.* They are each one sentence because I only try to capture an instant in them, where in other poems I try to cover vast amounts of time, to tie things together. In this I just want to take a photograph and that's all I want. So it's just a run-on; it's a gathering. The only important thing are the last three lines really. That is why I used no punctuation. It's supposed to be thin, like a tube.

MR. MOORE: Thank you. Drury College, do you want to ask questions on "I Remember" and / or "Young"?

YOUNG

> *A thousand doors ago*
> *when I was a lonely kid*
> *in a big house with four*
> *garages and it was summer*
> *as long as I could remember,*
> *I lay on the lawn at night,*
> *clover wrinkling under me,*
> *the wise stars bedding over me,*
> *my mother's window a funnel*
> *of yellow heat running out,*
> *my father's window, half shut,*
> *an eye where sleepers pass,*
> *and the boards of the house*
> *were smooth and white as wax*
> *and probably a million leaves*
> *sailed on their strange stalks*
> *as the crickets ticked together*

> *and I, in my brand new body,*
> *which was not a woman's yet,*
> *told the stars my questions*
> *and thought God could really see*
> *the heat and the painted light,*
> *elbows, knees, dreams, goodnight.*

Drury: One of the students asked that Mrs. Sexton give us a reading of one or the other of these that we might hear how she reads it.

MRS. SEXTON: I'd love to. Shall I do it?

MR. MOORE: Please do.

MRS. SEXTON: I'll read "I Remember." Now you're going to catch me because I don't read it the way it's written. But that's all right; it's good to catch poets. (Mrs. Sexton reads "I Remember.") That's the way it's supposed to be read.

Drury: Thank you very much.

Morehouse: We would like to ask a question about "Young" if we can also go back to "The Division of Parts." In "Young" there is this reference to "my mother's window a funnel / of yellow heat running out, / my father's window, . . ." We note a strange ambiguity of your grief in "The Division of Parts." We feel that it is ambiguity because of the double feeling you seem to be having toward your mother. Does this grow out of this past reference to the Freudian symbolism here in this line?

MRS. SEXTON: I think so, yes.

Morehouse: Then, is this a part of your dynamic? In "The Division of Parts" is the kind of guilt that you feel being unable to grieve?

MRS. SEXTON: Exactly, exactly. That's why you keep

writing these poems.

    MR. MOORE: Back to Stephens College. Do you want to take up "Flight"?

FLIGHT

Thinking that I would find you,
thinking I would make the plane
that goes hourly out of Boston
I drove into the city.
Thinking that on such a night
every thirsty man would have his jug
and that the Negro women would lie down
on pale sheets and even the river into town
would stretch out naturally on its couch,
I drove into the city.
On such a night, at the end of the river,
the airport would sputter with planes
like ticker-tape.

Foot on the gas
I sang aloud to the front seat,
to the slumps of women in cotton dresses,
to the patches of fog crusting the banks,
and to the sailboats swinging on their expensive hooks.
There was rose and violet on the river
as I drove through the mist into the city.
I was full of letters I hadn't sent you,
a red coat over my shoulders
and new white gloves in my lap.

I dropped through the city
as the river does,
rumbling over and under, as indicated,
past the miles of spotted windows
minding their own business,
through the Sumner Tunnel,
trunk by trunk through its sulphurous walls,
tile by tile like a men's urinal,
slipping through

like somebody else's package.

Parked, at last,
on a dime that would never last,
I ran through the airport.
Wild for love, I ran through the airport,
stockings and skirts and dollars.
The night clerk yawned all night at the public,
his mind on tomorrow's wages.
All flights were grounded.
The planes sat and the gulls sat,
heavy and rigid in a pool of glue.

Knowing I would never find you
I drove out of the city.
At the airport one thousand cripples
sat nursing a sore foot.
There was more fog
and the rain came down when it thought of it.
I drove past the eye and ear infirmaries,
past the office buildings lined up like dentures,
and along Storrow Drive the streetlights
sucked in all the insects who
had nowhere else to go.

Stephens: The last three lines of "Flight" seem to have a mixture of qualities of conflicting natures—generosity, despair, loneliness—are we correct in assuming that at the end of this poem you too feel that you have "no where else to go"?

MRS. SEXTON: Of course, and I don't think there's much generosity in it, except the image, the impulse to fly and then it becomes more and more depersonalized. It's sort of an image, "one thousand cripples / sat nursing a sore foot." They're frozen. And then I go past the eye and ear infirmaries, and buildings like dentures, all false, and then along the drive the streetlights suck in all the insects who have nowhere else to go just as I am sucked in, I have nowhere else to go. That is the very point in that image.

Stephens: And if we could have one last question then. Do you feel that the sea and the whole New England element are important to you in the creative process?

MRS. SEXTON: Yes. But that's because I happen to live right near the sea and love it. I think if I had grown up beside a cornfield it would have become very much a part of me; or the flatlands. Your region becomes imbedded in you.

MR. MOORE: Tougaloo College, on "Flight"?

Tougaloo: Yes. There are a number of rather startling similes in this poem, especially when you look at them at the ends of stanzas or the ends of lines and in some of your other poems too. Does your mind work this way, rather particularly with similes?

MRS. SEXTON: Yes, I think so. I think something that is more dissimilar is more shocking, brings you closer to the reality, the intensification, of the feeling. I have a great love of ending a stanza with a kind of "pulled-up" effect. This poem has no rhyme. Sometimes you can tie things together with rhyme and if you're not using it then you must use other methods.

Jackson: Just a general question: Is it implied in this poem that the adolescent is trying to reach out for understanding and not finding it in mother or father?

MRS. SEXTON: You mean in "Young"? No, because I think that the adolescent just glances at the windows, those strange windows or strange people. No, it's lying on the ground and asking questions of yourself. I would say the key lines are, "and I, in my brand new body, / which was not a woman's yet, / told the stars my questions." You see, it's this feeling of being outdoors and wondering, of thinking suddenly, "why I'm alive!" Your parents are very far away.

MR. MOORE: I'm terribly sorry our time is up. And

we've had a most wonderful morning and thank you very much for it.

MRS. SEXTON: Well, thank you.

Stephens: I hope that sitting in your living room you were able to relax and enjoy doing this enough that you will do it again sometime.

MRS. SEXTON (*laughter*): I'm not in my living room—I'm in my writing room with my feet up on the bookcase, with my chair tipped back, bare feet yet.

MR. MOORE: Thank you again.

MRS. SEXTON: OK. Thanks a lot. It was fun doing it. Good-bye.

April 13, 1964

Richard Wilbur

Richard Wilbur was born in New York City in 1921 and grew up in a pre-Revolutionary stone house which stood at one corner of a vast estate in New Jersey. He has spoken of the place as "a pocket of resistance to suburbia" which afforded him "a rural, pleasant, and somewhat solitary boyhood." He began writing poems early, and at eight produced his first, "That's When the Nightingales Wake." There were no nightingales on the New Jersey estate, but the young writer was already groping his way toward words and rhythms. His father was an artist who had come east from Omaha, Nebraska, and his mother was the daughter of an editor of the Baltimore *Sun*, whose father in his turn had founded some forty Democratic newspapers in his wanderings across the country. Young Richard Wilbur, who originally considered a career in journalism, wrote editorials for his high-school paper and at Amherst became editor of the college daily. During his summers he indulged in what he has called vagrancy: he traveled in freight cars to all the forty-eight states which then comprised the Union. When World War II came, he served in the 36th Infantry Division and was at Anzio and Cassino as well as on the Siegfried Line. From 1950 to 1954 he taught at Harvard while taking his M.A. degree, from 1955 to 1957 he was an associate professor of English at Wellesley College, and since then he has been professor of English at Wesleyan University in Connecticut. In 1960, Lawrence College at Appleton, Wisconsin, awarded him the L.H.D. degree. Mr. Wilbur's volumes of poetry include: *The Beautiful Changes* (1947), *A Ceremony* (1950), *A Bestiary* (1955), *Things of This World* (1956), *Poems, 1943–56* (1957), and *Advice to a Prophet* (1961). In addition to his original verse, he has translated Molière's *The Misanthrope* (1955) and collaborated with Lillian Hellman on the libretto for a comic-opera version of Voltaire's *Candide*. Mr. Wilbur has been awarded a Guggenheim Fellowship and has won numerous other distinctions; in 1957 his book *Things of This World*, received both the Pulitzer Prize and the National Book Award. In 1960 Mr. Wilbur was given the Prix de Rome. His poetry is somewhat

traditional in rhyme and meter, though as he says in the
following interview he constructs his poems as if they were
being written in free verse. His poems are immediate and
concrete, full of searching and finding, of expert observation and graceful wit. For the present occasion the poems
chosen were "Love Calls Us to the Things of This World"
and "Beasts." Mr. Wilbur added another during the conversation: "Seed Leaves," which is dedicated to Robert Frost.

MR. MOORE: I don't think Richard Wilbur needs any
introduction. I think you all know him as a poet. He has
won in a single year both the Pulitzer Prize and the National Book Award and he's won a number of other prizes
including the Prix de Rome. He has published several volumes of verse, and some remarkable translations of the
French of Molière. Professor Wilbur is speaking this morning from Portland, Connecticut. Will you come in, Dick?

MR. WILBUR: Hello! A few years back I got to go quite
often to poetry symposia, sit on the platform, listen to the
speeches, and wait for the question period. I remember that
in symposia there always comes the moment when the discussion is thrown open to the audience, and an irritable-
looking elderly man stands up and accuses modern poets of
a failure to communicate. I thought of that this morning,
because the telephone company has given me such a marvelous chance to communicate. I hope not to fail. It's exciting
to feel that you stand a chance of making sense in five states
at once!

I think I ought to begin by saying that I'm not a militant
member of any school of poets or poetry. I don't have any
poetic theories to sell. I don't feel any impulse to tell other
poets how they ought to write; I'd rather let them surprise
me. To listen to some of the critics nowadays, especially
those who write for the popular magazines, you'd think the
American poetic scene was a battlefield with beats and
squares and intermediate types all locked in deadly combat.
It's not really like that at all and, I must say, I don't think
much of critics who help make poetry exciting by means of

such a vulgar fiction. It seems to me that our best American poets as always are independent operators—what they call wildcatting in Texas—unaffiliated men and most of them quite generally responsive to good poetry of whatever kind. So, what I'm trying to say is that I haven't any pitch to make this morning; my poetic opinions are defensive weapons only. I hope people will attack me later on—I'll bring them up then.

I do, of course, have opinions on other things besides poetry. I'm for God and Lyndon Johnson and conservation and civil rights, city planning, the nationalization of the railroads, and a few other things. However, I think it's not generally for opinions and ideas that poets are interesting. Some poets are intelligent men, and they are entitled to their thoughts, but abstract argument and intellectual pioneering are not the special function of a poet. Aeschylus' *Oresteia*, for instance, wasn't a real contribution to Athenian legal theory; and Dante's *Commedia* gave us no new theology and neither did George Herbert; and Shakespeare's history plays added no fresh concept to the political thought of his age.

What poetry does with ideas is to pull them down off the plane of abstraction and submerge them in sensibility: embody them in people and things, and surround them with a proper weather of feeling—an appropriate weather of feeling—to let you know how it would feel to dwell in the presence of a certain idea—how the world would look if you had a certain idea in mind. It helps you to respond not merely with the intellect but with the whole being. I suppose you could say that one job of poetry is to test the ability of any idea, or ideas, to consort with human nature at any point in history.

Well, if I may, I'd like to present you now with a few samples of the kind of thinking I do best. I'd like to read you a new poem of mine which just appeared in *The New Yorker*, the last issue but one, I think (April 1964). This poem is called "Seed Leaves" and it's dedicated to Robert Frost. I dedicated this poem to him for several reasons—for one thing I was thinking of him as I wrote it, and wishing I could write a memorial poem for him. He got into this poem especially in the first two lines; they echo a couple of lines of his which you will possibly recognize. Then, too, this poem is in a meter which Frost favored. And finally, its subject—the subject of choice, of choosing—is one about which Frost wrote a great deal.

I imagine there are a couple of things I ought to say before I read this, since you're getting it by ear alone. Seed leaves are, as I'm sure you all know, the first leaves to appear above ground; and I'm sure you all know how a dicotyledonous plant first produces two leaves which really haven't the characteristic shape of the plant's leaf, but take their shape from the seed case. Then there's one other thing I ought to speak of. I mention in this poem the Life Tree, Yggdrasill, of Norse mythology. That's the cosmic tree, the Tree of Life, coextensive with the whole universe. Well, here's the poem.

SEED LEAVES
to R. F.

I

Here something stubborn comes,
Dislodging the earth crumbs
And making crusty rubble.
It comes up bending double
And looks like a green staple.
It could be seedling maple,
Or artichoke, or bean;
That remains to be seen.

II

Forced to make choice of ends,
The stalk in time unbends,
Shakes off the seedcase, heaves
Aloft, and spreads two leaves
Which still display no sure
And special signature.
Toothless and fat, they keep
The oval form of sleep.

III

This plant would like to grow
And yet be embryo;
Increase, and yet escape
The doom of taking shape;
Be vaguely vast, and climb
To the tip end of time
With all of space to fill,
Like boundless Yggdrasill
That has the stars for fruit.
But something at the root
More urgent than that urge
Bids two true leaves emerge,
And now the plant, resigned
To being self-defined
Before it can commerce
With the great universe,
Takes aim at all the sky
And starts to ramify.

I don't know how many of my hearers were familiar with the Life Tree, Yggdrasill. A difficulty for poets at all times is when to feel they're justified in making a difficult reference. You don't know nowadays what things people are going to recognize. It used to be that you could count on your readers, or hearers, to recognize biblical references, at least, but nowadays readers are likely to be affronted by the most obvious borrowing from Scripture, and take it for an obscurity. What I do, really, when confronted by a problem of this kind is to decide just how necessary to me the reference is. Now, in this case, Yggdrasill had to do with exactly what I wanted to say. The seedling of my poem wants to be unconditioned—it wants to avoid any kind of limiting choice. It wants to be the universe, and Yggdrasill is the plant of the universe. It's simply a great convenience to me to mention that mythical tree as a way of saying a whole lot in a little. If my readers don't catch it, it's their tough luck.

Robert Frost gave various definitions of poetry during his lifetime, mostly wicked and evasive ones, but one of the last ones he gave was this: "Poetry is what gets lost in translation." I hope that's not entirely so, because I've done lots of translation myself, but there *are* a couple of lines in this poem I just read which would probably get lost in translation into most languages. There's a line in which I say that the seed leaves of the plant still "display no sure and special signature." I hope that an English reader hearing that line, or hearing it for the second time perhaps, will hear the word "species" inside the word "special." It's making words work double which is one means the poet has of getting the kind of condensation he's after. I think that play between "species" and "special" might survive in translation into the Romance languages, but I imagine we'd lose it if this poem were taken over into Serbo-Croatian.

Well, I gather that some of you have been reading two of my poems, "Beasts" and "Love Calls Us to the Things of This World." If I can find the book, which I seem for the moment to have lost, I'll read those two poems to you.

I'll start with the poem "Beasts." Maybe I ought to say one thing about the very first line before I start, because I think a slight difficulty, or a slight question, in a first line is likely to put a reader off from the direction of the poem. I mean various things by that word "major" but the expression, "major freedom," comes from one of the church fathers—I forget which one. He distinguishes between major freedom and minor freedom and says that the saints enjoy major freedom because their wills are at one with God's will. They don't have to choose anymore. In this poem of mine I attribute that kind of freedom to the animal creation. Here is the poem.

BEASTS

> *Beasts in their major freedom*
> *Slumber in peace tonight. The gull on his ledge*
> *Dreams in the guts of himself the moon-plucked waves below,*
> *And the sunfish leans on a stone, slept*
> *By the lyric water,*
>
> *In which the spotless feet*

Of deer make dulcet splashes, and to which
The ripped mouse, safe in the owl's talon, cries
Concordance. Here there is no such harm
And no such darkness

As the selfsame moon observes
Where, warped in window-glass, it sponsors now
The werewolf's painful change. Turning his head away
On the sweaty bolster, he tries to remember
The mood of manhood,

But lies at last, as always,
Letting it happen, the fierce fur soft to his face,
Hearing with sharper ears the winds exciting minors,
The leaves' panic, and the degradation
Of the heavy streams.

Meantime, at high windows
Far from thicket and pad-fall, suitors of excellence
Sigh and turn from their work to construe again the painful
Beauty of heaven, the lucid moon
And the risen hunter,

Making such dreams for men
As told will break their hearts as always, bringing
Monsters into the city, crows on the public statues,
Navies fed to the fish in the dark
Unbridled waters.

Now I'll read you the other poem, "Love Calls Us to the Things of This World," and then perhaps we can get on to some questions or observations. This poem I always have to preface by a remark or so because it starts out abruptly. The title is taken from St. Augustine, I think from the *City of God*, and it has to do with the question of why, having had a glimpse of a momentary experience of, some transcendent spiritual happiness, one would turn around and come back to this grubby world. Augustine makes the motive love. Your situation as the poem begins is that you are waking up, oh, on the fourth or fifth floor of an apartment

house in some city, you are in the bedroom, of course. It is
about six or seven in the morning, depending on what city it
is, and as you look out the bedroom window the first laundry of the day is being yanked across the air. It's the
squeaking of the pulley that wakes you up.

LOVE CALLS US TO THE THINGS OF THIS WORLD

The eyes open to a cry of pulleys,
And spirited from sleep, the astounded soul
Hangs for a moment bodiless and simple
As false dawn.
                    Outside the open window
The morning air is all awash with angels.

Some are in bed-sheets, some are in blouses,
Some are in smocks: but truly there they are.
Now they are rising together in calm swells
Of halcyon feeling, filling whatever they wear
With the deep joy of their impersonal breathing;

Now they are flying in place, conveying
The terrible speed of their omnipresence, moving
And staying like white water; and now of a sudden
They swoon down into so rapt a quiet
That nobody seems to be there.
                            The soul shrinks

From all that it is about to remember,
From the punctual rape of every blessed day,
And cries,
            "Oh, let there be nothing on earth but laundry,
Nothing but rosy hands in the rising steam
And clear dances done in the sight of heaven."

Yet, as the sun acknowledges
With a warm look the world's hunks and colors,
The soul descends once more in bitter love
To accept the waking body, saying now

In a changed voice as the man yawns and rises,

> *"Bring them down from their ruddy gallows;*
> *Let there be clean linen for the backs of thieves;*
> *Let lovers go fresh and sweet to be undone,*
> *And the heaviest nuns walk in a pure floating*
> *Of dark habits,*
> > *keeping their difficult balance."*

MR. WILBUR: Now if people have some questions or observations I would love to hear them.

MR. MOORE: Thank you very much. That was very good. We appreciate getting that extra dividend of the new poem, too. Now we will have questions and take up these poems one at a time, beginning with "Beasts." Tougaloo, are you ready with a question on "Beasts"?

Tougaloo: Yes, we are! Is the purpose of this poem to emphasize the animal nature of man which often suppresses his human feelings or emotions, or is it considering just the relationship of man to nature and the animal world in general?

MR. WILBUR: Well, I think that the best thing I could refer to for the illumination of this poem is something of Pascal's, which I will probably misquote. He said somewhere that "man is neither angel nor beast, and when he tries to play the angel he ends up by playing the beast." I am talking, I suppose, about the uneasy relationship of man to nature in the largest possible sense. I present the animals in this poem as being helplessly in harmony with things, even in their acts of predation, whereas man is a torn creature—part angel, part beast—who finds it very hard to achieve perfect harmony, or a perfect sense of what he ought to be. He waivers between being a werewolf and a "suitor of excellence."

Drury: What is the purpose of the unusual line structure? The length of each line seems to be one of the formal characteristics of the poem. What part does this play in your mind?

MR. WILBUR: Well, although generally I use what is called the traditional meters, and care not to write in free verse and often go so far as to rhyme, I do approach the putting together of a poem in very much the way a free verse poet would do. I think that there are natural rhythms for the emotions, and that whatever subject one has chosen to write on is likely to have some kind of natural rhythm of its own. When I start out to write a poem I see how it wants to come out naturally, how the lines want to fall, and then if I manage to produce a first few lines or a first stanza in which the flow of the rhythm seems to me to interpret the feeling of the poem, or the matter of the poem, I continue to be faithful to that. I think that if one's poem isn't too long, this sort of strategy generally works out. Of course, in a very long poem the prevailing mood, or the matter, may alter so much that it may require a new rhythm.

Jackson: Do you mean to play *major* in the first line against *minor* in the eighteenth line, and is that an extended image of Ursa Major and Ursa Minor, the great bear and the little bear? Would you comment on that?

MR. WILBUR: Well, sir, I wasn't thinking of the great bear or the little bear; I was thinking of music. There is a good deal of music in the poem. Right in the first stanza one has "moon-plucked waves," and the word "guts," and together I suppose plucking at guts should make one think of a guitar. Then there is "lyric water" in the last line of the first stanza, and the poem goes on with various noises and suggestions of music. I guess what I'm trying to do is to suggest that you underline the harmony of the beasts with nature by making them *major* and by allotting a *minor* experience to man in his jangled condition.

Morehouse: Mr. Wilbur, we have been approaching your poetry from the point of view of imagistic analysis. In this way we arrived at the conclusion that it is possible that

"Beasts" might be rather satirical in that last stanza where you use the image of "monsters in the city" and "crows on the public statues" and "navies fed to the fish in the dark unbridled waters." Would you care to comment on our interpretation?

MR. WILBUR: Did you say satirical?

Morehouse: Satirical in the profound sense of being pessimistic.

MR. WILBUR: You know, I think that satirical would not correspond to my feeling about the close. That is, I didn't feel in writing this poem that I was defending a proper set of values and berating others for not sharing it. I was describing the potentiality of man for corruption and arrogance, and that's not a remediable condition. If you're talking about the *inevitable*, I don't suppose you can berate people about it.

Morehouse: What about ironic? Would that be a better term than satirical? Using Tate's interpretation of the word irony?

MR. WILBUR: Well, I'm sure that, in some sense, the word irony would suit; yes, sir.

Langston: We want to know whether or not the intention of the poem has to do with the beast and his ecological adjustment as contrasted with man and his ability to make ecological adjustment?

MR. WILBUR: Well, I suppose so. One would have to use that word ecological very broadly in speaking of the maladjustments of man which this poem describes; but I *am* talking about the difficulty man has in deciding what it is that he is, and how he ought to behave, how much perfection he can aspire to without becoming inhuman and violating his nature—that kind of thing. I suppose I'm thinking more in terms of man's inner experience than of his relations with the natural environment, and I describe his arrogance, especially at the close of the poem, in terms of sad, political consequences.

MR. MOORE: Thank you. Stephens College already has had an enormous discussion about this poem which took up all of one class period and they didn't get through with it, so they will probably ask a lot of fine questions. Incidentally, I think this is one of the most remarkable and outstanding poems of our time. It sums up our condition at the moment beautifully. For years this has been one of my favorite poems of the modern world. Now, Stephens, I know you have a lot of questions.

Stephens: A number of students have focused questions on the fifth stanza of the poem and particularly the phrase, "suitors of excellence sigh and turn from their work." I wonder if you might comment somewhat on that idea. The "suitors of excellence" for many of us is a broad phrase and might include a number of different groups of people or all people.

MR. WILBUR: I suppose that I wanted to be broad. I'm trying to paint a little picture there of someone like Milton's Platonist in his lonely tower. It could be almost any sort of aspiring man, assuming that he is hardworking, that he turns from his work out of weariness, that he turns to the contemplation of what is high. I then go on to say that it is the unhappy case that the highest dreams very often produce the worst and most ruthless consequences for society. There's a chapter in a book on the Renaissance called *The State as a Work of Art.* If a man aspires to create a state that is the work of art, he may end by creating something that is sometimes beautiful but, in the process, he will have killed a great many people getting rid of our natural human disorder. It is that sort of thing I am thinking of.

Stephens: In the stanza which precedes that, the use of the word degradation has caused considerable discussion. Would you comment on that?

MR. WILBUR: Well, that's the sort of word that's fun for me to write. I enjoyed panic also in the same line. Panic, of course, contains the god, Pan. The word degradation in its literal sense means going down steps, going down hill. I think it's always fun to take a word that has become abstract and use it in a concrete sense, restore it to its original vitality. Of course, I'm using it in both senses. I want the word degradation to suggest the emotional condition of the man who is giving way to this werewolf change and, at the same time, I simply want to say, in a rather heavy violent way, that the streams of his world are plunging down hill.

MR. MORE: Thank you. I wonder if we ought to try one or two more questions on this. Tougaloo do you have another one?

Tougaloo: Yes, and it leads directly out of the last one. One of the students has noticed the change in the water. In the beginning of the poem the water is "lyric" and at the end it's "dark and unbridled." I think the degradation is part of that process. Would you comment on that?

MR. WILBUR: What the student has noticed is quite right. I mean to start with the sort of water which goes with a harmonious world and close with the kind of disorderly, violent, and destructive water that goes with a jangled world. Both waters are, I suppose, rather subjective.

Morehouse: We have two questions: First, is the lucid moon that makes "such dreams for men as told will break their hearts as always" an ambiguous reference between moon and suitors of excellence?

MR. WILBUR: Excuse me, I've got to find my "moon" again.

Morehouse: That's in the fifth stanza.

MR. WILBUR: Initially I meant it to be the "suitors of excellence" who having construed heaven make such dreams for men as, told, will break their hearts. I imagine I may also want there to be a little grammatical uncertainty there so that the moon may seem to be influencing the suitors of excellence as it does the werewolf in the preceding two stanzas.

Morehouse: The second question concerns the word told. Do you mean told in the literal sense of prophecy and poetic visions of the good or do you mean in the sense of trying to put the dreams of excellence into action?

MR. WILBUR: I think it's implicit—I meant it to be implied—that the telling of dreams would lead to consequences.

Morehouse: The telling is a form of action or creating a form of action?

MR. WILBUR: Well, telling would be conducive to action. I think I have that in mind, since the following images are images of political disorder.

Langston: Would you please comment on what is meant by "he tries to remember the mood of manhood," the last line of the third stanza, please.

MR. WILBUR: You know, at about the time I wrote this poem I was very charmed with Anglo-Saxon poetry and it begins to sound a little Anglo-Saxon there. I think what I have in mind is that this man, struggling against the brutalizing influence of the moon but already partway gone toward wolfhood, is trying to pull himself back toward what has felt to him like the human condition. He is trying to recover his humanity, but of course, the process has gone too far.

By the way, I'd like to confess something about those central stanzas. People tend to think that the raw material of any poem must be dignified, but I confess that I got the material for stanzas three and four from the horror movie,

Frankenstein Meets the Wolf-Man, in which Lon Chaney, Jr. undergoes precisely the change that is described.

MR. MADDEN (*laughing*): I thought poets always wrote from experience.

MR. MOORE (*laughing*): A horror movie can be an experience.

Stephens: In the stanza that we were talking about earlier where there is the distinction between the work of men and making dreams—is there a strong distinction here? At first we had thought in "suitors of excellence" that you might be referring entirely to the creative individual rather than *all* men and found this distinction between work and the making of dreams interesting. Would you comment on that?

MR. WILBUR: Well, I suppose I'm assuming that a dream—the dream which leads perhaps to a poem—will, nevertheless, have consequences. I've never agreed with Mr. Auden's statement that poetry makes nothing happen. And then with that breath of the expression, "suitors of excellence," I was trying to include people like Karl Marx working in the British Museum, people whose work was spoiling to have consequences.

MR. MOORE: Thank you again. Now I wonder, before we go on to the next poem, if briefly you would like to comment, Mr. Wilbur, on anything we may have missed, or make any very brief statement about "Beasts" to sum it up?

MR. WILBUR: I think the questions were excellent. Before this conversation began I jotted down one or two things in the margin which I meant to bring up if nobody did, and they've all been said.

MR. MOORE: Good. Now we can go to this other excellent poem "Love Calls Us to the Things of This World." We'll begin again with Tougaloo.

Tougaloo: Yes. We heard this poem cold so to speak —it's one that we didn't have copies of—and I would like to say that the image, the key image of the poem, the line of laundry of angels, was an obvious and visible delight to the group.

MR. WILBUR: I'm very glad. I thought there was a slight laughter of protest from some of the girls. Are there girls, perhaps?

Tougaloo: Yes. Yes, there are.

MR. WILBUR: Well, I've noticed that there is sometimes laughter, a laughter of repudiation when those lines are said; and I never at all mind hearing people burst out laughing at those lines. It seems to me that if a poem as a whole is sufficiently serious it can risk the ridiculous somewhere in the middle.

Tougaloo: Yes. I've jotted down with a big question mark "all the world a laundry" and our question comes out of this. Are you saying that the human soul, like dirty clothes, can always go back for relaundering?

MR. WILBUR: No, I'm not so much saying that. I suppose what I'm doing is hedging like crazy in this poem. I think I'm writing a poem which starts with the feeling that laundry is very beautiful, and that angels must be like that. It is a poem which affirms the intuitions of the spirit, or however one wants to say that. It says that they are true, or may be true, but also resists the idea of any dissociated or abstract spirituality. The poem ends by asking that the laundry (which has come to be so angelic) be put to human use on this earth. I think that's the drift of the poem.

Drury: One of our students finds in both the means and substance of this poem a kind of objectivity and an affirmation that he feels is strongly reminiscent of Dylan Thomas. Is there anything to that?

MR. WILBUR: I think I'd probably be the last person to testify convincingly about what influences I may have suffered at one time or another. I don't think of Thomas as a poet of the very first rank, but I have enjoyed his work greatly. It may be that he has gotten into my poems here or there. There's one English word—that is to say English-English word—in this poem: ruddy. I did mean people to hear an Englishman cursing when that word ruddy appeared. That's the only thing which makes me think of Dylan Thomas, but others may have better answers.

Jackson: One student was very interested in your images, especially where you have in the first stanza "awash with angels," and in the fourth stanza "clear dances," and in the last stanza "difficult balance." The student wants to know whether he is really off the point or whether there's a possibility that you have a reference to the medieval debates of how many angels could dance on the head of a pin?

MR. WILBUR (*laughing*): I'm not aware of having had that in mind, but the fact that angels are said to dance in that debate may have helped me to imagine this wash as a dance of angels.

Morehouse: Mr. Wilbur are we to understand that the vision of the angels is at the same time the vision of this laundry billowing in the wind?

MR. WILBUR: Yes, that's precisely the thing.

Morehouse: If this is true, then the image "with the deep joy of their impersonal breathing" could have a double meaning of clothing on the line and the angel itself. Speaking of the angel element, would you say that this image means the *universal* ecstasy of the angel: joy but joy beyond the specific personality.

MR. WILBUR: Yes. Of course, the laundry is impersonal because there aren't any people in these smocks and blouses and so on. The angels would be impersonal in the sense of being joyfully free of self.

Morehouse: And also joyfully free of the waking body, of body, of flesh, of matter?

MR. WILBUR: Yes, they are free of the body.

Langston: Is your message in this poem that each morning man awakens in spirit but as the day progresses he becomes just as involved in worldliness as he has been the day before?

MR. WILBUR: I think I'm saying that, yes, but without the pathos that you find in some other treatment of the same idea. I think, for example, of a poem you may know, Elizabeth Bishop's poem, "Anaphora"—a beautiful poem which opens with the line, "Each day with so much ceremony begins." She describes the whole daily process from waking to sleeping again as a process of degradation, of compromise, of darkening. But I mean this process of accepting the body, of bringing the spiritual down into the ordinary, to be a cheerful and acceptable process. I think my feelings in this poem are rather like the feeling, the implicit feeling, of Robert Frost in his poem "Nothing Gold Can Stay." We hear at first a lament for the disappearance of everything pristine and early. But the poem turns out, after all, to think well of what happens to us after we fall from Eden, what happens to the trees after they lose their first gold.

Stephens: Perhaps because of the recent visit of Alan Watts to our campus and the phrase, "expanded consciousness," which has become a campus byword, the questions here focus on the matter that you seem to be, or the students seem to think that you are, separating the soul and body. My reading of the poem is one in which you are describing what we might call expanded consciousness in which the body or the material, realistic world takes on a new light. Would you comment on that?

MR. WILBUR: That's what I'm trying for—the latter. In

answer to a previous question I said that the angels and the laundry were the same and I really do mean that; but I think if this poem is asking for anything it's asking that angels and laundry not be separated. It's arguing for the kind of double vision that Blake asked for, and that the Zen masters have asked for as well.

Tougaloo: Could we ask a question on "Seed Leaves"?

MR. MOORE: Well, you might ask it, since it's on your mind.

Tougaloo: Are you equating the growth of the seed leaves with the growth of the creative process?

MR. WILBUR: I think I mean it to be more general than that. I think I mean my poem to be about people in general and the reluctance people have to accept any kind of identity by making limiting choices. It's something that I feel in my students all the time. They feel themselves forced at their freshman year to major in something; and then pretty soon they are deciding whether or not to go to graduate school and, if so, what school to go to; and they look forward resentfully toward all sorts of dreadful limitations like the necessity of marrying only one woman. I think everybody, not merely poets and artists, goes through it: this painful feeling that the world is insisting on narrowing one's possibilities.

Drury: The words "difficult balance" seem to sum up the whole problem of the poem: the balance between the soul and the things of this world. Do you mean to imply that this is more difficult for the nuns because they feel the balance more acutely?

MR. WILBUR: I'll tell you why my poem ends with nuns—it's because my city was Rome and, of course, the streets of Rome are full of monks and sisters. I think I can also say that it's always seemed to me that nuns have a particularly difficult job of balancing the claims of this world against the next.

Jackson: We would like to make an observation and ask a question. In the last stanza you have "ruddy gallows" and "clean linen" and "backs of thieves." Is there a possibility of a Christ reference?

MR. WILBUR: I think that I must somehow have been thinking of the crucifixion scene. I don't know whether I can at this moment justify my having had that thought. I hope that it isn't just distracting and misleading.

Morehouse: Could you comment on the list of thieves, lovers, and the nuns together? The "clean linen" by the way, could be burial cloth. But the thieves, the lovers, and the nuns—why this triangle? Why put them together?

MR. WILBUR: I'm not sure. It just seemed to me to be a summary way of indicating the diversity of human types. That's not a very satisfactory explanation to me, and probably isn't to you, but I can't do any better at the moment.

Langston: I would like you to comment on the third and fourth lines of stanza five, "The soul descends once more in bitter love / to accept the waking body."

MR. WILBUR: Well, I think that the man of this poem is a person in transition very much like that werewolf who was trying to remember the mood of manhood, and when we are moving from one feeling to another, even though we are moving for the better, we do so grudgingly because we are so given to inertia. I really want this soul to descend and to accept the body, but it does so with a certain reluctance. It surrenders its freedom with a certain reluctance. I'm reminded of a passage in St. Theresa's *Interior Castle* where she describes the soul as a butterfly which, once released from the cocoon, flutters desperately above the bushes and trees and flowers of the world, unable to decide where to light; but then, of course, it is unable to remain in flight perpetually. This soul is coming down with regret to some one plant.

Stephens: Does the same paradox exist in the phrase, "Let lovers go fresh and sweet to be undone"?

MR. WILBUR: Well, I'm playing around with the word undone, yes. And I'm simply consenting, as in the word thieves, to the idea that the world is going to go on very much as it has.

MR. MOORE: I think we are all very much indebted to Mr. Wilbur for a most satisfactory morning and for his brilliance as well as his good humor. Thank you, very much, Dick, and good-bye.

April 17, 1964

Vance Bourjaily

Vance Bourjaily was born in Cleveland, Ohio, in 1922, the son of Monte Ferris Bourjaily, a Lebanese immigrant who became a noted editor and publisher. Vance Bourjaily served with the American Field Service from 1942 to 1944 and in the Army of the United States from 1944 to 1946. Besides writing novels, he has been an editor, reporter, copy reader, and author of scripts for television. He was one of the founders of the literary magazine *Discovery*, on which he served as editor for six editions (1951–53). He went on a cultural mission to South America in 1959 under the auspices of the State Department. For some years he has taught in the University of Iowa Writers' Workshop under the direction of Paul Engle. Mr. Bourjaily began writing during World War II and has been highly praised as one of the important new voices to come out of that time, particularly by John Aldridge in his book *After the Lost Generation*. Commenting on Mr. Bourjaily's first novel, *The End of My Life* (1947), John Aldridge said, "No book since *This Side of Paradise* has caught so well the flavor of youth in wartime, and no book since *A Farewell to Arms* has contained so complete a record of the loss of that youth in war. Actually, Bourjaily has written the one-volume, contemporary equivalent of both." Mr. Aldridge went on to say, "*The End of My Life*, incidentally, is the only new novel which gives to books their true importance as source material for this generation's ideas and attitudes," referring to the volumes read by the main characters (at one point in the story, two football teams are imagined, composed of authors who are positive or negative, a "yes" team against a "no" team). Another of Mr. Bourjaily's notable novels is *The Hound of Earth* (1955), one of the early examples of what has come to be called "black" humor, the story of a scientist for whom the atom bomb is too much—he goes to work anonymously in a symbolic toy section of a San Francisco department store where one of his friends is a drunken Santa Claus. More recently, Mr. Bourjaily has attracted wide and favorable attention with his novel *The Man Who Knew Kennedy* (1967). Vance Bourjaily's other books include *The Violated* (1958), *Confessions of a Spent Youth* (1960), and *Unnatural Enemy* (1963); the first two of these are novels, the last a factual book about hunting. When Mr. Bourjaily was interviewed for the current series, he spoke from Mexico, where he was following the trail of one of his avocations, archaeology, and was also obtaining material for his imaginative writing.

MR. MOORE: Mr. Bourjaily is in Mexico on an archaeological expedition. He'll tell you something about that. You don't need any further introduction so we'll ask Mr. Bourjaily to come in and speak to us for about ten minutes, perhaps telling us what he is doing as well as commenting on his own work. Mr. Bourjaily.

MR. BOURJAILY: All right. Let me start, because you can hear me but not see me, by telling you what I look like and then I will describe where I am and so on. I am a forty-one-year-old man, about five feet seven inches tall, blue-eyed. I think of myself as having a pleasant manner. I don't think of myself as being a particularly polished speaker, but how speaking to you over the telephone will affect my relative degree of polish as a speaker I don't know. If I were there in person, you would probably get a certain impression of stammering and a feeling that I was not completely at ease in speaking to a group of more than five or six people. I believe perhaps this would disappear after a few minutes as I got warmed up to what I was talking about.

I am sitting in a telephone booth in a town called Tlacolula in the state of Oaxaca in Mexico. This booth has the only telephone in Tlacolula, and I have had to come here from the town of Mitla which is about ten miles away in order to get to a telephone at all. The telephone booth is located in a store, run by a man called Don Federico, which sells a few groceries. They sell mescal which is the local liquor. I see some bottles of sherry, quite a bit of rum around on the shelves, flashlight batteries, soap, and perhaps the most important thing in the store, the scales. They have three sets which they use to weigh out corn and beans and other dried foods that are the staples of the people who are in a village like this one.

Outside the store Tlacolula is fairly quiet this morning because it's Monday, the day of rest in Tlacolula. Monday is the day of rest because Sunday is traditionally market day. It has very likely been market day here for a thousand years. Generally the day on which market is held in this kind of Mexican town is the same day it was held in pre-Spanish times when the Indian civilizations were in power. It is precisely these Indian civilizations, or one of them, which we're investigating down here now, and which archaeology in Mexico concerns itself with. What we have been doing, up to now, and will continue doing this week, is a kind of archaeological work called site survey. It is a sort of reconnaisance in which we clomp around on roads that are hardly more than footpaths in a four-wheel-drive vehicle, getting ourselves into little towns which haven't been visited by archaeologists before. We try to form some estimate of what sort of ruins may be covered up in a particular town. The clues that lead us to these places are, generally speaking, sixteenth- and seventeenth-century Spanish documents which were written to describe new Spain to the rulers back in old Spain. Very often they were written by missionaries or bishops and from their descriptions of what these Indian towns were like then, four hundred or five hundred years ago, we estimate that this or that town may have been an important cultural center for the Zapotec or Mixtec civilizations which were the two groups here in the valley of Oaxaca.

At the end of this week we will begin excavation at a site called Caballito Blanco which we picked because considerable excavation has been done at surrounding sites. The surrounding sites represent all but one of the time periods into which we divide what we know of the pre-Spanish history of this valley. Previously excavated sites cover all except the second period. We believe, from certain evidence, most of it in the form of little bits of pottery that we picked up around Caballito Blanco, that it may be a second period site, and that through excavating there we may be able to fill in a little more knowledge of this particular period which is quite different from any of the others. However, we have another week of surveys to do before we start the excavation.

Now, let me go on from there to talk about why I'm doing this. I think the primary answer to that would be that I am doing it because I have a tremendous enthusiasm for it and a great amateur interest in it. This interest will be reflected in a novel I am currently working on called *Expedition* which is, in part, about a man who goes out on an actual archaeological expedition. However, it would be an over-simplification to suggest that I am here to gather materials for the novel. The fact is that the material of novels is very seldom in one's immediate experience. The particular expedition about which I shall be writing about which I have been writing actually—is one that took place ten years ago. The relation of what I am doing now to the material of the novel is, perhaps to some extent, to confirm an emotional sense toward the material, to reassure myself that my feelings about what goes on in these circumstances is exactly what I remember from ten years ago, perhaps to amplify these feelings and discover more about them.

As far as direct use of experience goes, I would find it very difficult to make direct use in the novel of anything happening as close to the time of writing the novel as this particular expedition is. I think one has to make a distinction between that and reporting, which, of course, you *can* do by walking around, looking around, making notes, and writing immediately what you've seen and experienced. I don't think much besides reporting can come from that. In general, I think one has to get somewhat remote from the experience one's going to use in fiction, both in time and in place. To write, in a way that will satisfy me, about Mexico I shall have to be several hundred miles away from Mexico and, as I already am, ten years away in time from the particulars that I am going to use in the book. I don't think I shall try to write things, in fact I probably won't even make any notes, until Mexico is a thousand miles away.

The reason for this is that the process of writing fiction is not a matter of describing directly a reality that one sees. It's much more often a matter of re-creating a reality which one recalls perhaps imperfectly which one remembers as having been in some way moving, and one almost has to re-create it in order to discover why it is that it still moves one to think about it.

Let me see if that doesn't lead us into a word or two about *The End of My Life*. That, again, was a book which I did not write immediately during the war, although I made a kind of start at it—I think it must have been in 1943 in Italy. I wrote what is now the next to the last chapter—the chapter in which Johnnie, the nurse, is killed—as a short story practically the day after a particular experience had suggested their story to me. This is something perhaps worth describing because this too has to do with how material becomes fiction. In this case I had done much what Skinner does in the book. I had met a nurse and she wanted to see the front so I drove her up a little way in my ambulance. We got somewhere around the artillery position and then I said, "Hey, let's turn around and go back," and she said, "Yeah, let's," and so we turned around and went back and nothing happened.

We went to a party that night and it wasn't until the next morning, waking up somewhat hung over and somewhat displeased with myself, that I began to have this masochistic fantasy of what might have happened, how things could have gone wrong. It became real to me. It really did. In a way the fantasy was more real than the experience of the day before had been. I kept torturing myself with these images of what might have happened to a point where I felt a kind of need to write it as a story, to write the fantasy as a story, which I then did. However, it wasn't a particularly good story and didn't lead anywhere at that time, and I put it away.

About three years later, in 1946, when I was finally discharged from the army I wanted to write a novel and I reread this, by then, old story about that old, by then, experience, and saw that in order to explain Skinner and the thing he did and the circumstances in which he found himself I would have to fill in a great deal more than simply what had happened on that particular day. That gradually led to the writing of a full novel about that character culminating in that particular experience. (*pause*) Excuse me. I've just stopped to light a cigarette.

Now the book that came out of the war, *The End of My Life* which you have been reading and which was written seventeen years ago—eighteen years ago, I suppose—is a certain kind of book. I think very much a young man's book. It's a book in a mood of romantic nihilism, I suppose, which is an appropriate enough mood for the age I was when I wrote it (twenty-four or twenty-five; I think I probably had a birthday while I was writing it so I was both twenty-four and twenty-five). The mood, then, still seems to me true. *The End of My Life* seems to me a reasonably accurate description of the way we felt about ourselves and the way we felt about that experience at the time. It doesn't seem to me an accurate book in the picture it gives of the war and of that kind of experience in an objective sense. It's a highly subjective book and like any highly subjective book, I think, limited. It was for that reason, the feeling that while I dealt with the emotional quality of the material, I hadn't really dealt with the war material in a way that satisfied me, that along about 1959 or 1960 I began to write *Confessions of a Spent Youth* in which I use the same material all over again. I think I use it in a very different way and in a very different tone. In my mind it wasn't until I had finished *Confessions* that I had really dealt with the war in a way that pleased me. In that sense *Confessions of a Spent Youth* could almost be read as a work of commentary on American first novels. What I tried to do throughout that much later book was to examine those experiences which are the standard—the set pieces—of American first novels; to hold the set pieces (I felt I had written some of them in *The End of My Life*) up against experience as recalled accurately and without the glow of romance and try to compare the convention with the reality. Having done this finally in *Confessions*, I felt that I was at last through with that particular body of material—the war, youth, and so on—and ready to go on and write novels about more mature experiences.

Well, I have used up my ten minutes and perhaps a bit more. I realize that it's *The End of My Life* you all want to talk about, so I think I'm now ready to answer questions.

MR. MOORE: Thank you very much for a fascinating presentation. You began giving us a wonderful sense of what the Mexicans call *ambiente*, the atmosphere of the surroundings where you are and that was extremely interesting. So was your discussion of these novels. We will now get to the questions, and the first question is from Jackson State College.

Jackson: This question concerns itself with the title of the novel.

MR. BOURJAILY: Did you say the title?

Jackson: With the title, yes. Must we assume that Skinner's death in prison was inevitable; that he also had already died spiritually at the end of the book?

MR. BOURJAILY: Well, I think I was certainly thinking in terms of spiritual death. The core of the human being was in some way exhausted and would have no further vitality. The particular personality which this human core had constructed in order to meet the war situation was no longer of use and I meant to imply a kind of rebirth. The Skinner who had lived through the events with Benny and Freak and Rod and so on was a useful enough personality with which to grow up and meet the war and endure it. But at the time of his emergence from prison he would have to be some different kind of man in order to be able to endure or even enjoy the different sort of world conditions which, you know, were then in the making.

Morehouse: I am of the opinion that the *Confession* can be seen as a sequel in a thematic sense to *The End of My Life*. If this is so, what major conclusions have you come to as to which book you like better in terms of thematic development, style, imagery, general accomplishment, development of character, and so on?

MR. BOURJAILY: All right. I think the two books are finally so different that I couldn't make a choice between them in terms of which I like better. First novels are like first loves, one is never able to reread them without becoming reinvolved in some way in the mood in which they were written. However, I think I feel that, for me at least, rereading *The End of My Life* is something that, when I do it, I have to make certain allowances for myself and my youth. I don't think I understood a great deal technically about fiction when I wrote it. And, in fact, most first novels are written within a kind of naïveté about the form. The stylistic influences and the conception one has of what a story is and how to tell it are much closer to the surface in a first novel than they are in later ones. I think that the two commanding figures were Hemingway and Fitzgerald for me. I felt both presences when I reread *The End of My Life*. It does, on the other hand, have a certain unity of effect it seems to me, because of the total predominance of that mood of romantic nihilism. It has a unity of effect which, I think, is a good quality and which I could not hope to reproduce again at this time, simply because it is no longer my own predominating mood.

I hope *Confession* is a wiser book, a subtler book, a more profound book. It certainly is a far more experimental book in form. It's conceived almost as a series of essays. The relationship of one chapter to the next in the way time is handled in that each overlaps the other. Any given chapter may start anywhere in time—that is, at any point in the hero's, or the protagonist's, life in which a particular subject becomes of interest to him. This chapter internally will then progress in time to a point which leaves the book a little more advanced than did the end of the preceding chapter. However, the organization of each of these chapters is topical. That is, there is one particular topic dealt with in each of these chapters and all the relevant experiences to the topic are contained in that particular chapter and excluded from the others. So that in this way, the book seems to me somewhat experimental in form, but I don't think I would be the appropriate person to comment on how successful the experiment is. The experiment probably caused me to lose some of the pure narrative drive of *The End of My Life* which is all written consecutively and in which the story is told in a rather straightforward way. There are no particular devices used except flashback. So that is the way that I would compare the two books. (*laughs*) I guess I will just refuse to make a choice between them.

Langston: This question is in two parts. First of all, none of the characters, except Benny, completed his college education before volunteering his services for the armed forces; yet all of the characters are portrayed as very intellectual. This is particularly noticeable in the dialogue used, though at times they tend to display a youthful irreverence. There is an implication, too, that the protagonist, Skinner, is in search of an escape from something and there is an implication that he desires to identify himself with something. I would like you to comment on these factors.

MR. BOURJAILY: Yes. Well, let me take the education question first and then perhaps we can get the part that deals with values. The war itself was perhaps our junior year in college for many of us. (Incidentally, I think that most of the people I had in mind when I wrote *The End of My Life,* or the base characters, did get back to college after the war and finished their education.) In the experience of going abroad and hearing other languages spoken there was a good deal of involuntary educating of oneself that went on. Even more important, however, in being thrown into war, into very intimate contact with a group where, from almost desperate necessity, one makes very close friends of one's own age but of somewhat different backgrounds, there was a kind of interchange among friends which perhaps takes place in the junior or senior years of college but which took place for us removed from educational institutions. However, we weren't removed from books and we weren't removed from the cultural experience of traveling and so on, and we taught one another. I think this must have happened quite commonly. In the group I was writing about for lack of any other teacher I suppose Benny becomes the teacher. I don't think I made much of this in the book. Benny was the teacher because he could draw upon his experiences in some ways; Rod is a teacher because he can draw upon a different kind of experience. And then Skinner has a somewhat teacherlike function in the group in that he becomes the mocking critic of the other teachers. What happens in a very imperfect way, I think, in such situations is that the educational situation which we institutionalize in colleges is simply reproduced within a little group of people of educable age; it is an imperfect way but not a way that fails to produce any results at all. I would guess that the same kind of educating even goes on in a group of men thrown together in prison. It must go on certainly in the army or abroad. It may not be all desirable education but it is what we mean by education nevertheless. Now, about the value question, can we find out a little more about what they want to know about that?

Langston: Was Skinner seeking an escape or some kind of identification with particular values?

MR. BOURJAILY: Well, I don't think he knew. I think he probably felt that he was trying to find values but that's really too abstract a way of putting it. I think Skinner was trying to find somebody *to be.* We use the phrase a search for identity about novels fairly often. It's not a very accurate phrase in my mind because it assumes that identity exists and that somehow one can find it as an accomplished and developed thing. Obviously identity doesn't exist somewhere to be found; identity—the feeling that one has achieved "self"—is something that develops very slowly perhaps through many years and through all one's youth. And identity is finally achieved, I think, from within rather than found somewhere without. Meanwhile, one is trying various systems of value; various ways of judging experience, various ways of estimating himself. These are suggested by the people we meet and the books we read and the things that happen to us and the things we cause to happen. I think Skinner in the book is probably ten years away, still, from finding himself in this sense. The book is only a partial record of his search for values or his search for identity, to fall back on those two phrases again.

Stephens: Our question is a follow-up on the last question. We especially enjoyed the football game created by Skinner and Benny and Cindy. Do you feel today that you would still use the same players on the same teams? (*laughter*)

MR. BOURJAILY: Oh wow! I'd have to have the book open in front of me to be able to say. Insofar as I can remember those lineups I guess they'd stand. I might make some substitutions this late in the game; you know, those players may be tiring a bit. (*laughter*)

Stephens: You wouldn't use the system of sending in a whole new team though?

MR. BOURJAILY: I don't believe I would have to send in a whole new team, no. No platooning. There are certain other writers I have read, studied and so on. Perhaps the most important (this is really a footnote) I forget whether Tolstoy is on one of those teams or not.

Stephens: No, he isn't. How about Camus?

MR. BOURJAILY: Camus would be an interesting player to contemplate, yes. I think I did use Dostoevsky. I would like to go on and say that perhaps the most important experience, a sort of mid-development for me as a writer occurred between the writing of my second book, *The Hound of Earth,* and the writing of my third, *The Violated,* which I think is probably the most successful of my novels in many ways. What happened was simply that I read two novels (or reread these novels—I had read them once before) and they became meaningful to me as a writer, meaningful to me as models, books to learn from, as they hadn't been when I had run into them for the first time. These two novels were *War and Peace* and *Tom Jones.* It seemed to me—this is a very subjective judgment and could not be

confirmed by a critic reading, say *The Violated* in comparison with *The End of My Life*—particularly, that reading, as
a writer, *War and Peace* made an enormous difference to
me as a novelist in opening my eyes to certain possibilities
of the form.

Like most twentieth-century writers, I had been brought
up on the work of Henry James and his followers down
through both Hemingway and Fitzgerald, and from this had
derived, I think, a very limited idea of the possibilities of
the novel as a form, without perhaps ever having thought
about point of view and about restricted point of view. I
just automatically felt that point of view should be restricted. This seemed the correct way. I don't think I even
knew at the time I wrote my first novel that Percy Lubbock
had codified the whole thing. Or that James had done so in
his prefaces, I read both Lubbock and the prefaces after I
had read *War and Peace*. I read them with a sense of rather
scoffing at them. They seemed rather silly to me. It seemed
to me that these were terribly useless books for a writer;
they might be useful for writers who had not been brought
up on this kind of work. The limits which James set, or
which Lubbock tried to set after James—I don't know if I
should accuse James of this—are artificial and pretentious,
and deny a great deal of the vitality which is possible to a
novel. It is the vitality which is so superbly present in *War
and Peace*. I'm getting pretty far away from the question
now, but Tolstoy would certainly have to go for me on
today's "Yes" team.

Stephens: Thank you.

Tougaloo: Two students of ours have asked whether
Skinner's nihilism is really genuine. One suggests that his
concern for people suggests not, the other suggests that he is
just punishing himself. Would you comment on this?

MR. BOURJAILY: Well, I'll try. I'm not sure that I can
successfully. Skinner's nihilism is genuine in that he seems,
to himself, to feel that way. I think looking at him (if I
could) as somebody else's character, I would say that there

is a perfectly obvious contradiction in his feeling that way. After having adopted the pose and having said "Life sure is a dreary affair," he is capable of going out and having a marvelously good time. However, while this contradiction exists in the character, it seems to me to exist as a kind of fraternal feeling in characters of that age and that temperament. Right down through history each generation exemplifies very much the same thing. It seems to me that you can go back decade after decade after decade and find this manifestation of the same combination: a kind of romantic nihilism and, at the same time, a considerable exuberance for life not only in its sensual aspects but in its intellectual aspects too. The fact is, when Skinner and his friends sit around contemplating how lousy life is, then, in a way, they are having a very good time. This is something I believe I dealt with in *Confession*.

Now, on the other hand, there is a point in the book at which Skinner becomes, I think, genuinely hopeless and with cause. That's the point at which he joins the pioneer regiment of Africa and this certainly is indicative of the situation to which these particular soldiers are subjected. It occurs in a much different way; in a way that he doesn't enjoy. Instead of being a kind of glowing melancholy, he is really severely depressed, genuinely without hope. Does that answer the question?

Tougaloo: Yes, thank you.

Drury: Do you mean to suggest that the kind of exuberance that dominates most of the scenes in the flashbacks is no longer possible for the Skinner who, in some kind of way, is going to be reborn at the end of the novel?

MR. BOURJAILY: Yes, that's a lovely question. As life implies death and happiness implies sorrow and so on, perhaps the nihilism and exuberance are really dependent on one another in a way. Therefore, when Skinner reemerges and is no longer the victim of one, he will no longer be able to produce the other. I think this quite possible.

MR. MOORE: Thank you again. I think we are all greatly indebted to Mr. Vance Bourjaily for a most illuminating morning. Thank you and good-bye.

April 27, 1964

Kay Boyle

Kay Boyle was born in 1903 in St. Paul, Minnesota, and grew up in Philadelphia, Atlantic City, and Cincinnati. She began writing as a small child, for, as she once told a reporter, "My sister and I had the idea that you made books for your family." Miss Boyle, who had traveled in Europe as a child, lived there for most of the period between the world wars, principally on the Left Bank in Paris and in Southern France; after World War II she lived for some years in West Germany, but has spent most of her time in the United States. Her early publications include *Wedding Day and Other Stories* (1929) and *The First Lover and Other Stories* (1932), as well as her first two novels, *Plagued by the Nightingale* (1930) and *Year Before Last* (1931). *Nightingale* reflects the experience of the author's early marriage to a Frenchman and her attempt to live in his family home. *Year Before Last* is the story of an American girl and an American poet who is dying of tuberculosis in Southern France. *Gentlemen, I Address You Privately* (1933) deals with an international group in Northern France, and *My Next Bride* (1934) tells the story of a young American woman staying in an art colony in Paris. With these books, Kay Boyle demonstrated that she was one of the finest new American writers. *The White Horses of Vienna and Other Stories* (1935) showed the author's concern with European socio-political matters; its title story won the O. Henry Memorial Prize. Besides her fiction, Miss Boyle has written poetry, which appears in *A Glad Day* (1938) and *Collected Poems* (1962); *The Youngest Camel* (1959) is a children's story. Her other novels include: *Death of Man* (1936), *Monday Night* (1937), *Primer for Combat* (1942), *Avalanche* (1943), *A Frenchman Must Die* (1946), *His Human Majesty* (1949), *The Seagull on the Step* (1955), and *Generation Without Farewell* (1949), the last reflecting the author's postwar experiences in West Germany, as do the stories in *The Smoking Mountain* (1951), the finest fictional interpretation of that place and time that has been written in English. *The Crazy Hunter* (1940) consists of three novellas, two of them reprinted in *Three Short Novels* (1958). Miss Boyle's latest collection of tales is *Nothing Ever Breaks Except the Heart* (1966). For the present conversation we chose her *Thirty Stories*, first published in 1946 and representing the range of her work until that time. Miss Boyle, now professor of English at San Francisco State College, is one of the most accomplished prose writers in English today; she uses the nuances of language to reach the hidden roots of character and to intensify the dramatic situations of her fiction. That she is a conscious craftsman with a luminous understanding of the art of literature manifests itself in the following conversation.

MISS BOYLE: When I start talking about writing I simply can't be stopped. There are so many things I want to say to the students who are listening that you will have to ring a bell to stop me.

I would like to talk a little bit about what writing means to me, if I may. There seem to me to be two things of equal importance in the matter of writing—I suppose I should explain, two things aside from the ability to write. The first thing, an acute awareness of words, of language, is almost a disease in itself, but it is seldom, unfortunately, a contagious disease. The other requirement as I see it, is an awareness of life, so pressing, so keen that it threatens with every instant to absorb all the time and energy which rightly should be given by the writer to writing itself. I think of James Baldwin instantly when I speak of awareness because he is to me the most exciting and the most interesting of our younger writers. He possesses not only a sense of language—an extraordinary sense of language—but also that remarkable sense of life. His passion for justice and eloquence on vital issues are constantly putting in jeopardy the writing of his books. Sometimes I deplore that this is so, but on the other hand I realize it must be so for him, for without that passion, that dedication, for the rights of man, his writing could never be what it is. It would be stripped of that fiery intention that we all pay homage to, and would be stripped of its admirable direction as well.

To my mind language can never be a matter of merely literary concern because language and content, form and subject matter, and I know we all agree, cannot be separated. They are one and the same thing. Language goes far deeper, almost more deeply than we realize. For instance, some psychologists would tell you that the lack of an adequate means of verbal expression plays a great part in the problems of juvenile delinquents, in the disturbed psyche, in the tragedies of all the outcast and all the lost.

There's a very good writer—a very good journalist—named George Steiner who has a great deal of value to say on the matter of language in present-day Germany, for instance. The linguists of the Nazi states, as we know, made a political weapon of the German language; a weapon more effective than any history had ever known before—a total weapon—that degraded the dignity of human speech to the level of baying wolves. Steiner believes, as does the remarkable young German poet, Hans Enzensberger, that the German language was so corrupted in Hitler's time that a great silence, a queer stillness (at least as far as the poets and all other writers are concerned, for the German politician, as we know, is still quite eloquent), a great stillness has now fallen on Germany. Steiner believes that the Germans must find a new tongue, a fresh, clear articulation, that not only communicates but creates the sense of communion before they can again be writers, poets, thinkers, passionate revolutionaries in the arts and letters and even on the political field of Germany.

Now I think of this because I think it applies to us, too, here in America. I had dinner recently with my publisher, Alfred Knopf, and there was another guest at the table who happens to be the owner of a great newspaper in Washington. She said, very bitterly, that she had lost her faith in the power of the word and that's a dreadful thing for the editor of a newspaper to say, but she said it with great emphasis. She said the word, for her, had been corrupted past all redemption by the Communists. Knopf retorted, with some annoyance, that the word had been corrupted right here on our own soil by Madison Avenue. He added it was more than ever the business of the writers to redeem the word. And this reminds me—this takes me back to our old days in Paris, in the twenties and thirties, when we wrote pamphlets on just this subject. We distributed them along the streets and in the café, treatises (no one would believe it now) on the revolution of the word. We recognized, with impatience and intolerance for almost everything that had been written in America, that the time had come to release the English language from the shapes and forms to which it had solidified on the printed page. I think this time has again arrived in our literary history here.

Our revolution, then, at that time, was against all literary pretentiousness, against weary, flowery rhetoric, against all the outworn literary conventions, and it should never be forgotten that it was a needed revolution. You people who are listening and writing should never forget that because it was so desperately needed, a sense of discovery and adventure animated the life of the writer at that time. The work of our nineteenth-century authors had never, for one instant, been free of the English literary tradition and we wanted to free it.

A very interesting philosopher called George Santayana in an essay on the moral background of our American literature speaks of our New England poets, historians, and orators (the writers of the middle of the nineteenth century) as harvesters of dead leaves. He wrote that sometimes these poets, these writers, made attempts to rejuvenate their minds by broaching native subjects. I really love this conception, this analysis, of our nineteenth-century American classics that we respect so much and are asked to read over and over again with a little misgiving. Santayana wrote: "They broached native subjects in an effort to prove how much matter for poetry the New World supplied and they wrote 'Evangeline' or they wrote 'Rip Van Winkle.' But their culture was half a pious survival, half an intentional acquirement. It was never for a moment the inevitable flowering of fresh experience."

Well, that shock of fresh experience which he referred to was what we wanted to find; it was what we were seeking to create, if we could, in Paris in the twenties and the early thirties. And, oddly enough, the sound of that clamor, the shock of the words which men and women wrote down on paper in those revolutionary days is still respected today. We paid homage to Joyce, we celebrated the short stories of

Sherwood Anderson; those short stories which Sherwood Anderson himself said were "a revolt against the cold, hard stony culture of New England in which gentility and respectability had become the pattern of our writing." We hailed the early work of Ernest Hemingway and the translations from the Chinese by Ezra Pound. We cherished the work and the spirit of William Carlos Williams. But T. S. Eliot and Henry James we discarded with vehemence. Gertrude Stein (without whom there might not have been as articulate a Sherwood Anderson and certainly no Hemingway) was very difficult to revere. She once remarked that nobody had done anything to develop the English language since Shakespeare except herself. Then, "Well, perhaps Henry James," she added, "just a little bit." She also was fond of announcing that the Jews had produced only three original geniuses: Christ, Spinoza, and herself.

It may be of interest to all of you to point out here that we expatriate writers, as we are called now—I'm not sure we were called that then, but we are called that now—were no more respected in our time than the beatniks are today. We are looked on with a curious respect now that we are all either dead or approaching the grave. In the twenties we were not considered of much enduring value, if of any value at all, by American critics or American editors or American publishers. Europeans, we like to think, had more perception; they took us much more seriously. And now, even at my time of life there are long periods when I feel that I am completely with and of the beatniks. The beats, for instance, are appalled by the materialism of contemporary life whether in our own country, or in the economic miracle of modern Germany, or anywhere else where material values are substituted for morality. I, too, am appalled by this. The beats, for instance, believe that our advertising and publicity media are corrupting the American language. I believe this too, and I believe that the corruption of its language is one of the most tragic things that can happen to a country. In Germany, as I have mentioned before, it was a fatal thing. William Shirer, among others, has made amply clear to us that writing under the Nazis became solely the entering into ledgers the names or numbers of the millions of dead, and speech was used for the specifications for gas ovens and the ordering of mass execution. The things that are said and written day after day in a country not only affect the character of that country but they shape its destiny. It is as serious as that.

I believe too, that one of the many functions of a writer is to create a public and a climate. Other functions of a writer are, to be sure, to be a poet, to be a philosopher, to be a historian, but the obligation to create an intelligent and aware public, an exhilarating climate for all of us to breathe in, is the responsibility a writer must accept from the outset as peculiarly his. Because I am deeply concerned with all the tasks of the writer, I feel that in our times it is not the writer who must seek to be accepted by the world in which he finds himself, but it is the world that must be transformed to acceptability by the higher standards of the individual. The writer's concern must always be not only with what is taking place, although that may be of necessity the framework within which to state the tenets of his faith, but his deepest concern must be, as well, with the dimensions of what *might* within the infinite capacities of man be enabled to take place. It is this high concern one finds expressed in the essays of James Baldwin which makes his work among the most important that's being done in America today. You'll remember that he wrote once: "Although we do not wholly believe it yet, the interior life is a real life and the intangible dreams of people have a tangible effect upon the world."

I tell my students that the awareness of these obligations of the writer must be present in every line of their work. I refer them to Albert Camus who in his life, as in his books, to the day of his death never ceased defining with quality and modesty the writer's predicament. He believed he had not the right, either as man or as author, to sever himself from the great issues of his time. He believed that those who *could* speak should give voice to those others who are inarticulate: the miner who was exploited, shot down, the slaves in the concentration camps and the slaves of the colonies—the legions of men throughout the world who are in such desperate need. Those who *could* speak, Camus said, and by that he meant the writers above all, should not through fear or through evasion or in judgment hold themselves apart. You will remember that Camus took part in French resistance; you will remember that Camus was fighting for the abolition of capital punishment. He took part in all the issues of his time that he could reach and even those that he could not reach. Camus explained with characteristic humility that it was not by nature but through affection and will power that he attempted not to separate himself from his times. That is, I believe, the great essential of the art of a writer even though it demands an effort of the will, as Camus says. The writer must recognize and must accept his commitment to his times. Well, I think that's about all I have to say on that.

MR. MOORE: Thank you very much. This is wonderful. Now we are ready for questions. Langston University?

Langston: In "Major Alshuster" why does the protagonist not have a realistic view in her relation to the major?

MISS BOYLE: Because she's a romantic. She was attempting, as I suppose I am in my work, to transform the world. She was trying to make Major Alshuster another and more fulfilled person.

MR. MOORE: Stephens College. Do you have a question?

Stephens: We have several. I hardly know where to begin there are so many. I think this has something to do with what Miss Boyle was talking about in her comments on language. In the story "The Canals of Mars," in the movie we have the following conversation:

"It's one o'clock," he said in the dark, "and they haven't reached civilization yet."

"This can't go on forever," she said.

"It can go on until they pitch camp," he said. "It'll have to go on until she's made the coffee and cooked potatoes in the ash." He had got to his feet now, and he said:

"You wait here while I ask. I don't want to have to see
them paddling into the sunset."

Is this simply descriptive or do you intend it, in that story,
to function as symbolic?

MISS BOYLE: No, it's not symbolic at all. It's simply a
story. Actually it happened exactly that way. One wanted to
save time and not see one of these travelogue things to the
very end. There's no symbolism in it, although if one looks
very hard one can perhaps find it there, which is quite
possible but certainly not valid.

Stephens: I think it's entirely possible to wonder
about whether or not we have reached civilization under the
circumstances of the story.

MISS BOYLE: Heavens, that had never occurred to me!

Tougaloo: We have a number of questions about the
balance of dream and reality in the stories. This would be
true of "Major Alshuster" and "Black Boy" and "Natives
Don't Cry." I wonder if you could comment on that, Miss
Boyle. How much dream and how much reality in your
stories?

MISS BOYLE: I think it's completely impossible to separate them, or to say where they are separated. They merge
into each other and in every instance (I suppose I am really
trying to be a historian) in every instance my stories are
based very, very, very deeply in fact. The characters are all
more or less recognizable. In fact, Major Alshuster recognized himself. I saw him only that one day but someone sent
him a copy of *Harper's Magazine*, I believe it was, or the
Atlantic Monthly, many years ago when the story appeared.
Someone recognized him who had not seen him in this light,
but still recognized him and sent him this story and said,
"Read this! This is perfectly outrageous! But this is certainly you." He wrote back a very angry letter to *Harper's*
and said he had never, never, never at any time not given his
sheep water. You may remember in the story that the sheep

are dying because they haven't been given water. So, in some strange way, even in the dream the reality does recognize itself.

Drury: In many of your stories you make use of insinuation or even silence instead of direct statements. In other words, it's often what the characters *don't* say that is most important. Would you comment on this technique in the light of your emphasis on the importance of language in writing. Is it also important to know what *not* to say in order to stir the reader's imagination?

MISS BOYLE: Well, I think the two things are very different. I think if we're interested in a cause we have to speak out about it. I think that's one side of our activities as writers. On the other hand, the subtlety in human relations is largely based on silence and what one does not say. I think that in having silences, in making implications, I'm simply recording what I've observed in life. In a family relationship (I have a great number of children) I never really like to give direct criticism or direct orders to them because it's just wrong. It rubs against the grain. Somehow, it is the *feeling* that they learn from day to day, what it is you really wish—although I don't mean I sit around brooding in silence or implying things—but when they really understand what you wish, deep down in you, and you understand what they wish, the whole thing works beautifully without outspoken declarations about it. This is *not* true about all the *causes* in which we believe; those we *must be* articulate about. You remember Camus wrote a very fine thing on capital punishment, and his letters to a German soldier, and all that sort of thing; these issues in which we are involved—we must speak up. Silence is not a position. We are trying to reach other people, we're trying to communicate things. Now, I think in human relationships—Henry James handles it so beautifully in his work, demonstrating how much we do have to rely on silence. In fact, in my creative writing classes at San Francisco State College I try to make them understand that the announced statement, the forthright statement, is not always true to life. They are not giving the feeling of the person when they do that. Does that answer?

Drury: Yes, I think so. Thank you.

Jackson: This is a general question. One of the students has suggested that there are influences of Katherine Mansfield and Virginia Woolf in your writings. Would you comment on that?

MISS BOYLE: Yes. All I can say is that I don't think that I am influenced by Katherine Mansfield and Virginia Woolf. I do think that at one time I was very much influenced by D. H. Lawrence, and I think I have been influenced by several of the French writers, but not Katherine Mansfield, whose work I have never, never liked at all because she had what I consider a very narrow feminine point of view—for instance, she uses the word little all the time, and various words which diminish her prose and her outlook on life. Also she had no connection with reality at all. I may be split and go half dream and half reality, but in her later years, as you may know, she lost touch with reality completely and she lived absolutely and wholly with the ghost of her brother who had died. I've never felt less in sympathy with anyone, either the spirit or the writing, than with Katherine Mansfield. Now Virginia Woolf—I never read her things very much but I think she's much more in the tradition of what we were fighting for, undoubtedly.

Morehouse: Because they were written over a long period of time the stories may not have a central unifying theme but do you feel in the larger sense that each group in this collection is unified?

MISS BOYLE: My stories? Do they have a unifying theme? No. Except inasmuch as every writer, I suppose, is writing the same story over and over with different figures and different plots and different scenes. I think probably that's the only thing. I know that I got so tired of writing things from the point of view of an American in Europe that my last novel I decided to write from the point of view of a German newspaperman. I rather got bored myself with my own point of view and so I projected myself into the mind of a German newspaperman whom I knew very well. I sent him the novel in its early draft and he pointed out things which he would not or could not have thought or which could not have happened in his past. So I think it's a pretty good representation of what he thought. No, they do not have a unifying theme, I think, except that I am always concerned with certain qualities in which I believe very strongly, the kind of morality that Baldwin is concerned with.

MR. MOORE: Thank you. That novel Miss Boyle was referring to is *Generation Without Farewell*, published in 1959 by Knopf. Now, Langston University.

Langston: Was there more in the love of "Wedding Day" than that of a brother and sister relationship?

MISS BOYLE: No. It was just a brother and sister relationship. A great many people have thought this was an incestuous story, but it was not. It was quite simply what it was.

Langston: We have one other question if there's time. Is your style influenced by your experiences in the different countries you write about? If so, to what extent?

MISS BOYLE: I think my style is influenced largely by my hope that I can write something that doesn't bore me and won't bore a number of readers. When I write a paragraph and I get all mixed up in sentences and everything seems to work out wrong, I know that will probably bore somebody else too. I think my style is an attempt to attain freshness and to retain that clamor of the spirit which Santayana referred to. Naturally, it is a little influenced—it must be—by the writers around you, French, German, or whatever they may be, but as one gets older one just struggles for this fresh spirit that one must express in a fresh way.

That's what I find very discouraging in my writing classes, the acceptance of the old ways of saying things. Now I have reached an age where I can be old-fashioned, and these young people must do the really remarkable and exciting things, if only to prove how really old hat I am. That's what I try to encourage in my classes.

MR. MADDEN: Along with Henry James, who also writes about the American in Europe, there seems to be a feeling in your writing that the American is shallow and phony. Would you like to comment on that, particularly in the light of our course title "American Life as Seen by Contemporary Writers?"

MISS BOYLE: You mean the Americans in Europe are depicated as shallow people?

Stephens: This is the implication of the question.

MISS BOYLE: Well, I think that Henry James's writing, great as it is, was limited by his social environment, was limited by his lack of adventurous spirit. I think that if James had gone into other milieus he would have written much more—how shall I say, not brilliantly, because he was very brilliant—he would have written in a wider, greater way than he did. I think there is a tendency to deal with the wrong people in his works. Now my writing about Americans abroad certainly was tempered by the fact that I was married to a Frenchman and I had a certain resentment against rich people who came over and lived there and did not understand the people. The Americans who came, like my American movie director in "Kroy Wen," could not possibly understand alien people. The American artists, writers in Paris—that was something else—the great ones were very lost and very unhappy people. There certainly was not a feeling of happiness among the exiles. There was a feeling of a certain accomplishment, at times, but they were exiles and they were working at great odds, I think. Everything was against them, really.

Stephens: In the light of recent events do you think the American abroad is in any way changed from the kind of person he was in the twenties?

MISS BOYLE: Well, yes, I think they've had to change. An interesting example of this is that a great many of my students here at State want to go abroad and bum around for a few years. I have to tell them that those days are gone—they're not past merely because I am older and see it with older eyes. Students say, "I've just read *Portrait of the Artist* and I want to go to Paris," but it just doesn't happen that way anymore. You really have to go, I tell them, within the framework of something larger now, like the Peace Corps, or in an educational position with UNESCO. The time has passed, things are too critical, to do it in the way that we did at the time we were staging our revolution.

Tougaloo: We have a double question about technique. One student asks about the ending of your stories, noting that they leave the reader to decide the outcome, if this is your concept of the short story? The other question notes that you handle very violent emotion in a short story, in "Winter Night" for example, and asks if this presents special problems.

MISS BOYLE: I don't quite understand what is meant by problems. What problems would be set by this?

Tougaloo: Problems of handling very violent emotions in a short space.

MISS BOYLE: Well, I think very violent emotions sometimes just take a very short space of time, don't you?

Tougaloo: Yes, that's true, only, it's sort of a bang and then you are left there. Do you leave it up to the reader to resolve at the end?

MISS BOYLE: The reader has to do a little bit of work. Yes. You mean that the reader has to work things out? I'm afraid I'm not understanding the question.

Tougaloo: That's O. K. You've understood, I'm quite sure. The reader has to work things out.

MISS BOYLE: The reader, one supposes, has had certain experiences and certain contacts with humanity, with people, and knows more or less. Now if the reader does not agree with the way I imply that it is going to end, then he may end it in any way he wishes. You remember Hemingway's bull fight story—a very good one.

MR. MOORE: *The Undefeated?*

MISS BOYLE: Yes, yes, it is. One doesn't know in the end whether the bullfighter dies or not. That story infuriates so many people because they want to be told. Did he or did he not die is really not important at all. He is undefeated anyway.

Stephens: Miss Boyle, I wonder if you could comment on the ending of "Winter Night." What *do* you see is happening there? Does the mother change her point of view?

MISS BOYLE: No. Impossible. And *The New Yorker* —when that story appeared in *The New Yorker*—showed me many of the letters, and I'm sure there were many more, that came in from people who were outraged by it: No, they had not visited Europe: no, they had not seen places bombed; no, they had not seen a concentration camp; but they had suffered and they refused to accept my judgment on this woman. The poor woman. She worked all day and she had a right to go out in the evening and it was *outrageous* the way this poor mother was depicted. No, she didn't change, I'm sure. In fact, she was more inured in her own way of living than before.

Stephens: Well, then, what kind of awareness comes about at the end of that story? The woman who had been in the concentration camp, we feel, is going to continue being the very kind and deep person that she is; the child responded to her immediately. What happens, as you see it, in that story?

MISS BOYLE: I really don't know. You see in the first place that woman would never have been able to tell the mother her story. She told the child. Now it might have been once in a million years that she would have been in a position to deal with a child of that age who responded to her. Maybe that woman will never tell that story again. She couldn't possibly go to baby-sit every night and tell that story. There wouldn't be the same situation or the same response.

MR. MOORE: Isn't the interest of the mother just ironic?

MISS BOYLE: Well, yes, there's irony in it, too, you know.

Jackson: One of the students has noted that the main characters in "The Canals of Mars" are not named. Is this a technique to make them symbolic of all love and farewell in wartime?

MISS BOYLE: No, that was not the intention. I didn't even remember they weren't named. No, that was certainly not the intention. It is not a symbolic story at all. It is a purely factual story.

Jackson: Jackson has another question. Three questions have been raised concerning "Natives Don't Cry" and they are the same. All of them concern the symbolism of the horses. Is there any symbolism there and if so, what is it?

MISS BOYLE: Oh, no, there's no symbolism there at all. That actually happened too. I was scared to death, no symbolism. There is symbolism in my "White Horses of Vienna" because they represent a time and a place and a kind of caste but those horses in "Natives Don't Cry"—no symbolism.

Morehouse: Morehouse has three questions. First of all, we notice the absence, except in the end, of scenes dealing with the American domestic situation. Is this because at the time of your writing you were more conscious of the European experience than the American experience?

MISS BOYLE: Well, you see I had to write about what I knew and I lived over twenty years abroad. I lived about twenty-five years abroad and obviously the scenes would have to be there where I was.

Morehouse: This was environmental rather than a matter of choice?

MISS BOYLE: Oh, yes. You see I married a Frenchman and went to France and stayed there. I didn't come back for almost a quarter of a century. I wrote about French people, my novels were about French people, and that's just where I was and what I was doing—that's all there was to it.

Morehouse: How would "Black Boy" fit into this pattern?

MISS BOYLE: Oh, that was when I was a child in Atlantic City.

Morehouse: A remembered experience?

MISS BOYLE: Yes, that was a remembered experience.

Morehouse: Thirdly, most of these stories have an oblique quality; the emotions come through in terms of personal relationships. If this is true, the story "Black Boy" would have both a social and a personal meaning. The social meaning comes through very clearly but what about the personal? What is the meaning on the level of particular instance itself of the relationship established between a young girl and the Negro boy?

MISS BOYLE: Yes, I got your words but I'm afraid I didn't get the sense of the question.

Morehouse: Is it supposed to be a sexual level or the level of love or affection?

MISS BOYLE: Oh, no, no. I think I was functioning then, at that early age, the same way I function now—in fact, I find it very convenient to have the same feelings now that I had when I was about eight or nine because I don't have to deny anything I ever wrote and say I didn't mean that. I think that I have that kind of mother-complex—that protective thing which has really been the motivation of my writing. I wanted other people to know what was going on in life: at least, how this person could be helped, or this person could be understood, or how awful the English are, how we must do something about enlightening and illuminating their spirit, you see. The crusading spirit, I'd say. Nothing, certainly, nothing to do with sex in that story.

Morehouse: The ending where he calls her his lamb is not to be taken as a feeling of affection on his part but simply as part of the story?

MISS BOYLE: Well, I imagine that someone who has been an outcast would respond with affection at a time when he feels he's being protected and championed. To me my grandfather represented—I loved him dearly but as I grew older we separated on nearly every issue in life—all that was evil and wrong in our civilization.

Stephens: One of the students notes that in "Wedding Day" the style, at times, has an almost poetrylike quality and she wonders if you would comment on your feeling about language in relation to that very early story and then the later stories. Do you feel that there is a change in style?

MISS BOYLE: Yes, I do, definitely. The thing is, I

started out as a poet and I wrote many, many volumes of poetry when I was a child. I kept on with that and my first things to be published were poems. In fact, William Carlos Williams, who was one of my very dearest friends, got very angry if anyone called me a prose writer. He always referred to me as a poet, and he said that it was just by mistake I had written prose. I definitely changed—tried to write less poetically in my stories—and I regret it in a way, and I feel now, in my dotage, that I am going back more to the poetic method.

Tougaloo: I wonder if you can say how you feel out and recognize something for a short story?

MISS BOYLE: Well, you just sort of get hit in the heart by it and you *have* to do it. Your breath is just taken away. You feel like, "my God, I must get that down. I must tell people that this happened." I might add that I had never read very much and so I didn't realize that many of the things I was writing had been written many, many times before. I try to discourage my students sometimes from reading *too* much because then they're not going to write.

Jackson: One student wants to know whether there is any significant meaning in the dance in "Wedding Day." Is it merely descriptive? He seems to think that it is suggestive of the state of turmoil and confusion that seemed to characterize the characters in "Wedding Day." Would you comment on that?

MISS BOYLE: You mean when the man throws the calling cards all around? Well, yes, I can see that it could have symbolic meaning. But it simply means he got completely and awfully fed up and decided to be violent. It's not symbolic of the confusion of the Americans in Paris or anything of that sort.

Stephens: Miss Boyle, you have rather consistently denied the symbolic content of your stories and I wonder if you would comment a little bit on how you see symbolism?

Do you see this as something laid over or something that emerges from particular situations? Would you comment on that?

MISS BOYLE: I think that symbolism does, of course, come into stories but usually quite unconsciously on the author's part, and I believe the critics who spend their time finding symbolic levels of meaning are doing themselves a greater service than they are the author. I think some definitions, for example, of what Joyce was saying on a deeper level in *Portrait of the Artist,* and in other books, have been intelligent and illuminating and have value. But I think in general it is perfectly ghastly. I have written what I call a phony analysis of *The Boarding House* of Joyce's and I use it in some of my classes, not telling my students it is a joke, and some of them are very impressed and are very irritated when I tell them afterwards that it is a joke. I don't have a very high opinion of this kind of analysis.

MR. MADDEN: All right. Thank you.

Morehouse: There would be a school that would argue that the intention of the artist is secondary to the effect of his work. Isn't it possible that in the use of certain images and certain references the author may be unconsciously and unintentionally bringing in a symbolic level?

MISS BOYLE: Oh, yes!

Morehouse: What would be the meaning of "The Canals of Mars" on all possible levels that you have in your mind when you use that expression?

MISS BOYLE: Well, I just recall a story that happened in a movie theatre. We had wanted to go to the planetarium and couldn't. But I remember another story which perhaps you are not familiar with called "His Idea of a Mother." A college boy came to me some years ago with a textbook that required an analysis of this story of mine and one of the questions was: "Why did Miss Boyle use nothing but feminine symbolism in the first paragraph?" Well, I was just flabbergasted! I didn't know that I had, and I looked at it and I *had!* I'd done it unconsciously but rightly, because the story was about a child's mother and everything in that paragraph was a feminine thing. It was very revealing to me that I had done it quite unknowingly. But "The Canals of Mars" is in no way a symbolic story. It was a story that I wrote very quickly and under great emotional pressure. Whatever symbolism can be read into it was purely unconscious.

Morehouse: It is therefore dealing with a superficial level as its only reality in terms of theme and idea? And the term "Canals of Mars" is not that which is distant and far away?

MISS BOYLE: No.

Langston: In "Friend of the Family" do you attempt to give us an attitude toward life or do you want us to observe a truth of life?

MISS BOYLE: The truth of life? Well, I don't think I actually thought it out that way. I just wanted to show a woman who is unsatisfied with her—well, almost like *Main Street*—an American wife is unsatisfied with her domestic life, she feels her husband is a businessman and not an artist, and she is very much drawn to the artist. I think that is all that's behind that.

Stephens: On the back of the New Directions paperbook the *San Francisco Chronicle* says: "These stories have none of the earmarks of feminine fiction," and you made some such distinction when you were talking about Katherine Mansfield. Do you think there is such a thing as feminine fiction?

MISS BOYLE: Yes, yes, I do.

Stephens: What are the characteristics of it?

MISS BOYLE: There's a feminine mistiness of view-point which I think can be a very dangerous thing; and I think you can usually see it in a piece of writing whether or not you know if the author is woman or man. I don't think women should try to write like men but I think they should try not to write like women. What I mean by that is: presenting the woman's instead of the human point of view. God knows there are two, or at least two, and maybe many more points of view, in any situation, but women writers tend to narrow down the choice.

MR. MOORE: Miss Boyle, we have only a moment or so but before we finish I wonder if you would tell the students about the story that you have just sold to the *Saturday Evening Post*.

MISS BOYLE: Yes, that's very interesting! I was recently asked to write a story for the feminine mystique number of the *Ladies' Home Journal* and so I wrote a feminine mystique story and they turned it down because it was too feminine mystique. It was solved by man and by love in the end. Then I was asked to write a story for *The Saturday Evening Post*, and I thought this was going to meet the same fate. I wrote about juvenile delinquents in Central Park. There's a rumble, and the hero gets killed. He's a Spaniard, and he gets knifed in the end. They have accepted the story to my great amazement, so I felt I should keep very far away from the feminine mystique and present the points of view of delinquents or other minority groups. (*laughter*)

MR. MOORE: Is there anyone else who would like to ask one more question? There's time for one more.

Tougaloo: Yes, we do at Tougaloo. The student says your titles are interesting. How do you get them?

MISS BOYLE: Well, sometimes I don't, sometimes the magazines put them on. This one I've just sold to *The Saturday Evening Post* I have no title for. I suggested the

"Ballet of Central Park" but I don't know whether they will accept that or not. Sometimes they prefer to find their own titles.

Stephens: This is Charles Madden. I have a question. How are the grandchildren?

MISS BOYLE: Fine! (*laughing*) I have one sitting on my knee now.

MR. MOORE: Thank you very much for a very profitable and interesting morning.

MISS BOYLE: Thanks to all of you. I loved it.

May 11, 1964